Religion, Education, Dialogue and Conflict

Religion, Education, Dialogue and Conflict analyses the European Commission-funded REDCo project, which addressed the question of how religions might contribute to dialogue or conflict in Europe. Researchers in education from eight countries – the UK, Estonia, France, Germany, the Netherlands, the Russian Federation, Norway and Spain – studied how young Europeans of different religious, cultural and political backgrounds could engage in dialogue in the context of the school.

Empirical studies conducted with 14-16 year old students included them offering their own perspectives and analyses of teaching and learning in both dialogue and conflict situations. Although there were some different national patterns and trends, most students wished for peaceful coexistence across differences, and believed this to be possible. The majority agreed that peaceful coexistence depended on knowledge about each other's religions and worldviews, sharing common interests and doing things together. The project found that students who learn about religious diversity in school are more willing to discuss religions and beliefs with students of other backgrounds than those who do not.

The international range of expert contributors to this book evaluate the results of the REDCo project, providing examples of its qualitative and quantitative studies and reflecting on the methods and theory used in the project as a whole.

This book was originally published as a special issue of the *British Journal of Religious Education.*

Robert Jackson is professor of education at the University of Warwick, director of Warwick Religions and Education Research Unit, and professor of religious diversity and education at the Council of Europe-related European Wergeland Centre in Oslo. He was editor of the *British Journal of Religious Education 1996–2011.*

Religion, Education, Dialogue and Conflict

Perspectives on Religious Education Research

Edited by
Robert Jackson

Routledge
Taylor & Francis Group
LONDON AND NEW YORK

First published 2012
by Routledge
2 Park Square, Milton Park, Abingdon, Oxon, OX14 4RN

Simultaneously published in the USA and Canada
by Routledge
711 Third Avenue, New York, NY 10017

Routledge is an imprint of the Taylor & Francis Group, an informa business

This book is a reproduction of the *British Journal of Religious Education,* volume 33, issue 2. The Publisher requests to those authors who may be citing this book to state, also, the bibliographical details of the special issue on which the book was based.

British Library Cataloguing in Publication Data
A catalogue record for this book is available from the British Library

ISBN13: 978-0-415-60431-4

Typeset in Times New Roman
by Taylor & Francis Books

Disclaimer
The publisher would like to make readers aware that the chapters in this book are identical to the articles as published in the special issue. The publisher accepts responsibility for any inconsistencies that may have arisen in the course of preparing this volume for print.

Contents

Notes on contributors

Aurora Álvarez Veinguer is associate professor in social anthropology at the University of Granada, Spain, and she completed her PhD thesis at the University of Wales, Bangor, UK. Her main research interests are processes of identities, (re)presentation, ethnicity, migration and gender. She is currently researching transnational migration and diversity.

Ina ter Avest is a senior researcher in religious education at the VU University in Amsterdam and a senior lecturer in religious education at the Utrecht University, the Netherlands. In line with the thoughts of Emmanuel Levinas and Hanna Ahrendt, and the concepts of umma (Islamic tradition) and ubuntu (African culture) with regard to the position of 'the other', the focus in her research is on processes of de- and reconstruction in (religious) identity development in a multicultural context – the role of religion in identity development of children, in professional identity development of teachers and in the development of identity of organisations/schools. Her key publications include: 'Dutch children and their God', (in *British Journal of Religious Education, 2009)* and *Classroom interaction: Analysis on (im)possibilities of diversity and dialogue in changing European countries* (with Dan-Paul Jozsa, Javier Rosón, Geir Skeie, eds., 2009).

Cok Bakker is a professor of religious education at the Faculty of Humanities, Department of Theology, Utrecht University, the Netherlands. His research concentrates on the religious and value dimension of educational processes, in the more restricted sense the subject of 'religious education' and in a broader sense by exploring the participants' perception of the religious dimension of (mainly) religiously affiliated schools. The core question is how in a context of a multiple diversity, which is reflected in daily school life, this diversity is perceived by the participants and how this influences contents and processes of education. His key publications include: 'Teachers in tension? Teachers between "the formal Christian identity of the school" and "Religious Diversity"' (in *Interreligious Learning. Series Bibliotheca Ephemeridum Theologicarum Lovaniensium*, 2007) and *Teachers responding to religious diversity in Europe: Researching biography and pedagogy* (with Anna van der Want, Ina ter Avest, and Judith Everington, 2009).

Gerdien D. Bertram-Troost's research focuses, both from a theoretical and an empirical perspective, on religious identity development of pupils and the impact of schools for secondary education on this development. She is especially interested in the effects of religious diversity in secondary education on pupils' knowledge, skills and attitudes towards religion and religious diversity in society. In her research, she uses both quantitative and qualitative methods (see, e.g., Bertram-Troost, de Roos, and Miedema 2009).

Gunther Dietz holds a PhD in social anthropology from Hamburg University, Germany, and is currently research professor in intercultural studies, Universidad Veracruzana, Mexico. Gunther Dietz works on intercultural and interreligious education, multiculturalism and social movements in Mexico and Spain. His most recent publication is *Multiculturalism, interculturality and diversity in education: An anthropological approach* (2009).

Judith Everington is associate professor in religious education at the Institute of Education, University of Warwick, UK. As a member of the Warwick Religions and Education Research Unit she was involved in the development of the Interpretive Approach to RE through a series of teachers' guides and pupils' books. For the past 10 years her research has focused on the relationship between beginning RE teachers' personal and professional lives. A series of publications based on life history studies of beginning teachers include articles in the *British Journal of Religious Education*, (Becoming an RE teacher: A life history approach, 2001) and in *Teachers and Teaching: Theory and Practice* (RE teachers do get drunk you know, 2004). More recently, her research has focused on the development of teacher education strategies that take account of teachers' personal lives and beliefs: publications include 'The use of the interpretive approach in the professional development of student teachers of religious education' (in Ipgrave et al., *Religious education research through a community of practice: Action research and interpretive approach*. 2009).

Bruce Grelle is religious ethicist at California State University in Chico, USA. He received his PhD in ethics and society from the University of Chicago Divinity School. He is an author and co-editor of *Explorations in Global Ethics: Comparative Religious Ethics and Interreligious Dialogue* (1998), and has penned essays on comparative ethics and interfaith dialogue as chapters for books or articles in scholarly journals. His areas of teaching and research are comparative religious ethics, religion and politics, and religion and public education. He is the director of the Religion and Public Education Resource Center (RPERC) at Chico State, and serves on the American Academy of Religion's task force on "Religion in the Schools" and on the statewide steering committee of the California 3 Rs Project (Rights, Responsibilities, Respect): A Project for Finding Common Ground on Issues of Religion and Values in Public Schools. He is past-president of the Chico Area Interfaith Council and serves on the steering committee for Chico's local "Celebration of Abraham" initiative. He teaches a variety of courses including Cross-Cultural Environmental Ethics; Jesus, Buddha, Marx: A Study in Comparative Ethics; Teaching About Religions in American Public Schools; and Approaches to the Study of Religion.

Robert Jackson is professor of religions and education in the Institute of Education at the University of Warwick, UK, and Director of the Warwick Religions and Education Research Unit (http://www.warwick.ac.uk/go/WRERU). He is also professor of religious diversity and education at the Council of Europe-related European Wergeland Centre in Oslo, Norway (http://www.theewc.org). He has undertaken various projects for the Council of Europe, the Organisation for Security and Co-operation in Europe and the United Nations Alliance of Civilizations programme, as well as taking a leading role in many research projects, including the European Commission project on religion, education, dialogue and conflict (REDCo). He is author of many publications in the field of religions and education, is co-editor of the book series *Religious Diversity and Education in Europe* and was Editor of the *British Journal of Religious Education* (1996–2011). His books include *Rethinking religious education and plurality: Issues in diversity and pedagogy* and *Religious education: An interpretive approach*.

Thorsten Knauth is professor for protestant theology and religious education at the University of Duisburg-Essen, Germany. He is director of the Centre for Inter-religious Learning at the Institute for Protestant Theology and currently also head of the Institute. His main research interests are on dialogical approaches in RE and qualitative empirical research with regard to religious learning in schools. His recent publications include: *Dialogue and conflict of religion. Studies of classroom interaction in European countries* (with co-editors ter Avest, Jozsa, Roson, Skeie) and *Gender, religion, Bildung. Beiträge zu Einer Religionspädagogik der Vielfalt* (with co-editors Pithan, Arzt, Jakobs).

Anna Körs has recently defended her PhD thesis at the Institute of Sociology, University of Hamburg, Germany, seeking to contribute to the 'spatial turn' in sociology by exploring the meanings of historical church buildings from the church visitors' perspectives at the present time. Currently, she is associate lecturer at the University of Duisburg-Essen and is going to teach at the Helmut Schmidt University, Hamburg. Her research fields include sociology of culture, sociology of religion, qualitative and quantitative methods. She has recently published on religious education including: *Jugend und Religion in Europa. Einstellungen zu Religion in Lebenswelt, Schule und Gesellschaft im Vergleich acht europäischer Länder*' (in Jozsa, Dan-Paul, Thorsten Knauth, Wolfram Weiße (eds.), 2009).

Fedor Kozyrev is professor of pedagogy and head of the Institute for Religious Pedagogy at the Russian Christian Academy for Humanities, St Petersburg. In addition to his participation in REDCo, he is a participant of interreligious hermeneutic practice of scriptural reasoning in the framework of the Cambridge Interfaith Programme. His main publications in Russian are two monographs on the developments of the theory and methodology of religious education and on the concept of religious education as one of the humanities. His English publications include: 'The roles of dialogue in religious education: A Russian perspective' (in *Education, religion and society: Essays in honour of John M. Hull*, ed. Dennis Bates, Gloria Durka, and Friedrich Schweitzer, 2006); 'Two concepts of religious education in postmodern age: "Humanitarian" versus "Holistic"' (in *Ecumenism of Life as a Challenge for Academic Theology: Proceedings of the 14th Academic Consultation of the Societas Oecumenica*, ed. Bernd Jochen Hilberath, Ivana Noble, and Peter De Mey, 2008); 'Towards a new paradigm of RE in Eastern Europe' (in *Religious education in a world of religious diversity*, ed. Wilna A.J. Meijer, Siebren Miedema, and Alma Lanser-van der Velde, 2009); and 'Religious education and religious freedom in Russia' (in *International handbook of interreligious education*, Part 1 (International

Marie von der Lippe is an associate professor in the Department of Archaeology, History, Cultural Studies and Religion at the University of Bergen, Norway, where she lectures in religious education on the teacher training programme, and formerly a researcher at the University of Stavanger, Norway. Together with Prof. Geir Skeie, Marie von der Lippe was responsible for the Norwegian research within the REDCo project. Her research interest is related to young people and religion in plural societies with a main focus on religion in education. She received her PhD in 2010 from the University of Stavanger for her research on the REDCo project. Her previous papers include: 'To believe or not to believe: Young peoples' perceptions and experiences with religion and religious education in Norway' (in *Encountering religious pluralism in school and society: A qualitative study of teenage perspectives in Europe*, ed. T. Knauth, D.P. Jozsa, G. Bertram-Troost, and J. Ipgrave, 2008); 'Scenes from a classroom: Video analysis of classroom interaction in religious education in Norway' (in *Dialogue and conflict on religion: Studies of classroom interaction in European countries*, ed. I. Ter Avest, D.P. Jozsa, T. Knauth, J. Roson, and G. Skeie, 2009); and 'Does religion matter to young people in Norwegian schools? (in *Teenagers' perspectives on the role of religion in their lives, schools and societies*, ed. P. Valk, G. Bertram-Trost, M. Friederici, and C. Beraud, 2009).

Bérengère Massignon is post-doctoral student at the Research Unit Group Societies, Religions, *Laïcités* (GSRL, France), University of Paris-Sorbonne, France, lecturer at the Institute for Political Studies (Sciences Po, Paris) and at the Catholic Institute of Paris. She has worked on the management of religious pluralism in French public schools. She is currently working on the relations between religions and European integration and churches lobbying in Brussels. She published, in French, *Gods and bureaucrats. Religions facing the stake of European integration* (2007). Her recent book, written with a journalist, Virginie Riva, *Europe, with or without God: Heritages and new challenges* (2010) deals with the new stakes faced by European members' states in relation to religious pluralism (e.g. Islam, cults controversies). It is based on her research and on the expertise gained as assistant researcher for the counsellor for religious affairs of the French Ministry for Foreign Affairs.

Ursula McKenna is a research fellow in WRERU and a part-time primary school teacher. She contributed to data collection and analysis of the qualitative and quantitative aspects of the European REDCo project. Her recent publications include: *Inter faith dialogue by email in primary schools: An evaluation of the building e-bridges project* (Religious Diversity and Education in Europe Series) (with J. Ipgrave and R. Jackson, 2008) and 'Personal worldviews, dialogue and tolerance: Students' views on religious education in England' (in *Teenagers' perspectives on the role of religion in their lives, schools and societies: A European quantitative study* (Religious Diversity and Education in Europe Series), ed. P. Valk, G. Bertram-Troost, M. Friederici, and C. Beraud) (with S. Neill and R. Jackson, 2009).

Joyce Miller is an associate fellow in WRERU and the deputy chair of the RE Council of England and Wales. She was part of the Warwick REDCo community of practice. Her research focus was an evaluation of the transferability of the interpretive approach to teachers' continuing professional development. Her recent publications include: ‘Raising humanities teachers’ understanding of their pupils’ religious and cultural backgrounds’ (in *Religious education research through a community of practice*, ed. J. Ipgrave, R. Jackson, and K. O’Grady, 2009) and ‘Responses of three Muslim majority primary schools in England to the Islamic faith of their pupils’ (2010) in *Journal of International Migration and Integration* (with J. Ipgrave and P. Hopkins).

Sean Neill is an associate professor at the Institute of Education, University of Warwick, UK, and a member of Warwick Religions and Education Research Unit. He has carried out quantitative analysis on a wide range of projects including the REDCo European religious education project.

F. Javier Rosón Lorente holds a PhD in social anthropology from the University of Granada, Spain. His main research interests are Muslim communities and interreligious relations in Spain.

Olga Schihalejev is a researcher and a lecturer in the Faculty of Theology, Tartu University, Estonia. She has worked as a teacher of religious education and has written teaching-learning resources for students in Estonia and been actively involved in improving the national syllabus for RE.

Anna van der Want is a PhD candidate at the Eindhoven School of Education, Eindhoven University of Technology, the Netherlands. She is a theologian and educational scientist with a special interest in teachers’ worldviews and the construction and development of teacher identity/identities. After completing an MA in theology at Utrecht University, she joined the research project featured in this article and played a key role in the reporting of the research in book form (van der Want et al. (2009) *Responding to religious diversity in Europe: Researching biography and pedagogy*). She is currently studying for a PhD and conducting a longitudinal study of teachers’ narratives and teachers’ views of teacher–student interaction in secondary schools.

Wolfram Weisse is director of the Academy of World Religions of the University of Hamburg, Germany, and professor of religious education and international theology. He has specialised in interreligious education and the dialogue of people with different religious backgrounds and world views. He has published extensively in German, and a few of his publications in English are listed in the references of this article.

Preface

Bruce Grelle

The issue of religion education (RE) is figuring ever more prominently on the world stage. Even before the events of 9/11 in the United States, there was growing recognition that knowledge about diverse religious and secular worldviews is indispensable for basic historical and cultural literacy as well as for the exercise of responsible citizenship in the era of globalization. After 9/11 discussions of RE in public schools took on a greater sense of urgency and began to attract the attention not only of scholars and educators but also governmental and inter-governmental organizations and policy makers.

The United Nations Charter and the Universal Declaration of Human Rights along with any number of subsequent UN covenants, conventions, and declarations make reference to 'the right to freedom of thought, conscience, religion or belief' and to the role of education in promoting respect for this right. The topic of RE *per se* was the focus of the International Consultative Conference on School Education in relation with Freedom of Religion and Belief, Tolerance and Non-discrimination which took place in Madrid in November, 2001.

UNESCO has emphasized the role of schools in promoting understanding among religious groups, and the Alliance of Civilizations is another UN initiative that has addressed RE directly.

As noted by Robert Jackson in his Introduction to this volume, despite substantial diversity in rationale and approach to RE in European countries, there have been several significant Europe-wide developments that aim toward the creation of a more general trans-national consensus regarding the justification and guidelines for RE in public schools. These include public statements and research activities sponsored by the European Union; projects and documents developed by the Council of Europe; and initiatives undertaken by the Organization for Security and Cooperation in Europe (OSCE). Perhaps the most significant of these initiatives is the OSCE's development of the *Toledo Guiding Principles on Teaching about Religions and Beliefs in Public Schools* (2007).

But against this background of scholarship, policy, and international diplomacy, one might wonder what public school *students* and *teachers* think about religion and religious diversity in the world today? How do young people (and their teachers) see the place of religion in their own personal lives and in the lives of their schools and societies? Do they think that learning about religions in schools can contribute to peaceful co-existence in religiously diverse societies?

These are among the questions addressed by REDCo – 'Religion in Education: A Contribution to Dialogue or a Factor of Conflict in Transforming Societies of European Countries' – a massive three-year research project coordinated by Professor Dr. Wolfram Weisse (University of Hamburg) and funded by a major grant from the European Commission. From 2006-2009 the REDCo project deployed an international team of scholars representing a range of disciplinary specializations in education, the humanities, and the social sciences. Focusing mainly on religion in the lives and schools of students in the 14-16 year age group with some attention to teacher attitudes and training and to classroom practices, this team carried out qualitative and quantitative research in eight countries: England, Estonia, France, Germany, the Netherlands, Norway, Russia, and Spain.

The present book reflects upon and extends the work of REDCo. It consists of chapters written especially for this volume by authors from all eight of the REDCo countries. Not only do these authors provide a snapshot of the current situation of RE in various locations throughout Europe, they also suggest lines of inquiry that can be applied or adapted to other settings beyond Europe. In so doing, they make a pioneering contribution to the emerging field of the comparative study of RE in public schools around the world.

There is considerable diversity in the way that RE is conceptualized, approached, and institutionalized both within and between the various countries of Europe, and this volume pays close attention to the historical and societal factors that help to account for this diversity. One sees this diversity in alternative ways of thinking about the aims of RE as educating 'into,' 'about,' or 'from' religion. Educating *into* religion involves a single religious tradition, taught by 'insiders,' with the aim of developing students' knowledge about and commitment to that tradition. Educating *about* religion involves a neutral description of religions in various historical and contemporary settings with the aim of cultivating cultural and historical literacy. Educating *from* religion encourages students' engagement with diverse perspectives on religious and moral issues with the aim of helping pupils develop their own points of view on religion and values.

These alternative conceptions of the aims of RE are linked in various ways to the manner in which states deal with religion in their school systems. In Spain and in parts of Germany and the Netherlands, there are 'confessional' systems where the state gives religious bodies responsibility for RE, although the nature and extent of this responsibility varies significantly from country to country. In France one finds a strictly *laïque* or 'non-confessional' secular system where religious bodies have no role in public education. There are also 'mixed' systems such as those in England and Wales where religious bodies may or may not have a role in RE depending on the degree of public funding received by the school (2007 p. 29).

In some countries RE is a stand-alone subject matter; in others it is integrated into history or other areas of the curriculum. In some countries it is compulsory; in others it is optional. In some countries (or regions within the same country), RE classes are segregated according to the students' own religious background; in others classes include students from mixed religious and non-religious backgrounds. REDCo's comparative approach is designed to highlight and clarify differences between countries while at the same time contributing to the development of a European perspective and identity, albeit one which is pluralistic rather than monolithic.

Beyond providing a rich introduction to the historical background, contemporary developments, and theoretical debates that set the context for RE in Europe, the REDCo project also provides a detailed picture of young peoples' perceptions of religion and religious diversity in their own personal lives, in their societies, and in their schools. The empirical findings generated by REDCo result from case studies in specific contextual settings rather than national surveys. Although the national samples are not representative, they do reveal tendencies in the ways that students from different personal and religious backgrounds in different countries think about religion as a potential factor in dialogue and conflict.

Among the project's central findings is that students are conscious of increasing religious diversity in society, and in general they are of the opinion that it is important to respect the religions of others. With regard to the role of religion in school life (e.g. wearing discrete or more visible religious symbols, absences for religious holidays, excusal from some classes for religious reasons) the studies document a range of different attitudes that appear to be determined largely by the students' own religious backgrounds (or lack thereof), by the role religion plays in (the history of) their respective countries, and by whether religion is more or less private and withdrawn from public life and discussion. While notions of freedom and tolerance are important, students also attach great importance to 'equal treatment' and are reluctant to change too much in school policy and curriculum for the sake of a particular group of students. While some students exhibit prejudices against the religions of others, especially with regard to Islam, they appear open to dialogue and hopeful that RE can contribute to the goal of peaceful coexistence.

As for religion in the curriculum, it appears that students in the European countries covered generally favour an approach to RE that provides objective information about different religions and their teachings rather than an approach that guides pupils toward religious beliefs. The majority of those surveyed appear to agree that school is a good place (and for some the only place) to learn about different religions and worldviews, and they generally regard RE as more relevant to cultivating respect for people of different religions and learning to live together than it is for learning about themselves and developing their own decisions about right and wrong.

The impact of the REDCo project beyond Europe has already begun to be felt. A recent issue of *Religion & Education* featured a special focus on how REDCo's approach and results might inform research on RE in South Africa, Turkey, and the United States.[1] REDCo has also been the topic of ongoing discussions among participants in the American Academy of Religion's Consultation on 'Religion in Public Schools: International Perspectives'. The present volume is suggestive of any number of theoretical-pedagogical and empirical questions that deserve further research in both European and non-European settings.

The theoretical and pedagogical framework for REDCo is provided by Robert Jackson's 'interpretive approach', which draws on ethnographic methods in its effort to help students gain a critical and reflective understanding of religions. The applicability of this approach in diverse societal and educational settings outside of Europe is worth sustained consideration. From a U.S. perspective, it would be especially interesting to compare the interpretive approach with the one recently set forth by the American Academy of Religion in its *Guidelines for Teaching about Religion in K-12 Public Schools in the United States* (2010).

REDCo also provides a wealth of empirical data that can inform ongoing discussions and future research on a whole range of questions including the relationship between organized and non-organized religiosity in contemporary societies; the relative influence of families, schools, religious communities, and the media in shaping student attitudes toward religions and religious diversity; the gap that often exists between the worldviews of teachers and those of their students; the relationship between RE and citizenship education; and the ongoing debate over the secularization vs. the desecularization of contemporary societies in Europe and elsewhere.

As the most recent outcome of REDCo, this volume is an admirable summary and elaboration of the project's research up to this point. It is also a stimulus to new research on RE in Europe and well beyond. I hope it receives the wide attention it deserves from scholars, teachers, and policy makers.

Religion, education, dialogue and conflict: an introduction

Robert Jackson

University of Warwick, UK

Especially in the years following the events of 9/11, 2001 in the USA, religion has become a major topic of public debate globally. In academic literature, there has been a growth in writing about the place of religion in the public sphere (e.g., Habermas 2006) and in policy development, at European and wider international levels, there has been close attention to education about religions and beliefs in schools. The Council of Europe completed its first ever project on the religious dimension of intercultural education, which includes a Recommendation by the Committee of Ministers – the Foreign Ministers of the 47 member states – that all young Europeans should learn about religious diversity (Council of Europe 2008). The Organisation for Security and Cooperation in Europe, the largest security organisation in the world, published the *Toledo guiding principles on teaching about religions and beliefs in public schools*, again arguing that education about the diversity of religions and beliefs in society should be a part of everyone's general education (OSCE 2007). The United Nations Alliance of Civilisations programme makes a similar recommendation through its education about religions and beliefs website (www.aocerb.org).

Consistent with this change in mood and policy, the European Commission funded a major project on religion and education in schools between 2006 and 2009 through its Framework Six programme. The full title of the project is 'Religion in Education: a Contribution to Dialogue or a Factor of Conflict in Transforming Societies of European Countries?' Known by its acronym REDCo, the project collected the views of adolescents from eight European countries on teaching and learning about religious diversity in schools. The REDCo project brought together educational researchers from universities in Germany, England, Norway, Estonia, France, Spain, the Russian Federation and the Netherlands. Meeting together regularly in each other's countries, the REDCo project team designed both qualitative (Knauth et al. 2008) and quantitative (Valk et al. 2009) studies and a classroom interaction study (ter Avest et al. 2009), all conducted by each national group in its own setting. In addition, there was a study of teachers from six of the countries (van der Want et al. 2009), plus a number of related studies conducted by particular groups (Ipgrave, Jackson, and O'Grady 2009; Álvarez Veinguer et al. 2009).

Co-ordinated by Professor Wolfram Weisse of the University of Hamburg, the REDCo project team worked to a tight timetable of research design, fieldwork, data analysis and report writing. The project spawned a new European book series entitled *Religious diversity and education in Europe*, published in Germany by Waxmann (http://www.waxmann.com/?id=21&cHash=1&reihe=1862-9547). At the time of writing, 19 books have been published in the series, nine of them specifically reporting research related to the REDCo project, the first an overview of the place of religious education within the educational systems of the participating countries (Jackson et al. 2007), the last an account of the Estonian research findings (Schihalejev 2010). The present publication offers a cross-section of the project's work, with new, specially written, contributions from authors in all eight of the REDCo countries. It thus provides an introduction to the wide-ranging work of the REDCo project as a whole.

The contributions are as follows. Wolfram Weisse provides an overview of the project, including his own personal retrospective reflections. The next four contributions provide examples of national studies. Marie von der Lippe from the Norwegian team, based at the University of Stavanger, focuses on Norwegian teenagers' discourse about Islam and Muslims, showing that young people need help from teachers in formulating their criticisms of dominant media discourses and in marshalling their own more independent ideas. The Spanish team from the University of Granada give a picture of the attitudes and experiences of young Spaniards in relation to religious diversity at school. Bérengère Massignon, from the French group at the Sorbonne in Paris, reports French teenagers' understandings of the concept of *laïcité*. Massignon illustrates how French secondary pupils share a *laïcité* of proximity – of being neighbours, of living together in community – which is different from the state interpretation and also from how the term is used in ideological debates in France. Pupils' view of *laïcité* is consistent with the idea of living together tolerantly and respectfully in a pluralist society, expecting equal treatment of different religions, and being open to dialogue with those who hold different views. Joyce Miller and Ursula McKenna, from the English team based at the University of Warwick, draw on two studies in order to compare and contrast the views of pupils and teachers in a school with a high population of Muslim students and a high number of non-Muslim staff.

The following four studies illustrate various methodological approaches and issues relating to the REDCo project. In the initial design of the project, Wolfram Weisse employed the interpretive approach (Jackson 1997) as a theoretical and methodological stimulus. My own contribution charts the use of the interpretive approach in the REDCo project, selecting some examples for discussion and illustrating some adaptations and developments to the approach. Thorsten Knauth and Anna Körs, from the Hamburg section of the German team, undertake a meta-analysis of the data collected by project partners for the qualitative study (Knauth et al. 2008). They take care to point out that national comparisons are not being made. Rather, particular contextual settings for religious education in the different countries, each shaped by national and regional traditions and structures, are being compared. The authors concentrate on four main issues, namely, the role of religion in school, the content of learning, the teacher's religiosity and learning models. Sean Neill from the Warwick group and Olga Schihalejev, from Estonia, illustrate the use of structural modelling techniques in exemplifying influences on English and Estonian students' views on religions and education. Judith Everington from the Warwick team and Ina ter Avest, Cok Bakker and Anna van der Want, from the Dutch group based at the VU University in Amsterdam and Utrecht University, summarise and outline the methodology of their study of religious education teachers' biographies conducted in six of the eight REDCo countries.

The final two contributions look back in a reflexive way at different aspects of the REDCO project. Fedor Kozyrev, from the Russian team, based in St Petersburg, reflects on the complex mixed methods methodology of the REDCo project. Recognizing the limitations of all research methods, and the inter-influence of research reports, he argues for the use of hermeneutical methods in interpreting mixed methods results, seeing this process as more like history or literary criticism than hard science. Revisiting data, in his view, should be seen as re-reading the story for a better interpretation. His re-reading of his own research studies in St Petersburg leads to his view that teaching which provides students with encounters with a plurality of interpretations of subjective knowledge, in dialogue with reflections on their own presuppositions, is likely to promote the development of both their critical thinking, and their capacity for impartiality. Finally, Gerdien Bertram-Troost, from the Amsterdam group, reflects retrospectively on ways in which, in a fast-moving project working to tight deadlines, longer and more focused conceptual preparation could have improved the quality of the quantitative questionnaire.

The contributions show the richness of the project and give a hint of the high volume of material produced by the REDCo researchers. The detail can be read in the volumes produced in the *Religious Diversity and Education in Europe* series. However, the project team were committed to disseminating research findings to potential user groups, including politicians, policy makers, teacher trainers and teachers. The presentations given at the European Parliament in December 2009, while acknowledging contextual differences between and within the participant countries, attempt a generic summary of project findings. These include the following:

- Students wish for peaceful coexistence across differences, and believe this to be possible

- For students peaceful coexistence depends on knowledge about each other's religions and worldviews and sharing common interests as well as doing things together
- Students who learn about religious diversity in school are more willing to have conversations about religions/beliefs with students of other backgrounds than those who do not
- Students wish to avoid conflict: some of the religiously committed students feel vulnerable
- Students want learning to take place in a safe classroom environment where there are agreed procedures for expression and discussion
- Most students would like the state-funded school to be a place for learning *about* different religions/worldviews, rather than for instruction *into* a particular religion/worldview

The various presentations at the European Parliament, plus summaries of findings, can be read at http://www.redco.uni-hamburg.de/web/3480/4176/index.html

Dissemination of the REDCo Project continues and the project team's thanks go especially to Claudia Lenz and her colleagues at the Council of Europe-related European Wergeland Centre, based in Oslo, who have organised dissemination workshops and conferences in Austria, Norway and Germany during 2010. A report on these activities can be read at http://www.theewc.org Dissemination work shows a particular synergy between the findings of the REDCo project and the Recommendation of the Committee of Ministers of the Council of Europe (Council of Europe 2008) and there is scope for developing materials and training programmes drawing on the REDCo findings and the Ministerial Recommendation.

Looking back, high points of the project include the wonderful educational and cultural experience of working in one another's countries and universities, resulting in the development of an international research community of friends and colleagues; reporting project findings at the Council of Europe in Strasbourg and at the European Parliament in Brussels; and sharing in the success of younger researchers who completed their PhDs during or soon after the completion of the project. The building of new capacity in European RE research has been a very important aspect of the project and a significant factor in the development of *collaborative* religious education research in Europe. The lowest point was the illness and death of the co-ordinator of the Estonian branch of the project and of the project's quantitative research. Dr Pille Valk died from cancer in September 2009, having managed to complete the editing of the quantitative book (Valk *et al.* 2009). Many REDCo researchers took part in a tribute to her at the University of Hamburg in November 2009, and attended the memorial conference held in her honour at the University of Tartu in September 2010. This publication is dedicated by all the contributors to Pille Valk's memory.

References

Álvarez Veinguer, A., Dietz, G., Jozsa, D-P. and Knauth, T. eds. 2009. *Islam in education in European countries: pedagogical concepts and empirical findings.* Münster: Waxmann.

Council of Europe. 2008. 'Recommendation CM/Rec(2008)12 of the Committee of Ministers to member states on the dimension of religions and non-religious convictions within intercultural education', available online at: https://wcd.coe.int//ViewDoc.jsp?Ref=CM/Rec(2008)12&Language=lanEnglish&Ver=original&BackColorInternet=DBDCF2&BackColorIntranet=FDC864&BackColorLogged=FDC864 (accessed 24 December 2010).

Habermas, J. 2006. Religion in the public sphere. *European Journal of Philosophy* 14, no. 1: 1–25.

Ipgrave, J., Jackson, R. and O'Grady, K. eds. 2009. *Religious education research through a community of practice. Action research and the interpretive approach.* Münster: Waxmann

Jackson, R. 1997. *Religious education: An interpretive approach.* London: Hodder and Stoughton.

Jackson, R., Miedema, S., Weisse, W. and Willaime, J.-P. eds. 2007. *Religion and education in Europe: Developments, contexts and debates.* Münster: Waxmann.

Knauth, T., Jozsa, D.-P., Bertram-Troost, G. and Ipgrave, J. eds. 2008. *Encountering religious pluralism in school and society: A qualitative study of teenage perspectives in Europe.* Münster: Waxmann.

OSCE. 2007. *Toledo guiding principles on teaching about religions and beliefs in public schools,* (Warsaw: Organisation for Security and Co-operation in Europe, Office for Democratic Institutions and Human Rights). (full text available online at http://www.osce.org/item/28314.html accessed 22 December 2010).

Schihalejev, O. 2010. *From indifference to dialogue? Estonian young people, the school and religious diversity.* Münster: Waxmann.

ter Avest, I., Jozsa, D.-P., Knauth, T., Rosón, J. and Skeie, G. eds. 2009. *Dialogue and conflict on religion: Studies of classroom interaction in European countries.* Münster: Waxmann.

Valk, P., Bertram-Troost, G., Friederici, M. and Béraud, C. eds. 2009. *Teenagers' perspectives on the role of religion in their lives, schools and societies: A European quantitative study.* Münster: Waxmann.

Want, van der A., Bakker, C., ter Avest, I. and Everington J. eds. 2009. *Teachers responding to religious diversity in Europe: Researching biography and pedagogy.* Münster: Waxmann.

Reflections on the REDCo project

Wolfram Weisse

Academy of World Religions, University of Hamburg, Von Melle Park 8, D20146 Hamburg, Germany

The REDCo project addressed the question of how study of religions and values in schools could contribute to either dialogue or tension in Europe. Researchers in the humanities and social sciences co-operated in order to gain better insight into how European citizens of different religious, cultural and political backgrounds could enter into dialogue which respected freedom of religion or belief. Empirical studies, targeting students in the 14- to 16-year age group, included a dual perspective of, on the one hand, the subjects' own perspectives and, on the other hand, analyses of examples of observed teaching. The project was funded by the European Commission for the period from March 2006 to March 2009 and was co-ordinated by the University of Hamburg. Eight European countries (Estonia, Russia, Norway, Germany, the Netherlands, France, England and Spain) participated. This contribution, by the project co-ordinator, provides an overview of the project and presents a personal evaluation.

Introduction

What is the secret behind the success of an international research project? As the co-ordinator of the EC-funded REDCo project, I am convinced that the following components provided the foundation of our research. The public and academic environment recognised the relevance of our research focus. The group of research leaders from the participating countries was regarded as strong, and the project attracted younger researchers with a high motivation to fulfil their task. The most important factor for our co-operative work was the good personal relationship between the project leaders and team members, including the younger researchers. In addition, we designed a challenging structure helping (and requiring) us to report both work in progress and results during the process of our work. This was the mix that ensured the success of the REDCo project, and I will now explain these points with a particular emphasis on the process of our study.

Background of public and academic esteem for the theme

For about 10 years, the dangers arising from religious and cultural isolation and confrontation and the instrumentalisation of religion for political purposes have become clear to a wider public, especially since 11 September 2001. However, religious values can also serve as the foundation for the peaceful coexistence of various religions and philosophies and to justify respect for the human dignity of others, regardless of their religious and political convictions. They can thus act as a pillar for civility.

In most European countries, we have assumed for a long time that increasing secularisation would lead to a gradual retreat of religion from public space. This tendency has reversed itself in the course of the past decade as religion has returned to public attention. Both throughout Europe and internationally, we are seeing a revitalisation of religion in both the individual and the public sphere. Even in states such as France, which has had a system of strict separation of state and church for more than a century, we can observe a new trend towards acknowledging religions' growing relevance 'dans la sphère publique' (Willaime 2008). Similar developments can be seen in other states and societies.

We can observe today how religions play an increasingly important role in European societies, both in dialogue between people of different faiths and in the context of social tension and conflict. This is as true in academia as in the public forum. Recent developments in the academic world are familiar. More and more scholars, who formerly did not touch the field of religion, are taking up this field, including colleagues from different disciplines, including political sciences, sociology, law and philosophy. An outstanding example is Jürgen Habermas. For decades, he refused to take religion into account within his thinking on communication. For some years now he has been writing more and more on religion and its role in mutual understanding (Habermas 2005). As an example from the political realm, I refer readers to a speech by former German chancellor Helmut Schmidt at the Hamburg town hall on 5 September 2008, in which he stressed that, in the context of core global policy issues, religious tolerance would be more vital for coexistence than ever in the twenty-first century.

In brief, there is a growing public awareness of the importance of seeking dialogue, with all that can aid us in preventing conflict and supporting peaceful coexistence in a multireligious and multicultural society. So, where are the theoretical underpinnings for the importance of dialogue, and what role has intercultural and (inter)religious education (RE) in this field?

Public responsibility for religious education

Regardless of the wide variety of conditions prevailing in different European countries, it appears increasingly important to study the factor of 'religion and religiosity' and its ambivalent potential for both dialogue and social conflict and tension. Education is a vital field within which this question can be addressed. The degree to which religion serves (or could potentially be made to serve) as a criterion of exclusion or prejudice in schools and universities should be investigated as well as to what degree religious discourse and dialogue in education can promote potentials for the peaceful coexistence of people in Europe. This is especially important with people of different cultural and religious backgrounds. A colleague from the University of Tübingen in the discipline of political sciences, Andreas Hasenclever, even claims that a positive correlation between religious education and political conduct can be shown: the lower the level of RE, the greater the potential for religious differences to be exploited as a tool for political mobilisation (Hasenclever 2003, 304). Whether this hypothesis is right or wrong, or to what extent it might be helpful to understand the correlation of RE and awareness in the political field, cannot be discussed here. But at least for European countries, we can say that, after a long period of public disinterest, RE and the responsibility for interreligious understanding in public schools are on the agenda again. The same is true for Eastern European states. After 70 years of Communism with its atheist ideology, religion is back: there is a serious academic and public debate on concepts of RE in public schools, and we have strong indications that RE will be a hot issue over the next few years, not only in Europe, but also in other continents (see, for example, UNESCO and Institute of Oriental Studies 2007 on central Asia and Moore 2007 on the USA).

The growing interest in religion and its relevance for intercultural and interreligious understanding (as well as its potential for destruction) is the background for recent programmes launched by international organisations such as UNESCO, the Council of Europe (2008a, 2008b) and the Organisation for Security and Cooperation in Europe (OSCE 2007). They have launched initiatives in the field of interreligious and intercultural dialogue with aims and recommendations that have synergy with the findings of our REDCo project.

The basic idea of REDCo

Religion in education was the thematic background of our REDCo project. REDCo stands for 'Religion in Education. A Contribution to Dialogue or a Factor of Conflict in Transforming Societies of European Countries?' It was part of the section 'Values and Religions in Europe' of the European Commission Framework 6 Programme 'Citizens and Governance in a Knowledge-Based Society'. This project was funded by the research department of the European Commission over a period of three years from March 2006 with a total of 1,188,000 Euros. Nine universities from eight different European countries participated (Weisse 2007).

The project's main aim was to establish and compare the potentials and limitations of religion in the educational systems of selected European countries.

Approaches and constellations that can contribute to making religion in education into a factor promoting dialogue in the context of European development were addressed through historical and contemporary studies (Jackson et al. 2007). The countries involved in our research were Estonia, Russia, Norway, Germany, the Netherlands, England, France and Spain.

We used the term *religious education* in a broad sense, to cover academic teacher training as well as both philosophical and practical aspects of religious and values education at school. Our main focus with regard to schools was the school subject religious education in one or other of its variants, but we also kept open the option of looking at religion and religiosity in other subjects.

When studying religion, we did not focus on abstract belief systems or homogenised 'world religions' but rather concentrated on the forms of religions and world views as presented by the adherents themselves. With reference to E. Levinas, we directed our attention to 'neighbour religions' (Weisse 2003), the views of neighbours in classrooms, in the region, in the state and the whole of Europe. The world religions are present in the 'neighbour religions', and thus our approach permitted us to study them in their current forms and potentials for dialogue and conflict. With a non-foundationalist view (Miedema 2004), we stressed the value of personal expressions and dialogue related to religious identity formation and identity management (Skeie 2001). In the context of these questions, we also covered gender issues.

Our main theoretical stimulus with regard to RE was Robert Jackson's interpretive approach to the study of religious diversity (Jackson 1997, 2004, 2011). The subject of our study can be best understood in the context of *citizenship education*. It has the potential to incorporate European and global ideas of citizenship and helping children debate issues relevant to a plural society (Jackson 2003, 67–92). Religious education, in the form of what in Germany is known as interreligious education, has shown itself to be able to contribute to intercultural understanding (Weisse 2003).

In all countries we used the same repertoire of methods. For textual analysis, we referred to mainly hermeneutical methods. Empirical methods included participant observation, semi-structured interviews, questionnaires (qualitative and quantitative) and videoing of RE lessons for interaction analysis. The data were analysed in a triangulation. All our projects looked at RE for school students in the 14- to 16-year age group in various countries. We combined analyses of concepts of RE with the concrete views of pupils: we observed pupils, interviewed them, asked for written answers in questionnaires and we analysed their interactions with peers and teachers. With this combination, we were able to capture both the perspectives from above and from below.

In both qualitative and quantitative studies, we recorded pupils' views on the societal function of religion, on their experience with religion in education and their wishes to include or exclude religion from education. All questions focused on the possibilities for dialogue and/or conflict. On the basis of the results of the qualitative analysis, we worked out questions for a quantitative survey, which was carried out in February and March 2008. All our projects examined classroom interaction in our various countries. On the basis of videoing RE lessons and/or participant observation, an analysis of interaction patterns in the classroom was possible.

Research group

The research group (consortium) was selected to take account of all our participating countries: Estonia, Russia, Norway, Germany, the Netherlands, England, France and Spain. All project leaders had previously co-operated fruitfully with some or all members of the group. Their respective disciplines (theology, Islamic studies, education, RE, sociology, political science and ethnography) complemented each other. In spite of a wide range of societal and pedagogical backgrounds, the research group shared the common view of the importance of the study of religion in European schools (see Council of Europe 2008a, 2008b; OSCE 2007). Apart from the project leaders,[1] more than 30 young researchers were employed thanks to the financial support given by the European Commission. This combination of experienced project leaders and young researchers contributed decisively to the success of our project. We managed to work together with a high level of dialogue, which included some conflict, but this was always directed to solving problems, not at individual persons. This was the basis for the community of researchers in our REDCo project: high productivity in the output of research and the growth of a community of committed researchers from different parts of Europe who greatly enjoyed meeting each other and thus succeeded in a time- and energy-consuming research process. Also, for many of the young researchers, the participation in the REDCo project was an important step in their academic career. In all of our countries, PhDs have been awarded to participants, and some researchers have attained lectureships or even professorships.

Process-orientated research

The process-oriented structure of our research and our obligation to write a large number of reports for the European Commission – on average one per month – gave the impetus to ensure regular output from our research group spread all over Europe. The reports (called 'milestones' and 'deliverables' in the language of the European Commission's research department) were a heavy burden for all of us but at the same time were the guarantee that we would agree on results and provide a basis for our publications. In the following, I will list the main activities carried out by the REDCo project in its first, second and third years.

First project year (March 2006 to February 2007)

Work in the first year included analytical work with regard to the role of religion in education in Europe, using documentary analysis and the development of a database. All partners wrote analyses on their respective countries focusing on the role of religion in education. The reports included information on the developments in recent decades, the special contexts, debates on religion and education and new challenges in the countries taking part in REDCo and in Europe as a whole and resulted in the publication of a book mapping the European scene for religion and education (Jackson et al. 2007). This study underpinned our ongoing research on the role of religion and education in Europe. Our ongoing work was also supported by a database including literature and different types of documents related to our REDCo theme.

The REDCo project's first book gave us the idea for a book series. After some discussion, we joined forces with the European Network for Religious Education through Contextual Approaches (ENRECA) to produce the book series 'Religious diversity and education in Europe' published by Waxmann. This series has included most of the main REDCo publications, plus a variety of other European research studies, including various edited books, conference proceedings and new research from PhD students in different parts of Europe. The series is growing rapidly, and, at the time of writing, 19 volumes have been published, with more on the way.

The first year's work also included the design of fieldwork and the start of the empirical work in all countries: our empirical work was discussed in detail. As a result, we wrote a fieldwork guide in which our common approaches and methods of data collection were recorded, and another report was produced including decisions on the detailed research design for our fieldwork. This guaranteed a common basis for our empirical research. Additionally, we began the fieldwork using different methods including participant observation, interviews and videoing in school classes. One major piece of qualitative research was done by use of a written questionnaire, which was completed by at least 70 pupils in the age group of 14–16 years in each participating country. On the basis of the data provided, preliminary reports for each REDCo country and comparative analyses of the results were drafted. These were revised and completed within the next half year and were also used to inform the design of our quantitative research, which was structured and organised over the six months following.

During the first year, theoretical issues were also raised, mainly in seminars, and this preparatory work was followed up more thoroughly during the second year. The debate about the interpretive approach as a common theoretical stimulus showed that there was a need to further develop the balance between the descriptive and the prescriptive aspects of the approach. Discussions of 'non-foundational education theory', 'neighbour religions', 'citizenship education' and 'identity formation' were included in the participants' deliberations.

Second project year (March 2007 to February 2008)

In the second year of REDCo, we deepened and extended our fieldwork by applying an appropriate set of methods. Our focus was on research using qualitative and quantitative methods and on video analyses of school lessons. Research using qualitative methods was conducted in all participant countries with a jointly developed qualitative questionnaire. The aim of this research was to gain insight into the personal views of pupils and their experiences with religion, into the social dimension of religion in their lives and into RE in school. The data we collected were published in book form (Knauth et al. 2008). On the basis of our qualitative analyses, we developed a quantitative questionnaire in English, which was translated into all REDCo languages. Our survey started in January 2008 and was completed in March 2008. In all countries, we achieved a minimum of 400 completed questionnaires from pupils in the age group of 14–16 years. In most of the countries, we collected 1000 or more questionnaires in order to create a sounder basis for our analysis. The data analysis was undertaken from April 2008 onwards. Other lines of fieldwork were also continued and deepened in the second year of our research. These focused mainly on classroom interaction and the role of teachers. Both areas of research were concluded in the third year of REDCo. We published our findings as a book (ter Avest et al. 2009) and in articles in refereed journals.

During the second year, we continued our research on theoretical issues. The debate about the interpretive approach as a common theoretical framework was completed thoroughly and productively. In successive discussions by the REDCo project team, a number of factors became clear: the interpretive approach was a theoretical ‘stimulus’, as indicated in the project proposal. The key concepts of the interpretive approach were used in field research in both methods and data analysis as well as in pedagogy. The project included scholars and researchers versed in a range of epistemological and theoretical positions and methodological approaches. This was regarded by the project team as very healthy and permitted a constructive dialogue on issues of epistemology, theory and method. The use of the interpretive approach was discussed in a milestone and a deliverable and subsequently an article (Jackson 2011). Other concepts were also addressed. The concept of ‘neighbour religions’ was used by participants to focus on local religious diversity and on neighbourhood interaction. The relationship between different forms of RE and education for democratic citizenship as well as the question of plural identities of young people remained ongoing issues under discussion by the project team.

We extended our dissemination activities considerably. A series of discussion and information forums for schools, teachers, pupils and parents was organised in all of our countries. The extent and intensity of the participation of REDCo members in conferences and public meetings dealing with religion in education increased considerably: we presented our project on 147 occasions in Europe, Asia, North America, Central America and Australia with a total outreach of about 40,000 participants. The number of articles and book chapters published by members of our consortium – about 100 – was also high. Plans were also being worked out to produce three films on REDCo, which could be used for public events and for seminars at schools and universities.

Third project year (March 2008 to March 2009)

During the final year, we gained a plethora of results from our empirical data working with both qualitative and quantitative approaches. With regard to qualitative research, at the beginning of the third year of REDCo, we published a comprehensive qualitative survey on the views of teenagers with regard to religious pluralism in school and society (Knauth et al. 2008). Throughout the third year, we continued our qualitative research work with regard to classroom interaction and the role of teachers in heterogeneous classes. Both avenues of research resulted in publications (Álvarez Veinguer et al. 2009; ter Avest et al. 2009).

With regard to quantitative research, the aim of our survey was to gain insight into the personal views of pupils on and their experiences with religion, into the social dimension of religion in their lives and into RE in school. The analysed data were published in book form. Our questions for the quantitative questionnaire were developed on the basis of our qualitative results. Throughout all REDCo countries, we deployed a total of more than 8000 completed questionnaires, so that we were able to create a solid basis for our research. The results showed that in all our countries, acceptance of religious heterogeneity is the mainstream position among youngsters in the 14- to 16-year age group. Nonetheless, the school has a central role to play in promoting learning about and from religions. This is necessary, as many of the pupils have wrong information or prejudices about other religions. Nevertheless, our findings are clear. Irrespective of their national and religious identity, pupils in Europe are open to a dialogue with different religious and cultural positions (see Valk et al. 2009).

We applied the following theoretical approaches intensively: the approaches of 'neighbour religions', 'citizenship education', 'non-foundational education', 'identity formation' and the 'interpretive approach'. Regarding 'neighbour religions', there was a development away from studying 'world religions' at a spatial and temporal distance and towards a concentration on the cultural and religious plurality in the home region or country. The commonly held opinion now is that it is vital for children from different world religions not to become 'alien' to each other, with all the stereotyping and divisions that entails, but rather to be seen as fellow humans and neighbours. The issue of citizenship education was also given considerable attention during the project. One of the reasons for this is, of course, that the diversity of political and societal systems had to be taken into account in terms of contextualising a particular country but also to be viewed from a comparative perspective. The explicit support of all REDCo researchers for non-dogmatic, open and dynamic theoretical approaches towards addressing world views and religions in an educational context is clearly expressed in our research. Non-foundational education stresses the value of personal expression and dialogue for personal religious identity formation and emphasises a concern for the otherness of the 'other' as a core element of every form of RE. This is especially the case with regard to the concept of religious identity formation. Using the latest insights from developmental education and developmental psychology, the religious identity development of youngsters in the 14- to 16-year age group was theoretically conceptualised in the very apt terms of exploration and commitment (identity formation). The debate about the interpretive approach as a common theoretical stimulus was continued thoroughly and productively. The key concepts of the interpretive approach were used in field research, in method development and in data analysis as well as in pedagogy.

In addition to the research with students, the Dutch team organised a study of teachers' responses religious diversity in Europe, which included some biographical study in six of the eight REDCo countries. The findings were published as a book (van der Want et al. 2009) and in various articles and book chapters.

With regard to dissemination, in addition to publishing more than 100 academic articles and even more presentations at conferences worldwide, we used three creative instruments and organised two especially high-level public events.

Our special instruments of dissemination work were three films produced on our REDCo work: one provides a condensed impression of the overall work, one is focused on classroom interaction in Europe and the last one presents a case-study from one of the members of the consortium. As elements for exhibitions, we also produced 14 roll-up displays based on our research results. Last, but not least, we formulated policy recommendations, which show the main results of our research in relation to requirements of European and international organisations as well as educational institutions at European as well as a national level.

We also had the opportunity to organise two high-level public events: one took place on 3 December 2008 at the European Parliament in Brussels (Weisse et al. 2009a). Commissioner Jan Figel gave an introduction, Member of the European Parliament, Vural Oeger, welcomed the REDCo researchers and three speakers from REDCo (Weisse, Jackson and Willaime) had the opportunity to present our findings. More than 120 people attended that gathering. The various presentations can be read on the REDCo website. The other event took place on 19 March 2009 at the Council of Europe in Strasbourg (Weisse et al. 2009b). The Director-General of Education, Gabriella Battaini-Dragoni, introduced the theme with a very positive acknowledgement of REDCo, and we once more had the chance to present our findings.

Overall research results and publications

Our project carried out joint, mixed methods research on RE in eight European countries simultaneously for the first time. Up to the end of our project in March 2009, we had successfully carried out research in the following fields:

- Addressing the increasingly urgent question of how dialogue between cultures and religions can be fostered and gaps bridged in the context of religion in education, including identifying effective pedagogical approaches and ways of dealing with religious conflict in educational settings.
- Formulating a view of the possibilities and limits of interreligious dialogue at the conceptual and empirical levels, with particular (though not exclusive) reference to the 14–16 age range.
- Combining national studies, with very different profiles, with agreed theoretical, methodological and thematic approaches from the outset.
- Including research and development partners in schools and maintaining dialogue with and providing information for stakeholders in our education systems, including various religious groups, the general public, the media and politicians.

Our work shows the value of exploring our theme in joint analytical publications. All in all, six books were published on the main results, by REDCo members, including a book specifically on the parts of the research dealing with aspects of Islam and another that dealt with the research on teachers.

The six books are:

Jackson et al. 2007. *Religion and education in Europe: Developments, contexts and debates.*

Knauth et al. 2008. *Encountering religious pluralism in school and society – A qualitative study of teenage perspectives in Europe.*

ter Avest et al. 2009. *Dialogue and conflict on religion. Studies of classroom interaction in European countries.*

Álvarez Veinguer et al. 2009. *Islam in education in European countries – Pedagogical concepts and empirical findings.*

Valk et al. 2009. *Teenagers' perspectives on the role of religion in their lives, schools and societies. A European quantitative study.*

Van der Want et al. 2009. *Teachers responding to religious diversity in Europe.*

Apart from these generic books, several national publications were produced. Some of these concentrated on REDCo results in a particular country (Béraud and Willaime 2009; Jozsa, Knauth, and Weisse 2009; Schihalejev 2010), while the Warwick Community of Practice book extended REDCo's work to include different action research studies in combination with the key concepts of the interpretive approach (Ipgrave, Jackson, and O'Grady 2009). This community of practice work continues to be extended by the Norwegian REDCo team.

During the third project year, we recorded an even higher research and dissemination output than within the first two years of the REDCo project. We wrote 26 reports, 21 of them deliverables and five of them milestones. In addition to the five books with the project results in whose production all partners were involved, several more were published of special analyses written by members of REDCo with reference to our research. In terms of dissemination, we continued our presentations in many parts of the world, produced three films on REDCo, one exhibition and wrote more than 100 articles in journals and books. All of our research results are focused in our policy recommendations, which were thoroughly discussed during the last months of our REDCo project and in a final plenary meeting at Klingenthal (near Strasbourg) on 19 March 2009.

European perspectives

As mentioned above, we formulated policy recommendations on the basis of the findings of REDCo. Our research results underlined the great relevance of dialogue at classroom level. This has been the reason for our suggestion to enhance the opportunities for dialogue and discussion between different religious and non-religious world views in the classroom.

On the basis of our research in the REDCo project, the following points from our policy recommendations should be taken into account both when addressing different national contexts and at the European level:

(1) *Encouragement for peaceful coexistence*: Education policy development and implementation need to focus on the transformation of abstract (passive) tolerance into practical (active) tolerance.

(2) *Promotion of diversity management*: Citizenship education tends to focus on homogeneity, but in turning from passive to active tolerance, it is necessary to value religious diversity at school as well as at university level.

(3) *Including both religious and non-religious world views*: School is a place where all students' right to freedom of religion or belief must be respected. Religion is important to some of the students, and their beliefs must not be allowed to become an obstacle to their academic progress.

(4) *Professional competence*: No changes can be made without education of the professionals and the required competence on their part. Such education would be needed both at initial training level and in the continuing professional development of teachers.[2]

Beyond the individual study results, our project opens perspectives for international research. Our findings can put the differences between countries and their main emphases into sharper profile, thus improving our understanding of the path to developing a European identity. 'Identity' must be understood as plural and dialogical rather than monolithic (Peukert 2005). The need for this is evident not least from the appeals from various European institutions. Developing education for democracy has been a vital issue in more than 50 years of history of the Council of Europe. Within this context, education for democratic citizenship and, more recently, intercultural and interreligious education have been playing increasingly important roles. As the most important examples I refer to the *White paper on intercultural dialogue* (Council of Europe 2008a) and the Recommendation CM/Rec(2008)12 of the Committee of Ministers to member states on the dimension of religions and non-religious convictions within intercultural education (Council of Europe 2008b), both endorsed by the Foreign Ministers of the 47 member states of the Council of Europe. These documents emphasise the great importance and relevance of learning about religions as part of intercultural education and of interreligious dialogue: 'Interreligious dialogue can contribute to a broader consensus in a society on the solutions of social problems' (Council of Europe 2008a, 23).

This is particularly important for school students still in the process of forming their opinions, for whom encounters with people of different religions and philosophies can be an important step towards:

- respecting other positions (even in disagreement) rather than privileging one's own opinion,
- not regarding religion and culture as monolithic but rather as determined by a multiplicity of human beings in daily practice and changeable, and
- establishing bars against the ideological abuse of religion and its instrumentalisation for political conflict.

For the future development of all countries, in Europe and elsewhere, the peaceful coexistence of people with different cultural, religious and philosophical backgrounds is not only a social necessity. In modern states, its influence extends well into the economic sphere. A 'creative class', necessary to boost economic development, is more and more attracted by regions where differences of all sorts have become part of daily life (Florida 2003). Thus, our aim of fostering and/or introducing the study of religion into public school curricula in Europe not only offers the potential for better interpersonal relations; it can also contribute to the overall pace of innovation and growth of society. Political and societal stakeholders should utilise this experience to open up schools for the growing awareness that dialogue is a most fascinating issue.

Our goal in our REDCo research was to contribute to intercultural understanding, the respect for otherness and coexistence with the help of interreligious dialogue in the public schools of Europe. We focused our research on

Europe, being aware of the fact that the new discussion on religion in education has world-wide dimensions.

The contributions in this publication show some of the analyses created in the course of our REDCo project. They can be seen as examples of our research and may provide stimuli for further discussion.

Notes

1. Wolfram Weisse [University of Hamburg (Germany)], Robert Jackson [University of Warwick (GB) (UK)], Jean-Paul Willaime [Sorbonne University, Paris (F)], Siebren Miedema and Ina ter Avest [Free University Amsterdam], Cok Bakker [University of Utrecht (the Netherlands)], Geir Skeie [University of Stavanger (Norway)], Pille Valk [University of Tartu (Estonia)], Muhammad Kalisch and Dan-Paul Jozsa [University of Münster (Germany)], Vladimir Fedorov [University of St Petersburg (Russia)] and Gunther Dietz and Aurora Alvarez Veinguer [University of Granada (Spain)].
2. See the policy recommendations of REDCo in eight languages on webpage: www.redco.uni-hamburg.de.

References

Álvarez Veinguer, A., G. Dietz, D.-P. Jozsa, and T. Knauth, eds. 2009. *Islam in education in European countries: Pedagogical concepts and empirical findings.* Münster: Waxmann.

Béraud, C. and J.-P. Willaime, eds. 2009. *Les jeunes, l'école et la religion.* [Adolescents, school and religion] Montrouge Cedex: Bayard.

Council of Europe. 2008a. *White paper on intercultural dialogue: 'Living together as equals with dignity'.* Strasbourg: Council of Europe Publishing.

Council of Europe. 2008b. Recommendation CM/Rec(2008)12 of the Committee of Ministers to member states on the dimension of religions and non-religious convictions within intercultural education (adopted by the Committee of Ministers on 10 December 2008 at the 1044th meeting of the Ministers' Deputies). https://wcd.coe.int//ViewDoc.jsp?Ref=CM/Rec(2008)12&Language=lanEnglish&Ver=original&BackColorInternet=DBDCF2&BackColorIntranet=FDC864&BackColorLogged=FDC864

Florida, R. 2003. Cities and the creative class. *City & Community* 2, no. 1: 3–19.

Habermas, J. 2005. *Zwischen naturalismus und religion. Philosophische aufsätze.* Frankfurt am Main: Suhrkamp. [English translation: Habermas, J. 2008. *Between naturalism and religion. Philosophical essays.* Cambridge: Polity Press.]

Hasenclever, A. 2003. Geteilte werte – gemeinsamer frieden? Überlegungen zu zivilisierenden kraft von religionen und glaubensgemeinschaften [Shared values –

common peace? Reflections on the power of religions and religious communities in civil society]. In *Friedenspolitik, ethische grundlagen internationaler beziehungen,* ed. H. Küng and D. Senghaas, 288–318. München: Piper.

Ipgrave, J., R. Jackson, and K. O'Grady, eds. 2009. *Religious education research through a community of practice: Action research and the interpretive approach.* Münster: Waxmann.

Jackson, R. 1997. *Religious education: An interpretive approach.* London: Hodder and Stoughton.

Jackson, R. ed. 2003. *International perspectives on citizenship, education and religious diversity.* London: RoutledgeFalmer.

Jackson, R. 2004. *Rethinking religious education and plurality: Issues in diversity and pedagogy.* London: RoutledgeFalmer.

Jackson, R. 2011. The interpretive approach as a research tool: Inside the REDCo Project. *British Journal of Religious Education* 33, no. 2: 187–206.

Jackson, R., S. Miedema, W. Weisse, and J.-P. Willaime, eds. 2007. *Religion and education in Europe: Developments, contexts and debates.* Münster: Waxmann.

Jozsa, D.-P., T. Knauth, and W. Weisse, eds. 2009. *Religionsunterricht, dialog und konflikt. Analysen im kontext Europas* [Religious education, dialogue and conflict. Analyses in the context of Europe]. Münster: Waxmann.

Knauth, T., D.-P. Jozsa, G. Bertram-Troost, and J. Ipgrave, eds. 2008. *Encountering religious pluralism in school and society – A qualitative study of teenage perspectives in Europe.* Münster: Waxmann.

Miedema, S. 2004. Beyond foundationalism. A plea for a new normativity in the philosophy of religious education. In *Towards a European perspective on religious education,* ed. R. Larsson and C. Gustavsson, 36–45. Stockholm: Artos & Norma.

Moore, D.L. 2007. *Overcoming religious illiteracy. A cultural studies approach to the study of religion in secondary education.* New York: Palgrave Macmillan.

OSCE. 2007. *Toledo guiding principles on teaching about religions and beliefs in public schools.* Warsaw: Organisation for Security and Co-operation in Europe, Office for Democratic Institutions and Human Rights. http://www.osce.org/item/28314.html

Peukert, H. 2005. Identität [Identity]. In *Neues Handbuch theologischer Grundbegriffe* [New handbook of basic theological terms], ed. P. Eicher, 184–92. München: Random House.

Schihalejev, O. 2010. *From indifference to dialogue? Estonian young people, the school and religious diversity.* Münster: Waxmann.

Skeie, G. 2001. Citizenship, identity politics and religious education. In *Towards religious competence: Diversity as a challenge for education in Europe,* ed. H.-G. Heimbrock, C. Th. Scheilke, and P. Schreiner, 237–52. Münster: Lit Verlag.

ter Avest, I., D.-P. Jozsa, T. Knauth, J. Rosón, and G. Skeie, eds. 2009. *Dialogue and conflict on religion. Studies of classroom interaction in European countries.* Münster: Waxmann.

UNESCO and Institute of Oriental Studies. 2007. *Intercultural dialogue and cultural diversity.* Almaty: Daik Press.

Valk, P., G. Bertram-Troost, M. Friederici, and C. Béraud, eds. 2009. *Teenagers' perspectives on the role of religion in their lives, schools and societies: A European quantitative study.* Münster: Waxmann.

Van der Want, A., C. Bakker, I. ter Avest, J. Everington, eds. 2009. *Teachers responding to religious diversity in Europe.* Münster: Waxmann.

Weisse, W. 2003. Difference without discrimination: Religious education as a field of learning for social understanding? In *International perspectives on citizenship, education and religious diversity,* ed. R. Jackson, 191–208. London: Routledge.

Weisse, W. 2007. The European Research Project on Religion and Education 'REDCo'. An introduction. In *Religion and education in Europe: Developments, contexts and debates,* ed. R. Jackson, S. Miedema, W. Weisse, and J.-P. Willlaime, 9–25. Münster: Waxmann.

Weisse, W., R. Jackson, C. Rudelt, and J.P. Willaime, eds. 2009a. Religion in education – A contribution to dialogue or a factor of conflict? The REDCo-project. Paper presented at the European Parliament, December 2008, in Brussels. www.redco.uni-hamburg.de

Weisse, W., I. ter Avest, G. Battaini-Dragoni, J. Ipgrave, C. Rudelt, and J.-P. Willaime, eds. 2009b. The relevance of interreligious dialogue for intercultural understanding. The White Paper 'Living together as Equals in Dignity' of the Council of Europe and the principal findings of the European research project REDCo. Documentation of a public event in the Council of Europe, March 2009, in Strasbourg. www.redco.uni-hamburg.de

Willaime, J.-P. 2008. *Le retour du religieux dans la sphère publique. Vers une laicité de reconnnaissance et de dialogue.* [The re-emergence of religion in the public sphere. Towards a laic system of recognition and dialogue]. Lyon: Editions Olivétan.

Young people's talk about religion and diversity: a qualitative study of Norwegian students aged 13–15

Marie von der Lippe

Department of Archaeology, History, Cultural Studies and Religion, University of Bergen, N-5020 Bergen, Norway

This paper focuses on how young people talk about religion and diversity in a multicultural society. More specifically, it focuses on how students speak about Islam and Muslims. In analysing interviews with students, a main interest has been to examine the relationship between the students' speech and dominant discourses in Norwegian society represented in the media and public debates. This paper has the following structure. First, the theoretical basis of the research is explained and how Gerd Baumann's terms 'dominant' and 'demotic' discourse are understood and employed in this study. Then, the project is contextualised within the Norwegian debate about plurality. Further, methods and analysed data are presented. In the main analysis, there is a focus on some of the students' statements and the discourses they seem to activate. In conclusion, the consequences that the analysis has for school and the subject of religion in general, and for religious education teachers in particular, are discussed briefly.

Introduction

How do young people talk about religion in a multicultural society, *what* are they talking about and *why* do they talk the way they do? This paper attempts to answer these questions through an analysis of interviews with students aged 13–15 years. The focus is on discourses that students appear to be drawing on: one marked by openness and a mainly positive view of the multicultural society; and the other marked by scepticism and sometimes fears of immigrants in general, and Islam and Muslims in particular. The research questions raised in this paper are: Which discourses seem to be available for students when talking about religion and diversity? How do the students draw upon these discourses in the interviews? Which discourses seem to be dominant and what correlation is there between students' statements and discourses at the macro level? I use discourse analysis as a theoretical and methodological approach in order to relate the students' conversations at the individual level to more overarching discourses in Norwegian society, and my main conceptual tools are 'dominant' and 'demotic' discourse, based on Baumann's research (1996).

Theoretical basis

Dominant and demotic discourses

In his ethnographic study of a multi-ethnic district in London, Southall, Gerd Baumann investigates how people switch between different discourses when they talk about culture, community and various identities. Instead of focusing on one ethnic group, Baumann (1996) highlights the interaction between different ethnic groups and individuals in the same district. He shows how the terms 'culture' and 'community' hide differences across groups and individuals. Although residents use the terms, the conceptual content varies in two systematic and different ways. Partly, they draw on a dominant discourse related to the cultural community, and partly they establish an alternative discourse where the relationship between culture and community is problematised, and sometimes even rejected. This alternative discourse is what Baumann calls a 'demotic' discourse (1996, 10).[1]

The dominant discourse related to culture and religion exists both on macro and micro levels. It is used, amplified and reproduced, in the media and by politicians. However, in some cases, Baumann believes that the residents of Southall, deliberately and in their own self-interest, also use the dominant discourse and identify themselves with familiar categories such as Sikhs, Muslims, Punjabis or whites. In other situations, the categories are used much more flexibly, when the residents take part in other communities across ethnic and cultural divisions. Baumann ascribes to his informants a dual discursive competence, where culture and community are defined and redefined based on what belongings they want to emphasise. Cultural and ethnic categories and so-called 'imagined communities' are sometimes maintained, while in other cases they are dismissed as useless categories (1996, 190). This gives reason to assume that the informants not only are constituted by the dominant discourse, but also appear to be agents who can change this discourse by denying a particular relationship between culture and community. A key question is to what extent the participants have the opportunity actively to participate in discourse production. In order to examine these opportunities and the relationship between actors and structures, discourse theory is a useful approach.

Discourse theory

Baumann uses the term 'discourse' well aware of the vagueness of the concept, and shares Lutz and Abu-Lughod's (1990) understanding and use of the term: 'One is to help focus the analysis of language and other social practices on pragmatics, rather than semantics, and the other is to relate these "large-scale pragmatics" to the efficacy of power relations' (Baumann 1996, 10). Discourse is thus related both to language acts and to structural power relations. According to Jørgensen and Phillips (1999), there is no real agreement about what a discourse is or how to analyse discourses. They suggest a minimum definition where discourse is understood as 'a certain way to speak about and understand the world (or part of the world)' (1999, 4). Different discourse theories share the understanding that representations of reality are constructed through language, and that some of these representations stand out as more obvious and 'natural' than others. What Baumann calls 'the dominant discourse' is an example of this.[2] Discourses are closely linked to historical, social and political conditions, and only effective within specific and limited social space. The purpose of discourse analysis is usually to identify such 'natural' ways of talking about the world, and to reveal the exercise of power legitimised by these discourses (Gullestad 2002, 47). It also strives to illuminate how social actors shape and are shaped by the discourses, and how knowledge, identity and social practice are transformed and reproduced both at the individual (micro) and the societal (macro) level.[3]

This dialectic is not only to be found in prejudiced statements, but is also reflected in the language of people who stand out as having little prejudice, as will be shown in the later analysis. The point is that the dominant discourse serves as a backdrop of many utterances (Vassenden 2008, 49). Put simply, the dominant discourses are shaped at a structural level (media, politicians, etc.), whereas the demotic discourses are formulated at the individual level, based on a kind of everyday experience, expressed in an everyday language. Seen from a discourse analytical approach, this sociological division into a micro level and a macro level is appropriate, particularly because it may show the relationships between the different levels of speech. As language users, we are social actors who speak both as community members, members of various groups and communities, and out of personal experience. Utterances can therefore be analysed at different levels, and seem to belong to different discourses. In order to analyse the discourses the students draw on and the repertoires that are available to them, it is, therefore, necessary to say something more about the national debate about the multicultural Norwegian society.

The Norwegian debate

Debates related to Norway as a multicultural society have long been politicised and polemical. In a recent report, controversies in the field are analysed and largely related to the interpretation of racism and discrimination in Norwegian society (Rogstad and Midtbøen 2009). When events in the public sphere are interpreted as expressions of racism or discrimination, sharp debates often occur, and the boundaries between academia, politics, morals and experiences are challenged. In the report, Rogstad and Midtbøen discuss 'the double-edged refusal of the new Norway' (2009, 1). On one hand, there is a majority population that discusses and understands itself as open and welcoming and definitely not racist, but with some pretty clear ideas about so-called Norwegian values. On the other hand, we find a diverse minority population who seldom claim that they are subjected to racism, but where the life stories of individuals tell another story. The Norwegian debate about racism within the social sciences has been little oriented towards international research. To the extent that the scientific debate has been concentrated around prejudice and 'race', this has largely been tied to a traditional concept of racism[4] (Gullestad 2002, 152). Gullestad has criticised research colleagues, politicians and the media for producing and maintaining the notions of 'us' and 'the other' as two disparate entities, and finds it to be particularly important that the majority population is willing to see itself as the majority, in order to advance the discussion about multicultural Norway (2002).[5]

From my point of view, there are several, and not just one dominant discourse prevailing in the Norwegian public debate. While Baumann writes about *the* dominant discourse, I will apply the term 'dominant discourses' to indicate that there are parallel and competing hegemonic discourses that influence individuals on the micro level. This understanding forms part of the background for my investigation of how young people talk about religion and religious diversity, and in particular Islam and Muslims. The point of my analysis is to show how discourses on the structural level in various ways are included in the students' repertoires and frames of interpretation.

Sampling and data

My research is based on interview material that was collected in 2007/2008 as part of the REDCo project, a large European project related to young students' perceptions about religion and diversity in multicultural societies.[6] In addition to two comprehensive surveys where around 850 Norwegian students in total participated,[7] I conducted semi-structured interviews with a smaller sample of students. The following discussion is based on data acquired from a total of 20 individual interviews with students aged 13–15 years. The students come from four different schools in Bergen (three public and a Christian private school) and have Christian (8), Muslim (6) and non-religious backgrounds (6). The sample consists of 11 girls and 9 boys with various national and ethnic backgrounds (Norwegian, Iraqi, Kurdish, Somali, Philippine, Yemeni, Creole, Zanzibaran and some with mixed Norwegian and non-Norwegian backgrounds). A theme-based interview guide was used to ensure that important topics and questions were addressed in a semi-structured way. Thus, it was possible to follow up many sidetracks during the interview and made it work more like a conversation. The intention was that students should be encouraged to give their perceptions and opinions about the various topics, and also have an opportunity to influence the conversation development (von Brömssen

2003, 114–5).[8] This strategy is common in discourse analytical work, where the purpose is precisely to uncover patterns and relations, but also ambiguities, contradictions and competing discourses activated by the informants. The overall theme for the conversations, was their perceptions and attitudes towards religion and religious diversity, divided into several sub-topics. A main finding was that religious diversity was mainly related to Islam and Muslims. In the following I have used both shorter and longer excerpts from conversations with three students, not as representatives of young students in general, but in order to illustrate my analysis of emerging dominant discourses.[9]

Examples from the student interviews

'They are all a bit racist – I am not!'

The example that follows is an excerpt from an interview with Rachel (15 years).[10] Rachel has a white majority background. She is a Christian charismatic and goes to a Christian private school. Unlike many of the other students at her school, Rachel has many friends outside of school with different ethnic, religious and cultural backgrounds. According to Rachel, there are many racists in Norway, and she also describes her own parents as prejudiced and racist:

> Rachel: There are very many racists, for example, my mother and my father. They are really bad. I will not even say what they do. But, I'm just glad that I am not like them. They are all a bit racist – I am not!
> Marie: No. Can you give some examples of what they say?
> Rachel: Yes, mom, she said, it was like, you know those who wear a lot of clothes. Then my mom says, well there walks a whole lot of nice curtain fabric. Things like that. It is completely unnecessary.

Rachel here refers to an episode with her mother a few days before the interview, when they were in Oslo to attend a meeting within the Pentecostal movement. The mother then complained about all the foreigners in the capital, and commented on a Muslim woman's dress. Rachel experienced the situation as uncomfortable. She did not share her mother's scepticism, and has repeatedly tried to get her to change her opinion, but according to Rachel her mother does not want to listen. She believes one of the reasons why she and her mother have different views on issues surrounding multi-culture can be related to her mother's lack of personal experiences with difference, while Rachel has many friends with diverse backgrounds:

> Rachel: I've seen that they are normal people; they can be just as Norwegian as the rest of us. Just because they have a different skin colour it does not mean they have less value. But I do not think mom understands that.
> Marie: Does she know your friends?
> Rachel: She knows at least who they are, but she doesn't like them really.

The point here is not whether the mother's statement is racist or not, or whether Rachel's mother is a racist. The main issue is how Rachel is positioning herself: 'They are all a bit racist – I am not!'. Calling others and their views racist is often used strategically in political debates to identify the opponent, and to promote one's own political views (Gullestad 2002, 143). In recent times, however, several examples from media and public debates have shown that it is almost impossible to accuse anyone of racism in Norwegian public discourse.[11] It is therefore rare to hear statements like Rachel's. At the same time, expressions like 'I am not a racist, but…'[12] are frequently used to legitimise criticism of immigrants, Muslims, etc. without being branded as racist. This discourse is found among politicians and academics, as well as among ordinary people.

In the second quotation Rachel explains why she is more open towards diversity than her mother, by referring to the fact that she has seen that 'they' (friends) are 'normal' people and can be just as Norwegian as 'us'. 'Norwegian' is here understood both as something homogeneous and also as the general norm. Two discourses are reflected in this; one where Rachel rejects what she perceives as her mother's racist attitudes, and another where her own language is communicating a certain ethnocentrism; 'the others' are measured up against 'the Norwegian'. Whiteness, in contrast to other skin colours, is here somehow connected to Norwegianess. In a similar manner to the way masculinity and heterosexuality is understood as 'the normal', whiteness seems to have a hegemonic and privileged position. This is in line with so-called *whiteness studies*, which have contributed to the understanding of the white majority (see, among others, Doane and Bonilla-Silva 2003; Frankenberg 1997).

Rachel appears to be trapped between racist and anti-racist discourses. This becomes even clearer later in the interview when she is asked if she perceives Bergen as a multicultural city. She answers 'yes, but not as much as in Oslo'. She finds the number of immigrants in the capital to be almost frightening, and says:

> It has sort of become like the capital of Africa, or something. Or the capital of Iraq. Yes, yes, if Iraq, Baghdad, suddenly had more Norwegians than Iraqis, it would have been wrong. It had become imbalanced. Of course one thing is that we have different cultures here, but not so many that we are outnumbered by foreigners. I do not like that.

Here Rachel draws on a common populist discourse where the number of 'foreigners' is frequently used as an argument in the political debate about the negative effects that immigration has on society and Norwegian values, often exemplified with the increasing of crime and so-called Islamisation.[13] When Rachel was asked to explain what she considered to be Norwegian, she answered that Norwegianness was related to the number of Norwegians. Like her mother, she thinks that there are too many foreigners in Oslo: 'It has sort of become the capital of Africa or something.' In the first quotation Rachel's intention is to distance herself from her mother's racist remarks, and she draws on an anti-racist discourse. She is also activating a more demotic discourse where she refers to her own positive experiences with diversity. In the last quotation, however, Rachel draws on a common populist discourse where the numbers of immigrants is seen to threaten Norwegian society. Unconsciously, Rachel reinforces images of the 'the other' as the other, even when 'they' are seen as equal to 'us'. In this way, the polarisation between 'us' and 'them' is reproduced, even when Rachel clearly wants to distance herself from what she perceives as racism. There is a widespread trend to present the dominant in-group (majority population) in positive terms, whereas the dominated out-group (minority population) consistently is described more negatively (van Dijk 2005).

'It is not true that all Muslims are terrorists'

Christian (15 years) has a white majority background. He calls himself an atheist, but has no other relation to this category except not believing in God. He is an extrovert teenager, and has many friends both in and outside the average public school he goes to. His friends as well as other acquaintances come from different places in the city, and have various backgrounds, including Muslim. He seldom speaks with them about religion. Part of what Christian says may appear as contradictory and ambiguous, but it may also reflect that he is trying out different positions during the interview and by this he employs different discourses. Christian reads newspapers every day and sometimes he watches the television news:

Christian: We get a lot of information from the media and things like that. For my part, I read the newspapers almost every day, and sometimes I watch the news too.

Marie: But do you think that the media always gives the right image?

Christian: That is not true. It's not true that all Muslims are terrorists for example.

Marie: No.

Christian: Sometimes they [media] give that impression. 'And today there was a Muslim suicide bomber, which blew up 10 people in the air.' And things like that, and ... but...

Marie: What comes to your mind when you hear those things?

Christian: It's not okay. Eh ... I can't understand what they give to Allah by blowing themselves up in the air, somehow. I can't see the point in it. It is really just insane.

Marie: Does it make you more, or does it give you any prejudices? Do they destroy in a way?

Christian: Yes against those people who do it, but not against other Muslims. OK, there are some Muslims who are like that, but that does not mean that everyone is like that.

Christian's statement is an example of how links between media, Islam and terrorism are formulated on the micro level. Christian believes the media to be an important source of information, but, at the same time, much of this information gives a distorted image of reality: 'it's not true that all Muslims are terrorists.' According to Christian, there is a disparity between representations in the media and 'facts'. But rather than elaborate on this discrepancy, Christian is more concerned to say what he thinks about Muslim suicide bombers: 'I can't understand what they bring to Allah.'[14] He qualifies the statement by adopting so-called enhancers: 'I can't see the point in it' and finally: 'it is really just insane.' Here Christian is giving an assessment of Muslim suicide bombers where he connects a certain type of action and behaviour with a particular religion, which is inconsistent with his own norms and values. By doing this, he contributes indirectly to a positive self-presentation. At the same time, Christian shows that he is aware of the stereotype he presents by moderating his statement: 'OK, there are some Muslims who are like that, but that does not mean that everyone is like that.' Christian demonstrates that he knows where the stereotype is coming from, and that he will not fully accept it. At the same time, he is primarily relating the negative actions to Islam, and not to political conflicts, for example.

Negative portrayals of Muslims in the media have been dominant for a long time. Christian is clearly aware of this, by criticising the media, but he is also affected by it. In contrast to Rachel, Christian does not express a particular position, but seems to draw on both dominant and demotic discourses simultaneously: (1) Muslims are responsible for negative actions and (2) Muslims are not a homogeneous group. It is well known and documented that the media are an important opinion producer in society. In a study of majority Norwegians in the multi-ethnic residential areas in Oslo, the sociologist, Vassenden, found that several of his informants were aware of how the media greatly influenced their opinions and attitudes towards ethnic minorities, immigrants and Muslims (2008, 254). As in the example of Christian, this illustrates how narratives on the macro level are reappearing at micro level through linguistic representations, even though the actors are highly aware of it.

'In a way skin colour has been replaced by religion'

Aisha has a black African minority background. She is a Muslim and, during the interview; she repeats several times that she is proud of her African background, skin colour and religion. She has many friends from different backgrounds, and spends a lot of her spare time together with friends in the city centre. She believes there should be room for different Muslim identities, and says: 'You do not have to be really, really, really Muslim, just try to be a Muslim.' Aisha wants the freedom to define who she is – both in the role of girl, Muslim and African. She does not feel Norwegian, but also has no desire or need to be Norwegian. In the interview with Aisha, the conceptions of 'us' and 'them' have switched positions. Whereas Muslims for Rachel and Christian belong to the category 'them', Aisha is part of the Muslim 'us'. On the question whether she experiences prejudices against Muslims, as a Muslim herself, Aisha responds:

> Yes, for example when they talk about Taliban or people who kill themselves and stuff, it is very much like Muslims have done it. Why should you say Muslims? It bothers me a bit. Why should you say Muslims? There was a man, OK fine, he was a Muslim. But it was not just because he was Muslim, that he did it. He did it because he wanted to do it. He would do it for his country, right. Bombard anything, for example. But I do not understand why they should take the religion. If he had been a Christian they would not have said a Christian, da-da-da … I think people are very much against Muslims. And they should not be because they do not know if I had been a Christian, and I had a bomb and killed me. So they had not written a Christian man killed himself … They had said that a man killed … but of course when it is a Muslim they take a Muslim man, da-da-da . I think that is very sad. Because it is not about the religion when you kill yourself or take a bomb or … It does not say in the Qur'an that one should take a bomb in 2007 and kill yourself, and … it's just nonsense. It is in the Qur'an, it says that you should not kill yourself, so what they are doing is illegal. So I think it's stupid that they connect this with religion.
>
> Marie: Yes. What can be done, then, to reduce prejudices?
>
> Aisha: You know what? I don't know, but what might have helped is that those who are Muslims must cease to let people have reason to talk about Muslims. For example, they need to stop blowing themselves up, what good is it in it? To kill others? There are people, innocent people who die. There are innocent people who die. They must think of that too. And for example planes, many things like that. What is it good for? Kill people? It's not good, you do not kill people. It's illegal to kill people. So they must not give people reason somehow. They must open their eyes and then … be whatever they want to be.

As the quotation demonstrates, the question is no longer about utterances about Muslims as 'the other', but how Aisha expresses her perceptions of how other people are talking about her and her likes. In other words, it reveals some sort of 'perceived discourses', where Aisha is analysing how 'the others' (non-Muslims) are talking about Muslims. As with Christian's statement, Aisha refers to the Taliban and suicide bombers, and in this way she activates the same dominant discourses. However, Aisha's own Muslim background places her utterances in a different context. The way Aisha expresses herself clearly shows that the theme engages her personally. She repeats both whole sentences and words several times, and uses other amplifiers in the language like: 'I think people are very much against Muslims.' She also comes with statements like, 'I think this is very sad,' showing that she is really affected by the problem. Her statements can be read as a double criticism: one is aimed at how the Muslims are portrayed in the media and by the Norwegian majority population; the other is directed at Muslims who participate in violent actions.

In the first part of the quotation, Aisha criticises the media and the Norwegian majority population. She does not mention the media directly, but uses formulations like: 'why are you saying Muslims?' and 'they had not written'. The formulations refer to media expressions about Muslims, but the use of pronouns like 'you' and 'they' shows that the criticism is also directed towards the majority population more generally. Aisha is not only pointing to the existence of prejudices against Muslims, and that Muslims are associated with terrorism, but also reveals how these prejudices are expressed and reinforced through the language. According to Aisha, the media consistently mention Muslim identity, while Christian identity is omitted: 'So, they had not written a Christian man killed himself … They had said that a man killed … but of course when it is a Muslim so they take a Muslim man'. Aisha finds that in the media the classification as Muslim often is the only and overriding identity, but when Christian identity is mentioned, this is usually presented as just one of several identities. Thus, the category 'Muslim' appears to be less complex than the category 'Christian', and in this way dominant discourses about Muslims are reproduced.

In the second part of the quotation, Aisha does not know initially how to answer the question about whether there is something one can do to reduce prejudice. A little later she presents her second criticism – this time directed towards Muslims supporting terrorist attacks. In this, she confirms the dominant discourse (terrorist + Muslims = true). However, as with Christian, she is moderating the discourse by adding 'some Muslims'. At the same time, she denies that suicide bombings may be linked to Islam by referring to the prohibition against suicide in the Qur'an (Islam + suicide = forbidden). Whereas Christian links suicide bombings directly to the 'cause of Allah', Aisha rejects this link by referring to the Qur'an. She problematises the relationship between terrorism, suicide bombings and Islam, and tries to establish an alternative discourse in which these relationships are questioned and rejected through a deconstruction of the dominant discourses. This alternative discourse, where Aisha deconstructs Muslims as a unified group and denies the connections between Islam and terrorism, can be understood as a demotic discourse.

Unlike Rachel and Christian, Aisha is directly affected by the dominant discourses about Muslims and terrorism. She experiences prejudices that previously were directed at skin colour, which now have been replaced with prejudices against religion:

> People see us differently. See us in a negative way. And I think there must be an end to it. It is … In a way skin colour has been replaced by religion, to put it that way. So I think it's terrible.

This shift from classical racism based on biology and race theories to a new racism rooted in culture and religion, has also been emphasised in the academic debate about the multicultural society (see, among others, Eriksen 2001; Gullestad 2002; Jackson 1997, 2004). The new form of racism 'may include both people who are considered visibly different and people who are not considered visibly different, but whose culture and religion are deemed to be foreign' (Gullestad 2002, 149, my translation).[15] There is no reason to believe that Aisha refers to the academic discourse about racism and the new form of racism. Rather, she gives expression to a type of experience she possesses, where her religion, not her skin colour, is the one that stigmatises her. At the same time, Aisha says that she has experienced negative statements about her skin colour, and the turn from classical racism into a new form of racism should not be overstressed, but rather seen as two parallel discourses. One of Aisha's strategies to meet these prejudices is to emphasise that she is not Norwegian, but proud of being a black African Muslim girl in Norway. In a recent study of the interplay of ethnicity, race and religion among young people in Oslo, the sociologists Andersson and Vassenden (2009) found that whiteness tends to hide information about faith, whereas non-whiteness signifies 'religious'. Today, it is less legitimate to discriminate someone out of skin colour, while negative statements related to religion (in particular Islam) have become more common. At the same time, skin colour seems to be an indicator of whether someone is perceived as religious or not, and dark skin is often associated with Muslims. Thus, many Muslims are in danger of being stigmatised on the basis of both skin colour (race) and religion.

Discussion

The cultural sociologist, Michele Lamont, talks about different rhetorics in her analysis of how the terms 'racism' and 'anti-racism' are used in France and the USA (Lamont 2000). According to Lamont, who studied the situation of North African immigrants and African-Americans, the rhetorics of racism and anti-racism are framed in universalistic terms, and at the same time they are related to broader moral systems and to the wider cultural context in which these rhetorics are formulated. Comparing repertoires of arguments among workers in France and the USA, she analyses cultural differences in the two societies (2000, 26). In each society, a variety of arguments are used to describe 'the other' in either a racist or anti-racist way but, according to Lamont, there are also major differences in the cultural tools that the French and Americans have at their disposal (2000, 45). Whereas the respondents in the USA often explained racial differences in terms of biological, historical, economic and/or psychological characteristics, the French respondents were more likely to explain these differences with reference to cultural and religious variables. These repertoires exist in the cultures of which they are a part, and their views are based on the discourses which are available to them. This strongly correlates with my own findings, and support my statement that the young students' language, to a large extent, is influenced by the culture they are a part of, and that their different statements about Islam and Muslims are related to the cultural repertoires and discourses to which they have access.

Religion has largely been 'Islamicised' in the media and, not unexpectedly, Islam is in focus when the students are asked to talk about religious diversity and related topics. The fact that the students to some extent activate the same dominant discourses, regardless of ethnic, religious and cultural background, is perhaps more surprising, but supports the idea of hegemonic, dominant discourses in the society. In Norway, the media are clearly an important provider of cultural tools, and often tend to spark processes in which prejudices are amplified rather than analysed. The same trend is also visible in Norwegian politics and public debates. When it comes to Islam, prejudices are related to fundamentalism and terrorism, which in turn are related to religious and cultural practices. When students talk about Islam and Muslims, their language is characterised by dominant discourses, and they often, more or less consciously, switch between different discourses in the interviews. This shows how difficult it is to break with the dominant discourses, as showed in the case of Rachel, who wants to position herself as an anti-racist. Still, this does not mean that it is impossible to develop demotic discourses. At first glance, it appears that Aisha, like Christian, activates the same dominant discourses in which terrorism and suicide bombings are linked to Islam and Muslims. The micro-analysis of the interview shows, contrary to this, that Aisha is trying to deconstruct these connections. Probably there is more at stake here for Aisha as a Muslim, than for the two students with majority backgrounds, and therefore the need (and creativity) to find alternative ways to talk about Muslims is more crucial to her.

Conclusion

I have shown how students' talk about religion in multicultural Norway is related to overarching macro structures. Their language is to a large extent influenced by dominant discourses in Norwegian society. Young people meet these discourses mainly through the media and political debates, where Islam has been particularly focused in recent years. One particularly interesting finding is that, what may appear to be ambiguities, contradictions and competing discourses on the individual level, are established as a pattern when the interviews are seen as a whole. Further, Baumann's concepts of 'dominant' and 'demotic' discourses have been useful in the analysis of the various discourses among the students. However, one of the findings in my own material is that there seem to be a number of discourses at play when students talk about religion and religious diversity. It therefore seems appropriate to speak about 'multiple dominant discourses'. Baumann's positive view regarding the actors' agency and their ability to switch between dominant and demotic discourse for their own purposes is less supported by my data than in his study in Southall. I find more resonance in Fairclough's statement that there is an existent potential to change the structures, but at the same time, this potential should not be over-stressed (2003, 9).

I hope that my findings will contribute to academic understanding of social and cultural processes, but also be of interest for schools and educators in general, and teachers and researchers in religious education in particular, as they raise questions about how different religions and worldviews are represented in the media and public debates, as well as among students. The results from the research indicate that religious education should have a focus on how issues of religion and culture are represented in public media. If this knowledge is used in making students more aware of *how* they talk about others, *what* they talk about and *why* they talk like they do, it is also possible to make them aware of what consequences this may have for those affected by prejudices. Both teachers and researchers may contribute to developing and establishing alternative discourses,[16] by focusing more on students' own experiences with religious and cultural diversity. If negative stereotypes are not challenged in school, dominating images of 'the other' may easily be reproduced.

Notes

1. *Demotic*: popular, 'of the people'. The term refers to the ordinary, everyday, current form of a language, and pertaining to ordinary people.
2. Other terms for the same can be 'the established discourse' or 'the hegemonic discourse' (Laclau and Mouffe 2002). Gullestad (2002) uses the term 'national order' to describe a similar issue.
3. Norman Fairclough discusses this as a dialectical relationship and relates it to other social structures (Fairclough 2003), and also Teun A. van Dijk finds that discourses related to ethnic minority groups can be understood in this dual perspective between a micro and a macro level (van Dijk 1987).
4. The traditional concept of racism refers here to racism based on biology and former race theories.
5. Gullestad received strong reactions to her critique, especially from those who had been subject to her criticisms. One possible reason for these reactions may be that 'the real discomfort occurs when the responsibility is placed in the broader segments of the population, or, even more so, when responsibility located in the linguistic practices and interpretation framework shared by the entire population' (Hagelund 2004, 22, my translation).
6. Religion in Education: A Contribution to Dialogue or a factor of Conflict in transforming societies in European countries? (REDCo). The REDCo project was funded through the EC's 6 Framework Programme for the period 2006–2009.
7. The results of the surveys are published in *Encountering religious pluralism in school and society* (Knauth et al. 2008), and in *Teenagers' perspectives on the role of religion in their lives, school and society* (Valk et al. 2009). For more about the Norwegian results, see von der Lippe (2008) and Skeie and von der Lippe (2009).
8. In a reflective perspective, there is much to say about the interview situation, and the contents of the talks. To what extent can the students' statements be related to the expectations of the interview, how much do they want to give the 'right answers', how politically correct are their responses, etc. The format of this paper does however not provide room to expand these questions more here.
9. The quotations are translated from Norwegian into English, and mildly edited for clarity and readability.
10. All names of interviewees are anonymised.

11. The Norwegian law on racism, §135, was introduced in 1970 to prohibit discriminatory and hateful remarks in the public related to skin colour, ethnicity, nationality, religion or sexual orientation, but has rarely been used in Norwegian criminal law.
12. The Norwegian social scientist, Ottar Brox (1991), published his study *Jeg er ikke rasist, men ... Hvordan får vi våre meninger om innvandrere og innvandring* (I am not a racist, but ... How do we get our opinions about immigrants and immigration). Brox used a traditional definition of racism and found that few Norwegians are racists despite their negative attitudes towards immigrants. Their negative attitude was, according to Brox, not based on race but referred to immigrants' cultural and religious practices.
13. In a speech to the Norwegian Progress Party in 2009 at an executive committee meeting, the leader Siv Jensen warned against what she called 'sneaking Islamization' in the Norwegian society. This turned into an intense debate in the media where both politicians and academics attended the battle. See for example http://www.dagbladet.no/2009/02/21/nyheter/politikk/innenriks/frp/siv_jensen/4966977/
14. Another possible explanation is that my question, 'what comes to your mind when you hear those things?', is so imprecise formulated that Christian does not perceive that it is related to his perceptions of the media, but rather understands it as a question about what he thinks of suicide bombers.
15. Samuel Huntington's much discussed book *The clash of civilizations and the remaking of world order* (1996) can be considered as a typical example of 'the new racism' where cultural differences between the Western and Islamic world are considered to be so different that they stand out as incompatible.
16. See more on this topic in von der Lippe (2009).

References

Andersson, M., and A. Vassenden. 2009. The interplay of ethnicity, race and religion in an urban space. Paper presented at the 14th International Metropolis Conference. National responses to cultural diversity, September 15, in Copenhagen, Denmark.

Baumann, G. 1996. *Contesting culture.* Cambridge: University Press.

Brox, O. 1991. *Jeg er ikke rasist, men ... Hvordan får vi våre meninger om innvandrere og innvandring?* [I am not a racist, but ... How do we get our opinions about immigrants and immigration?]. Oslo: Gyldendal norsk forlag.

Doane, A., and E. Bonilla-Silva, eds. 2003. *White out: The continuing significance of racism.* London: Routledge.

Eriksen, T.H., ed. 2001. *Flerkulturell forståelse* [Multicultural understandings]. Oslo: Universitetsforlaget.

Fairclough, N. 2003. *Analysing discourse: Textual analysis for social research.* London/New York: Routledge.

Frankenberg, R., ed. 1997. *Displacing whiteness. Essays in social and cultural criticism.* Durham: Duke University Press.

Gullestad, M. 2002. *Det norske sett med nye øyne* [The Norwegion seen with new eyes]. Oslo: Universitetsforlaget.

Hagelund, A. 2004. Anstendighetens utside: 'Rasisme' i norsk innvandringspolitisk diskurs [The outside of decency: 'Racism' in Norwegian immigration policy discourse]. *Tidsskrift for Samfunnsforskning* 1, no. 45: 3–29.

Huntington, S.P. 1996. *The clash of civilization and the remaking of world order.* New York: Simon & Schuster.

Jackson, R. 1997. *Religious education: An interpretive approach.* London: Hodder and Stoughton.

Jackson, R. 2004. *Rethinking religious education and plurality: Issues in diversity and pedagogy.* London: RoutledgeFalmer.

Jørgensen, M.W., and L. Phillips. 1999. *Diskursanalyse som teori og metode* [Discourse analysis as theory and method]. Roskilde: Roskilde Universitetsforlag.

Knauth, T., D.P. Jozsa, G. Bertram-Troost, and J. Ipgrave, eds. 2008. *Encountering religious pluralism in school and society: A qualitative study of teenage perspectives in Europe.* Münster: Waxmann Verlag.

Laclau, E., and C. Mouffe. 2002. *Det radikale demokrati: Diskursteoriens politiske perspektiv* [The radical democracy: The discourse theoretical political perspective]. Roskilde: Roskilde Universitetsforlag.

Lamont, M. 2000. The rhetorics of racism and anti-racism in France and the United States. In *Rethinking comparative cultural sociology. Repertoires of evaluation of France and the United States*, ed. M. Lamont and L. Thévenot, 25–55. Cambridge: Cambridge University Press.

Lutz, C., and L. Abu-Lughod, eds. 1990. *Language and the politics of emotion.* Cambridge: Cambridge University Press.

Rogstad, J., and A. Midtbøen. 2009. *Rasisme og diskriminering: Begreper, kontroverser og nye perspektiver* [Racism and discrimination: Concepts, controversies and new perspectives]. Oslo: Norges forskningsråd.

Skeie, G., and M. von der Lippe. 2009. Does religion matter to young people in Norwegian schools? In *Teenagers perspectives' on the role of religion in their lives, schools and societies*, ed. P. Valk, G. Bertram-Trost, M. Friederici, and C. Beraud, 269–301. Münster: Waxmann Verlag.

Valk, P., G. Bertram-Trost, M. Friederici, and C. Beraud, eds. 2009. *Teenagers perspectives' on the role of religion in their lives, schools and societies.* Münster: Waxmann Verlag.

van Dijk, T.A. 1987. *Communicating racism: Ethnic prejudice in talk and thought.* Newbury Park: Sage.

van Dijk, T.A. 2005. Critical discourse analysis. In *The handbook of discourse analysis*, ed. D. Schiffrin, D. Tannen, and H.E. Hamilton, 352–71. Oxford: Blackwell.

Vassenden, A. 2008. *Flerkulturelle forståelsesformer: En studie av majoritetsnordmenn i multietniske boligområder* [Multicultural ways of understanding: A study of majority Norwegians in multiethnic neighbourhoods]. Oslo: Institutt for sosiologi og samfunnsgeografi. Det samfunnsvitenskapelige fakultet, University of Oslo.

von Brömssen, K. 2003. *Tolkningar, förhandlingar och tydstnader: Elevers tal om religion i det mångkulturella och postkoloniala rummet* [Interpretations, negotiations and silences: Pupils' talk about religion from within multicultural and post colonial spaces]. Acta Universitatis Gothoburgensis.

von der Lippe, M. 2008. To believe or not to believe: Young peoples' perceptions and experiences with religion and religious education in Norway. In *Encountering religious pluralism in school and society: A qualitative study of teenage perspectives in Europe*, ed. T. Knauth, D.P. Jozsa, G. Bertram-Troost, and J. Ipgrave, 149–72. Münster: Waxmann Verlag.

von der Lippe, M. 2009. Scenes from a classroom: Video analysis of classroom interaction in religious education in Norway. In *Dialogue and conflict on religion: Studies of classroom interaction in European countries*, ed. I. Ter Avest, D.P. Jozsa, T. Knauth, J. Roson, and G. Skeie, 174–93. Münster: Waxmann Verlag.

Under the shadow of Al-Andalus? Spanish teenagers' attitudes and experiences with religious diversity at school

Aurora Álvarez Veinguer[a,b], F. Javier Rosón Lorente[b] and Gunther Dietz[c]

[a]*Department of Social Anthropology, University of Granada, Granada, Spain;* [b]*Laboratorio de Estudios Interculturales, Instituto de Migraciones, University of Granada, Granada, Spain;* [c]*Instituto de Investigaciones en Educación, Universidad Veracruzana, Xalapa, México*

Religious education (RE) is a persistently 'hot topic' in contemporary Spain. Although nominally Catholic, majority Spanish society tends to be sharply divided with regard to the issue of religion in education: more conservative and Church-attending parents approve of the still overwhelming presence of Catholic teachers, trained and chosen by the Catholic Church, who teach (confessional Catholic) religion in both public and confessional primary and secondary schools. More liberal or progressive parents reject this 'intrusion' of the Church as reminiscent of 'national Catholicism' and favour a strict state–Church separation similar to the French *laicité* model. This bipolar conflict has become more complex recently. The current dynamics of pluralisation of confessional RE at school, which is currently being implemented in several pilot primary schools in districts with high percentages of Muslim (particularly Maghrebien) as well as Protestant (increasingly Latin American) immigrants, meets strong resistance, not only from the Catholic Church, but also from those who struggle for a completely 'laicist' solution. The following analysis of qualitative and quantitative questionnaire data designed and collected in the frame of the comparative REDCo project ('Religion in Education: a contribution to Dialogue or a factor of Conflict in transforming societies of European Countries, sixth framework programme') presents an approach to youngsters' attitudes and experiences with confessional RE.

Introduction

Religious education (RE) in contemporary Spain is still heavily shaped by two long-lasting traditions: firstly, the self-perception of Spanish society as being homogeneous in religious terms, and, secondly, the close interrelation and frequent institutional overlapping between the Catholic Church and the Spanish nation state. Both traditions are deeply rooted in historical continuities, which still have strong consequences for present-day societal and educational reforms. Spanish society has been predominantly Catholic. Back in 1994,[1] 81.2% declared themselves to be Catholic, whereas only 4.6% identified themselves as non-believers; furthermore, 32.1% of the population identified as non-practising believers. Nowadays, the majority of Spaniards, about 75.5%, identify themselves as Catholic, although the percentage of non-believers has risen to 13.4% and in general ever more people identify as non-practising believers.[2] According to a poll carried out by CIS in February 2010, 57.6 % of those who declare themselves to be part of a religious tradition do not practise their religion at all.

In the educational domain, certain features have persisted since the Franco regime, particularly the existence of a mixed, three-fold school system which reflects the deeply rooted tradition of transferring educational competences to the Catholic Church. For the compulsory school years (primary and secondary education for students aged 6 through 16 years) and for the non-compulsory pre-university *bachillerato* (16 through 18 years), there are three school types: public schools, which are originally owned and run by the central state, but which in ever more regions are now transferred to the autonomous communities' governments; state-subsidised private schools, which are mostly owned and run by Church institutions, congregations or orders, but which are nearly completely subsidised by the state or the regional government; and completely private schools.

Until very recently, and despite Spain's rich history of religious pluralism (cf. Dietz 2007), as a result of the long lasting tradition of state and Church induced homogenisation described above, non-Catholic religious communities hardly existed in contemporary Spanish mainland society. Although Protestant, Jewish and Muslim communities have slowly started to (re)settle in several Spanish cities since the 1970s, they were not visible until the 1990s, when this type of movement began to grow, thanks to the international impact of migration. This is the case for the Protestant communities, who are currently the most successful non-Catholic congregations with regard to their internal organisation, their broader claims and their access to RE. In addition, Muslim communities are the most important, most visible and most stigmatised communities in contemporary Spain. According to unofficial estimates, based above all on the predominant 'religion of origin' of mainly Moroccan and Algerian immigrant populations, approximately 1,000,000 people may identify themselves as Muslims.

These demographic changes, which pluralise the 'religious landscape' of the country, are forcing the Spanish state to reconsider the privileged treatment it concedes to the Catholic Church and its relationship to non-Catholic denominations in all societal domains. Throughout this very recent process, the legal framework of religious pluralism is being modified, which requires changes both in the Spanish Constitution of 1978 and subsequently in the 1980 Law on Religious Freedom and in the cooperation agreements with religious denominations.

RE in Spain: 'past and present'

Reflecting the slow 'transition' towards de-monopolising the position of the Catholic Church in public schools, RE as a subject has been reformed step by step through each new educational reform (Gasol 1997; Llerena Baizán and Llerena Maestre 2002). Since the beginning of the Civil War in 1936 until 1977, RE, understood only as Catholic RE, had been a compulsory main subject of instruction during the primary, secondary and pre-university levels (Rodríguez Sanmartín 1988; Dietz 2007). The legal situation changed with the 1978 Spanish Constitution. Its Article 16 guarantees religious freedom, which makes compulsory religious instruction unconstitutional; on the other hand, Article 27 of the same constitution emphasises the right of all parents 'to obtain for their children a religious and moral instruction which is coherent with their own convictions' (Constitución Española 1991). Although the parents' right to obtain RE for their children does not imply necessarily or automatically that it has to be delivered in public schools (Tarrés and Rosón 2009, 181), *de facto* it does, ever since it has been interpreted as a state obligation. This interpretation is consistent with the Church's educational privileges, as included in the 1979 Concordat.

Currently, the legal situation of the subject is being reformed and counter-reformed. The former Conservative government had tried to fulfil its promise towards the Catholic Church to strengthen the position of RE by abolishing the non-religious alternative and by plainly integrating two alternative subjects into the core curriculum: both the confessional subject of *Religión* (católica) and the non-confessional subject of *Hecho religioso*, conceived as an introduction to the history of religion (Llerena Baizán and Llerena Maestre 2002; Esteban Garces 2003). Subsequent debates, mainly emphasising above all the presence of the crucifix in the classroom, have been among more or less secularised Catholics. The landslide victory of the Socialists in the elections held in the shadow of the 11 March Madrid bombings paralysed this conservative reform, which is now being replaced by a new educational law. This maintains the current practice of RE, but – for the first time – explicitly states that RE will be taught 'in compliance with all signed agreements', not only with the 1979 Concordat. Furthermore, the distinction between a confessional and a non-confessional subject of RE is adopted from the conservative draft regulation, but is supplemented by a third subject, citizenship education,[3] which will be compulsory during one year in primary and two years in secondary education.

Since this reform process of the 1990s, politicians, Church authorities, teacher unions and parents' associations have continuously debated the problematic aspects of the position of RE in public schools (*Comisión Episcopal de Enseñanza y Catequesis* 2005): the concrete conditions and ways of integrating RE into the overall curriculum, the subject's equal or unequal treatment in relation to other subjects, its numerical impact on the grade average and the role, choice and payment of RE teachers. Despite these debates, from a formal point of view, RE is today taught from the first grade of primary education (six years old) until the first grade of post-secondary education (*bachillerato*; 16- to 17-year-old students).

With regard to the different school types, from a total figure of 5,009,178 students,[4] about 1,041,208 attend subsidised Catholic schools, representing approximately 20.8%[5] of all Spanish students attending compulsory and pre-university educational levels. Of all private and subsidised schools, 79.1% are owned by members of the *Federación Española de Religiosos de Enseñanza-Titulares de Centros Católicos*, which transfers the school administration to another Church-run entrepreneurial organisation, called *Educación y Gestión*, which administers 2082 schools and employs approximately 77,998 teachers;[6] 6261 of these teachers (8.03%) are members of religious orders.[7]

Mostly Spanish middle and upper class parents send their children to these schools, which are generally not considered of better 'teaching quality' (Fernández Enguita 1990); in interviews conducted in southern Spain, the main reasons mentioned by parents for choosing these schools are always the same: that they are supposed to be 'better equipped' and that they are more selective and socially more homogeneous than public schools. The strong presence of the Catholic Church is, however, not limited to its educational engagement through its own schools. As many teachers of public schools have been educated themselves in Catholic schools and/or have been trained as teachers in Church-run pedagogical teacher training schools, they tend to be very receptive and tolerant towards Catholic elements of 'moral and value education' in public schools. Consequently, even public schools show an overt presence of Catholic religious symbols, liturgical traditions, practices and festivals.

Besides, in all public schools, Catholic RE is plainly and autonomously designed, organised and offered by the Spanish Conference of Bishops' Commission for Education and Catechesis. Catholic RE is still chosen by a huge majority of students, but the percentage of involvement has been constantly diminishing over the past few years: in primary education, it has decreased from 90.82% (academic year 1996–1997) to 76.44% (academic year 2007–2008) of all students, in secondary education, Catholic RE only reaches 61.5% of all students, and in pre-university level only 51.31% of all students attend Catholic RE, while 48.63% of students choose 'study activities' (cf. INE *curso* 2007–2008).[8]

Analysing in depth the most recently available figures, provided by the Spanish Ministry of Education and Science for the academic year 2007–2008,

Table 1. Religious education and its alternatives in the different school levels.

	Primary level			Secondary level				Pre-university level
Subjects	1st and 2nd	3rd and 4th	5th and 6th	1st	2nd	3rd	4th	1st
Shared			Education for citizenship and human rights (50 h)	Education for citizenship and human rights			Civil-ethic education	Philosophy and citizenship (70 h)
Free choice	(105 h) RE Educational support	(105 h) RE Educational support	(105 h) RE Educational support	(105 h) RE alternatives: –Religion –History and culture of religions Educational support			(105 h) RE alternatives: –Religion –History and culture of religions Educational support	–Religion

only 0.68% of the total number of 2,607,384 students attending Spanish schools were receiving a minority confessional RE in primary school: only 7040 students were receiving Protestant RE, 10,430 Islamic RE and 261 Jewish RE, whereas 1,993,084 took Catholic RE and 596,569 participated in the alternative 'assisted study activities'. In secondary and pre-university levels, only Catholic RE (for 1,125,373 secondary school students, i.e. 61.50% and for 300,005 pre-university students, i.e. 51.31%) and alternative assisted activities (for 653,448 secondary school students, i.e. 35.72% and for 284,336 pre-university students, i.e. 48.63%) were offered. This means that in the final school years of bachillerato, the non-Catholic confessional RE was nearly completely absent: 0.06% (350 students) both in Islamic and in Protestant RE, while Jewish RE did not exist at all (0.01%) at this level (cf. INE *curso* 2007–2008).

An empirical research study of RE

In the context of these slow, but ongoing transformations with regard to RE and religious diversity in contemporary Spanish society, we have carried out between 2006 and 2009 the Spanish part of the European project 'Religion in Education: A contribution to Dialogue or a factor of Conflict transforming societies of European countries' (REDCo; www.redco.uni-hamburg.de). The main aim of the project was to establish and compare the potentials and limitations of religion in the educational fields of selected European countries and regions in order to identify approaches that can contribute to making religion in education a factor promoting dialogue in the context of European development. For this reason, we used quantitative and qualitative research methods, with the aim of having a detailed portrait of young people's attitudes and opinions. We were sympathetic to the ethnographic grounding of the interpretive approach, which was a stimulus to REDCo research (Jackson 1997). A relevant point of departure for our research was the fact that the ultimate target and supposed beneficiary of RE, Spanish youth, are very rarely consulted about their views, opinions and perceptions on religion or on learning about religion at school.

For practical as well as empirical reasons we decided to focus on those sites where we were conducting ethnographic fieldwork in the framework of our local REDCo project. Therefore, both the quantitative and qualitative questionnaires were distributed in secondary schools in three regions or 'autonomous communities': Andalusia, Murcia and Melilla. The regions were chosen in order to diversify the sample internally with respect to the following bases of comparison: (1) urban versus rural (Granada and Melilla versus Murcia); (2) emerging versus established region of immigration (Murcia versus Granada); and (3) strong tradition of mono-religious presence versus long existing religious diversity (Granada and Murcia versus Melilla). In broad terms, the data collected in the rural and urban, public and private schools on the Iberian Peninsula reflect typical features and trends of contemporary Spanish society, both with regard to gender, social class and religious belief. The Melilla data, on the other hand, are exceptional in the sense that they do not reflect the overall Spanish situation, basically because autochthonous Spanish Muslims are nearly nonexistent in mainland Spain. Nevertheless, for the central issues of this project the situation in Melilla constitutes – for good or bad – a 'social laboratory' of future Spanish multi-faith society, which is why we included such a large 'extreme group' sample from this population.

In our qualitative sample, four schools were chosen in Granada and Murcia: one Catholic confessional school in Granada, one public school in Granada and one public school in Murcia. Only four Muslim students of Moroccan origin participated in the mainland Spanish questionnaires, so the large majority (88.88%) hold Spanish citizenship, are monolingual in Spanish and come from a Christian-Catholic background. In the case of Melilla, three schools participated in the qualitative questionnaire: one mixed public school and two public schools. Nearly half of the interviewees are male and half are female. Both majority religions present in Melilla were included in the sample: 46.88% of the participating students were Muslim and 43.75% were Catholic. Only 9% declared themselves as non-believers, atheists or *mestizos*, a term used in Melilla for children from mixed, Christian–Muslim marriages. All interviewees hold Spanish citizenship (a post-dictatorship achievement for the Melilla and Ceuta Spanish Muslims), and most of their parents were also born in Spain. Only 9.45% of the parents were born outside Spain, mostly in northern Morocco. Nevertheless, in sharp contrast to the mainland Spanish sample, half of the students speak Chelja/Tamazigh or another oral variant of the so-called Berber or Amazigh languages.

The qualitative research was done using a written questionnaire, which was completed by 113 pupils in the age group of 14–16 years: 81 in Murcia and Granada, of whom 53 were female (65.43%) and 28 male students (34.56%); and 32 in Melilla, of whom 17 were female (53.13%) and 15 male (46.88%) (Dietz, Rosón, and Ruiz 2008).

On the basis of our qualitative analyses the REDCo team developed a quantitative questionnaire (cf. Valk et al. 2009). Our survey started in January 2008 and was completed in March 2008. In Spain, we selected six schools in Andalusia, one in Murcia (a total of seven schools in the Peninsula), and seven in Melilla,[9] and samples of 14- to 16-year-old students in their second or third year of secondary education. These schools follow different RE models, have different gender balances and present different levels of ethnic-religious diversity. We feel, therefore, that they reflect the religious and social plurality of Spain. The sample includes the opinions of 381 female (56.1%) and 298 male students (43.9%) from a total of 679 surveyed (one no answer) (Rosón and Álvarez Veinguer 2009).

Teenagers' attitudes towards inter-religious cohabitation: 'reproducing confessional models'

If we analyse the result from the qualitative questionnaire, often echoing the debate which is currently going on in Spanish politics and media about the future of RE, the main reason the students express themselves in favour of maintaining religion as a subject in school consists in the necessity to 'know about one's own religion' (MUSfch).[10] The respondents emphasise the aspect of information and knowledge. In other cases these arguments are often extended to the necessary knowledge of 'religions in general' and of 'other people's religions and customs', which seems to be an argument expressed particularly in public schools, not in confessional ones. Students believed that learning about different religions helps them to learn about their own religion (mean = 2.2).[11] Whereas some students stress the 'right to know from which religion they come' (MEEmch), others suggest maintaining and expanding RE in order to 'have some place pupils get information about topics of religions, living together, etc.' (GRLmch). Several students make the point that religious knowledge should be shared by all students, independently of their own belief. The necessity of recognising all religions and not only Catholicism in RE is particularly often pinpointed by Muslim students, both by migrant students living in the Spanish peninsula and by native Muslims in Melilla.

Nearly all of them indicate that 'if there are classes of Christian or Catholic religion, then classes for Islamic religion are also to be allowed'. In their view, 'either all religions are offered or none of them' (MEEmmu). Two kinds of reasons are mentioned: on the one hand, it would be discriminatory if Muslims were prevented from having their own RE classes; on the other hand, these RE classes should provide information and knowledge about each other's beliefs as well. However, this potentially inclusive and inter-religious character of RE is not agreed by all interviewees. Although they are generally positive about RE, for them RE is synonymous with Catholic RE – a subject which should never be compulsory, neither in public nor in Catholic schools, and which should be offered only to 'Catholic believers'. In their opinion, atheists, Muslims and others should attend alternative classes of 'ethics' or 'other subjects'.

This broadly positive view of RE contrasts with a rather strong minority of students, who strictly oppose any RE at school. In the context of increasing religious pluralism and diversification, some interviewees, mostly Muslim ones, argue that precisely because society is increasingly diverse and people from ever more religions coexist, the school should not offer a place for any faith at all. For them, introducing the different religions into the school would create more barriers among students. Some Catholic students, as well as many Muslim ones, suggest that in order to avoid conflicts and barriers at school, the family and particularly the parents should be in charge of religious instruction, not the school. An Amazigh Muslim girl from Melilla proposes that 'Castilian religion [sic!] should be taught at school, but Islamic religion as well. And as they won't offer all religions, the best thing is that we learn about our religions at home and so we save hours for other things at school' (MEEfmu).

In the quantitative analysis of this point we observed that for the majority of students, RE classes help them to understand others, live together and learn about different religions. This forms part of what is desirable in RE classes. However, it does not specifically correspond to the national model where RE classes, as we previously mentioned, mostly focus on the religion itself as the only alternative (Catholic religion). This was seen more clearly in the qualitative analysis in relation to what contents should be included in RE; overwhelmingly, the contents of RE are conceived of as knowledge, as information to be transferred from the RE teacher to the students. This cognitive approach reflects the prevailing didactic practice of (Catholic) RE in Spain. The interviewees can be classified into two groups: on the one hand, those who propose confessional and mono-religious contents, and on the other, those who suggest either supra-confessional or multi-confessional topics. It is difficult to generalise from the sample which group might be stronger, as they seem nearly to be of the same size (Dietz, Rosón, and Ruiz 2008).

Multi-confessional claims are well illustrated with the following sentence: 'they should stop forcing us towards one religion through their talks, which in my opinion are deceitful' (GRImnr), as explained by an atheist boy attending a Catholic confessional school. 'Knowledge about other religions' and 'the history of all religions' should be included in RE. Islam, Judaism, Hinduism and Buddhism are mentioned as 'religions we have to learn about'. Students are particularly interested in these religions' 'customs' and 'feasts', in 'their Gods', 'their beliefs' and their 'current situation in their countries' (GRCmmu).

We need to emphasise, however, that most students deemed it necessary to obtain objective knowledge of world religions (mean = 2.3),[12] as well as to learn about and understand their teachings (mean = 2.4), so that they can converse on religious topics (mean = 2.4).[13] Finally, the model where all religions are represented in one classroom was not considered positive (mean = 3.5), but the extreme variability of responses restricts the significance of this result (SD = 2.4). The variability was related to non-believers who, while rejecting this model (mean = 3.7) more than believers, varied extremely in their responses (SD = 3.7) (Rosón and Álvarez Veinguer 2009).

In relation to students' opinions on whether the teacher should be 'religious', our research found rather opposed views. A huge group of students, particularly the most convinced and explicit believers, could not think of an RE teacher who 'does not practise what he teaches'. In their shared view, somebody who does not believe will not be able to transmit his or her knowledge about the particular religion and will not 'convince us'. These interviewees conceive the RE classes in confessional, catechism-like terms: 'a teacher of Catholic religion has to be a Catholic, of course' (GRLmch), one pupil states. Another half of the sample, however, expresses the opposite opinion. In the view of these pupils, teaching RE is like teaching any other subject; therefore, in order to be able to teach about religion, 'you should know about religion, not believe in it' (MEEfch).

One reason the interviewees argue against using only believers as RE teachers is the increasingly pluri-confessional composition of many classrooms. As pupils will often come from Catholic, Muslim or atheist families, a teacher who openly shows he/she is from one belief may create problems among the class or in his/her relation with the parents.

In our research we also asked students what model of RE they preferred, a confessional model where they are taught RE in separate groups according to their affiliation or a non-confessional model where they are taught RE together. The answers given by the pupils with regard to the preferred 'model' reflect contemporary debates in broader society. It is precisely this question where few pupils express a mere lack of opinion; the huge majority seems to have a firm stance on this issue.

If we analyse our quantitative data in relation to preferred models of RE (see Figure 1), we perceive that, firstly, students preferred a model where RE is optional (mean = 1.7). Moreover, they somewhat agreed that RE should be separated by religion (mean = 2.5), but the answers varied considerably (SD = 1.3). This would correspond with the current situation. We stress, however, that

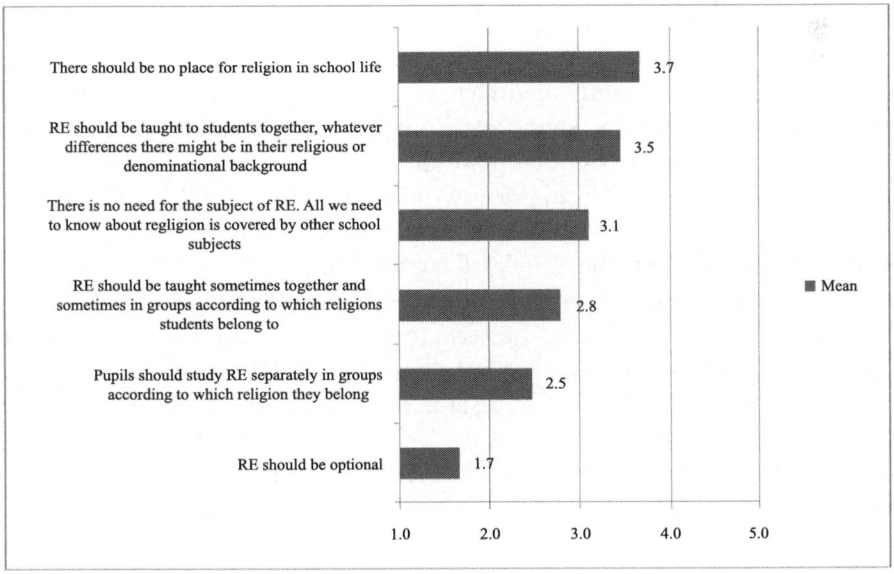

Figure 1. Preferred models of religious education.
Note: Means of estimates, scale from 1 – strongly agree to 5 – strongly disagree.

most[14] students deemed it necessary to obtain objective knowledge of world religions (mean = 2.3), as well as to learn about and understand their teachings (mean = 2.4), so that they can converse on religious topics (mean = 2.4).

Likewise, we should underline that most interviewees are in favour of maintaining or reintroducing (in secondary level) religion as a subject at school. This opinion is expressed by both pupils attending Catholic confessional schools, where Catholic RE is obligatory, and those attending public schools, were Catholic RE is optional.

However, they 'neither agreed nor disagreed' that learning about religion is necessary to solve social problems (mean = 2.7). As for a model which would include both joint and separated education they 'neither agreed nor disagreed' (mean = 2.8). Finally, the model where all religions are represented in one classroom was not considered positive (mean = 3.5), but the extreme variability of responses restricts the significance of this result (SD = 2.4). The variability was related to non-believers, who while rejecting this model (mean = 3.7) more than believers, varied extremely in their responses (SD = 3.7).

In the quantitative analysis of this point, a minority of respondents approve of joint and shared RE classes where they could learn together about religion, in general, and different religions, in particular. The arguments given in favour of this model are of two different kinds. Most of the proponents of this approach reflect the above-stated interest in 'knowing more' about other religions. Apart from knowledge-related arguments, several pupils express concern about possible consequences arising from confessionally separated classrooms. 'I would not like being put apart' or 'I would feel bad if I have to leave in the religion class' are preoccupations often shared. However, this opposition towards separate religion classes is not shared by the huge majority of respondents. Most pupils prefer being taught about their own religion separately from pupils pertaining to different faiths. The first argument against shared religious instruction is provided particularly by those pupils who are atheists and/or who express laicist positions with regard to religion in school. In their view, common RE classes would imply that they end up being 'compulsory' for any student, even those who are 'just not interested' in religious matters. Reflecting the poles of current public debate, focused on the compulsory versus complementary nature of (Catholic) RE and on the existence of non-religious educational alternatives such as 'ethics' or 'citizenship education', several pupils understand that shared RE would be not only compulsory, but also implicitly confessional – classes in which the RE teacher anyway would go on 'professing his faith'.

This rejection of common, inter-faith RE classes is also found in the case of those students who approve of and enjoy current confessional Catholic education. In their view, forcing 'a Muslim or an atheist' to participate would be 'rather violent' or 'a real mess' for all. As the objective of RE is still conceived as a matter of the promotion or affirmation of one's own faith, the presence of non-believers is seen as a merely disturbing factor inside the classroom. In the opinion of a Catholic girl, 'it is better independently, not because of racism, but for better comprehension. If not, it would be more a debating class, not a class of religion' (GRIfch).

The defenders of confessionally segregated RE tend to suppose that pupils from other creeds will not be interested at all in 'other people's faith'. This attitude favouring non-mixed classes seems to reflect an essentialist notion of 'religion' and 'belief'.

Finally, there is a tiny minority who disapproves of the distinction between common versus separate classes for RE. Several students insist that it depends on the content and the nature of each class to be taught. They propose having shared classes providing information about different religions, their history and customs, but to separate pupils according to their particular faith for confessional classes.

We emphasise that the majority of those between 14 and 16 years old have not known or been able to opt for any religious instruction/education other than Catholicism. Likewise, they have not known until recently any educational model other than the traditionally implemented.[15] In this context, it stands to reason that most of these students associate religion and RE classes with their own faith, and from this point of view, consider that the most appropriate model is the one currently being carried out: confessionally separated RE.

Nonetheless, examining the responses obtained within the framework of the project, it is interesting to note that most students considered that learning about religion helps to understand others, live peacefully together and better understand the history of their country. This suggests that the harmony and coexistence sought by multicultural societies (through dialogue, respect and tolerance) contrasts with the values of the very religions whose disagreements these societies seek to overcome. In this case there is little real coexistence and interaction with the 'other', seeing that religion classes are segregated by faith.

Given the above, the first noteworthy finding was that most Spanish students 'agreed' that at school they learn about different religions and this helps them to live together (mean = 2.3). Likewise they agreed that they learn to respect others regardless of religion (for believing students, mean = 1.7; for non-believers, mean = 2).

Conclusions

Although a huge group among the interviewees demands further information and deeper knowledge, of both their own religious traditions and particularly about other faiths, many pupils – consciously or not – still stick to a confessional, nearly catechism-like notion of RE. Both Catholic and Muslim students perceive the official recognition of religious diversity in the classroom and its potential treatment by confessionally neutral teachers. Furthermore, as our context data from ethnographic interviews show, the solutions proposed and the approaches preferred by the interviewees, reflect a strong influence by their parents as well as by the currently ongoing media debate on variants of and alternatives to confessional Catholic RE.

Most Spanish interviewees are in favour of maintaining or reintroducing religion as a subject at school (not only Catholicism, but also Islam), at secondary level. They consider that students should be taught in separate groups. Some of the respondents envisage changes toward a multi-religious class. A minority of adolescents expressed a *laïcite* point of view, considering religion to be a private matter. An important proportion of the Spanish students (half of the sample) want to learn about their own confession, which indicates confessional tradition and heritage in student conceptions of RE.

As far as teaching methods are concerned, the views of the Spanish interviewees mentioned knowledge and information delivered by teachers to students. They are not used to sharing their personal religious experiences with their classmates and do not seem comfortable with that kind of approach. As far as religion and education are concerned, Spanish adolescents appear to be quite conservative. Most of them promote the model of teaching they have experienced: confessional RE in Spain. Different national models appear here as a product of a long history of relationships between state, Church and school, and students have internalised them (Álvarez Veinguer and Béraud 2008).

Notes

1. According to the CIS poll from October 1994.
2. As this poll does not distinguish between different religions, the percentage includes believers from different religious backgrounds without regard to any specific denomination.
3. This new subject, called 'education for citizenship and human rights' or 'civil-ethic education', according to the different grades, was introduced in the sixth grade of primary school and is being taught throughout all secondary school grades (cf. Table 1).
4. Cf. Statistics and Archive Services of FERE-CECA and EyG (2008–2009).
5. The percentage rises to 21.25% in the case of the compulsory educational levels.
6. In total, there are 95,353 teachers in these schools, of whom 7039 (7.38%) are members of religious orders. Of these the church-run schools have 77,998 teachers, of whom 6261 (8.03%) are members of religious orders. Cf. Statistics and Archive Services of FERE-CECA and EyG (2008–2009).
7. With regard to the number of pupils in these Catholic schools, in primary education there are 535,483 in total, of whom 444,425 (83%) attend these schools. In secondary schools, there are 415,602 pupils, of which 347,902 (83.71%) attend these schools. Finally, at pre-university level, from a total number of 103,203 students, 84,308 (81.69%) attend these schools. Cf. Servicio de Estadística y Archivos FERE-CECA y EyG (2008–2009).
8. Instituto Nacional de Estadistica. La enseñaza de la religión. Curso 2007–2008 [National Statistics Institute. The teaching of religion. Year 2007–2008]. For more details see http://www.ine.es (p. 6).
9. With the aim of guaranteeing the anonymity of the schools, we eliminated names and explicit references to them from the discussion of the research findings.

10. For the interviewee acronyms, see the explanation in the Appendix.
11. Means from here on are calculated on the Likert scale: 1 = strongly agree, 2 = agree, 3 = neither agree nor disagree, 4 = disagree, 5 = strongly disagree.
12. Means of estimates, scale from 1 – strongly agree to 5 – strongly disagree.
13. Standard variation for these figures is 1.0 with a low standard deviation. This indicates a small degree of dispersion in the answers and a general average close to the central value (agree).
14. This means that 61.3 % of the students strongly agree or agree and that only 8.5% disagree, 5 = strongly disagree. Similar levels apply to other questions where 'most' is used.
15. Ethics, 'society culture, religion', education for citizenship, religious facts, etc., have been the only non-confessional alternatives.

References

Álvarez Veinguer, A., and C. Béraud. 2008. Religion and education in the French and Spanish context: Distant cousins. In *Encountering religious pluralism in school and society: A qualitative study of teenage perspectives in Europe,* ed. T. Knauth, G. Bertram-Troost, J. Ipgrave, and D.-P. Jozsa, 357–68. New York/ Münster: Waxmann.

Comisión Episcopal de Enseñanza y Catequesis. Secretariado. 2005. *50 preguntas a la enseñanza de la religión católica en la escuela: Todo lo que debe saber sobre la enseñanza de la religión católica en la escuela* [50 questions on Catholic religious education at school: All you need to know about the teaching of Catholic religion at school]. Madrid: EDICE.

Constitución Española. 1991. Constitución Española. In *Declaración Universal de las Derechos Humanos – Constitución Española – Estatuto Autonómico de Andalucia* (Málaga, Arguval) [Universal Declaration of Human Rights – Spanish Constitution – Status of Autonomy of Andalusia (Malaga, Arguval)], 17–105.

Dietz, G. 2007. Invisibilizing or ethnicizing religious diversity? The transition of religious education towards pluralism in contemporary Spain. In *Religion and education in Europe: Developments, contexts and debates,* ed. R. Jackson, S. Miedema, W. Weisse, and J.-P. Willaime, 103–31. New York/Münster: Waxmann.

Dietz, G., J. Rosón, and F. Ruíz. 2008. Religion and education in the view of Spanish youth: The legacy of mono-confessionalism in times of religious pluralisation. In *Encountering religious pluralism in school and society: A qualitative study of teenage perspectives in Europe,* ed. T. Knauth, G. Bertram-Troost, J. Ipgrave, and D.-P. Jozsa, 21–49. New York/Münster: Waxmann.

Esteban Garcés, C. 2003. *Enseñanza de la religión y ley de calidad* [Religious instruction and the quality law]. Madrid: PPC.

Fernández Enguita, M. 1990. *Juntos pero no revueltos: Ensayos en torno a la reforma de la educación* [Together but not mixed: Essays on the educational reform]. Madrid: Visor.

Gasol, R., ed. 1997. *La enseñanza religiosa escolar* [School religious instruction]. Barcelona: Edebé.

Jackson, R. 1997. *Religious education: An interpretive approach.* London: Hodder & Stoughton.

Llerena Baizán, L., and J.E. Llerena Maestre. 2002. *La calidad educativa, compromiso de la educación cristiana* [Educational quality, a commitment for Christian education]. Sevilla: Consejo Interdiocesano para la Educación Católica en Andalucía.

Rodríguez Sanmartín, A. 1988. *La presencia de la iglesia católica en el sistema educativo español, según las bases legales (1953–1980)* [The presence of the Catholic church in the Spanish educational system: Legal foundations (1953–1980)]. Madrid: Universidad Complutense, Facultad de Filosofía y Ciencias de la Educación.

Rosón, J., and A. Álvarez Veinguer. 2009. Spanish youth facing religious diversity at school: Findings from a quantitative study. In *Teenagers' perspective on the role of religion in their lives, schools and societies. A European quantitative study*, ed. P. Valk, G. Bertram-Troost, M. Friederici, and C. Béraud, 357–88. New York/Münster: Waxmann.

Tarrés, S., and J. Rosón. 2009. La enseñanza de las religiones minoritarias en la escuela: Análisis del caso de Andalucía [The teaching of minority religions at school: An analysis of the case of Andalucia]. *Ilu. Revista de Ciencias de las Religiones* 14: 179–97.

Valk, P., G. Bertram-Troost, M. Friederici, and C. Béraud 2009. *Teenagers' perspective on the role of religion in their lives, schools and societies. A European quantitative study.* New York/Münster: Waxmann.

Appendix. Details of questionnaire coding and interviewee features

City and school	Gender	Religion
GRI = Granada Catholic confess. school	f = female	mu = Muslim
GRC = Granada public urban school	m = male	ch = Christian
GRL = Granada public semi-urban school		nr = no religion
MUS = Murcia public rural school		me = *métis*
MEV = Melilla mixed public school		
MEJ = Melilla Muslim majority public school		
MEE = Melilla Catholic majority public school		

Example: MEVfmu = Melilla – mixed public urban school – female – Muslim
MUSfch = Murcia – public rural school – female – Christian

Laïcité in practice: the representations of French teenagers

Bérengère Massignon

GSRL (Groupe Sociétés, Religions, Laïcités), University of Paris-Sorbonne, UMR 8582, 59-61 rue Pouchet, Paris 75849, France

Focusing on the results of the REDCo (Religion in Education: a Contribution to Dialogue or a Factor of Conflict in Transforming Societies of European Countries) research, this publication sets out how French pupils conceive of *laïcité*, both generally and in school. It also explores pupils' perceptions of the 2004 law banning the wearing of ostentatious religious symbols in state schools and their perceptions of the current arrangements for dealing with pupils' religiously motivated requests (e.g. absence for religious reasons, religious dietary requirements in school canteens). Finally, questions concerning if and how pupils have interiorised the principle of *laïcité* are considered. Does it still have a militant tone, with a kernel of anticlericalism and often anti-religious views? To conclude, it is shown that secondary pupils share a '*laïcité* of proximity' which is neither how the state interprets *laïcité*, nor how it is used in ideological debates.

Laïcité appears as a cardinal value in French political culture. The word, which is difficult to translate into English, appears in all the social and political debates concerning religion in France. It indicates one of the boundaries that cannot be passed, that which separates public and private space: the public arena within which one's role as a citizen is exercised, as opposed to the more intimate space in which particular features of one's identity are shown, notably religion. It is particularly associated with the state school, as the place for the transmission of knowledge and also as the special arena for the development of future citizens. In fact, the word is equivocal, since it has had different meanings in the course of the great debates which have punctuated its history. Furthermore, at any given moment, there have always been different conceptions of what it should be (Baubérot 2004). Different facets of this notion, which is at the same time both venerated and controversial, are considered here and defined as necessary to better contrast them with the views of young people.

Numerous philosophical, historical and sociological writings have contributed in recent years to give a renewed vision to the notion of *laïcité*, particularly in schools. The REDCo (Religion in Education: a Contribution to Dialogue or a Factor of Conflict in Transforming Societies of European Countries) project offered the opportunity for an in-depth study of young people's understanding and opinions, that is, *laïcité* seen from below. The qualitative and quantitative investigations led by the French REDCo group are drawn upon. These cover the whole of mainland France, are of adolescents of between 14 and 16 years old and were originally published in French (Massignon 2009). The qualitative investigation concerned 103 young people in state school between 2006 and 2007 (described more fully in English in Béraud, Massignon, and Mathieu 2008); the quantitative investigation covered 851 adolescents in state and private Catholic schools, between 2007 and 2008 (described more fully in English in Béraud et al. 2009). The word *laïcité*, being hard to translate and rooted in the French context, did not appear in the REDCo questionnaires. However, the data on this are rich. Pupils evoked it spontaneously. Furthermore, even in the absence of the term, certain questions relating especially to expressions of religiosity by pupils in the school environment and other questions on the role of religion in society related to it fairly directly.

What conceptions do adolescents have of *laïcité* in general, and how do they formulate them in their own words? More specifically, what vision do they have of it in the school setting? According to numerous voices in the educational system, the law of 15 March 2004 forbidding the wearing of religious symbols has calmed the conflicts in school caused by the expression of religious affiliation by certain pupils (hereafter, the '2004 law'). Thus, the national Inspector General of Education, Hanifa Cherifi, noted problems at the start of the school year in 2004 in some schools, for example, in Strasbourg, Caen, Lyons and Creteil. However, these qualitative data show overall a clear reduction in issues concerning the wearing of the *hijab* from before the law (1994–1995) and after the law (2004–2005) (Chérifi 2005, 44). Nevertheless, one can ask whether the question should not be focused on other issues (religious dietary requirements in canteens, absenteeism for religious reasons), indeed for other more serious consequences (racist, sexist or anti-Semitic comments and behaviours) (Wieviorka 2005; Dhume-Sonzogni 2007). How do pupils of different religions, particularly Muslims, judge this law? The qualitative and quantitative data provided here supplement earlier studies.

Laïcité in general as seen by the pupils

For the pupils interviewed, *laïcité* is associated with a collection of values. It can also be correlated to the kinds of behaviour that favour the ability to live together in a pluralist society. More unexpectedly, pupils appealed to the notion of *laïcité* to criticise the media. Finally, one can ask to what extent it is possible to deconstruct the connections between French *laïcité* and anticlerical, or even antireligious, attitudes.

The values of laïcité

Laïcité can be defined in relation to three points: freedom of conscience and religion; the equality of different religions; and the neutrality of the state – defined as the reciprocal non-interference of the state and religious institutions in their respective spheres of activity. The pupils, from their own experience, highlight above all the values of freedom and equality and reformulate them in their own vocabulary. First and foremost in the comments received by the qualitative investigation, the pupils' keywords are 'respect' and 'tolerance'. Tolerance is associated with freedom of thought. It is at the same time not only the positive acceptance of difference, but also a right not just to difference, but to a lack of difference:

> It's a question of tolerance; everybody has the right to think what they want and not be judged on the basis of their religious beliefs. It just means putting aside our differences and accepting the other person for what they are. (Boy, Jewish)

Laïcité is associated with equal treatment of different religions:

> at school when you go through the front door of the *lycée*, you aren't a Christian or Muslim anymore. Everyone is the same. (Boy, Catholic)

Furthermore, to the open question in the qualitative enquiry, 'do you think that people from different religions can live together?' the pupils replied very stereotypically, giving evidence of having absorbed the norms of pluralism as a result of *laïcité*. They claimed to have classmates of different religions (agree: 72%; disagree: 13%) and rejected the idea of living only with people of the same religion as them (84%; only 5% giving the opposite point of view).

Finally, French pupils set out a *laïcité* of dialogue and even a vision of the world (whether religious or not) which did not put itself forward as possessing the monopoly on truth. In effect, in the qualitative data, pupils illustrated a religiosity that was open to discussion. Faced with a classmate's attempt to convert them, the majority would be open to discussion (86%) without seeking to convince the classmate that he or she held the truth (74%). Twenty-five per cent put forward the opposite point of view, and most considered that they would not be influenced by this attempted proselytisation (90%).

Living together in community and laïcité *of proximity*

Laïcité, in as much as it sets up a neutral space guaranteeing freedom of belief and convictions, and equality between religions can be seen as a value that favours the pupils' ability to live together with different religious or non-religious points of view. What did the adolescents in the research think?

For the qualitative respondents, the principal precondition for living together between people of different religions is doing things together (82%). Some other preconditions for peaceful living together were put forward by the pupils: knowing the other's religion (74%), and having a '*laïcité* of intelligence' rather than of abstention, to use Debray's (2002, 43) formulation. To clarify, this expression primarily has a sense that is more cognitive than relational, even if one can hope for some connection between the two. The third prerequisite comes from personal knowledge of people of different religions (70%). Fourth was the fact of sharing common interests (68%). The role of the state appears to be secondary to pupils who responded very little to the proposition that the state has strong laws about the role of religion in society (41% had no opinion). Thus the pupils identified themselves in a *laïcité* of proximity, of being neighbours, lived out and practised in day-to-day life, rather than in a *laïcité* of the state which seemed to them more distant or was not part of their experience.

The formulation par excellence of *laïcité*, in as much as it illustrates the ideal of a strict separation between the public and private, is: 'if everyone keeps to their own religion in private'. This view received divided opinions in the quantitative questionnaire. One should clarify that *laïcité* defined as separation is not the only way to understand it. Barbier contrasts two concepts of *laïcité*: *laïcité* of separation, which was dominant in France from the time of the 1905 law until the 1980s and *laïcité* of neutrality, putting forward the primacy of religious freedom. This contrast is born from the appeasement of the 'war of the two Frances', one Catholic and one Republican, opposed over the very definition of the French nation during the nineteenth century. The first put forward the religious dimension of France, while the other made reference to the principles of the French revolution. The *laïcité* of separation is anticlerical, while the *laïcité* of neutrality is more liberal; the latter prevailed in 1990s (Barbier 1995, 84–90). This tallies with a large quantitative survey by Barthélémy and

Table 1. The conditions for living together: a *laïcité* of proximity.

Question: There are people from different religions living in every country. What do you think would help them to live together in peace?

	Yes (%)	No (%)	Without opinion (%)
If they do something together	82	9	9
If they know about each other's religion	74	16	10
If they personally know people from different religions	70	18	12
If people share common interests	68	16	16
If everybody keeps their own religion in private	46	24	28
If the state has strong laws about the role of religion in society	29	28	41

Michelat (2007), which found that 41% of the population aged 18–25 adopted a *laïcité* of separation, associated with leftist, non-religious views. Nevertheless, for a section of French people, *laïcité* remains understood as separation; so, it is interesting to measure adolescents' ideas against this view. Amongst the pupils interviewed, only 46% on average accepted this prerequisite for living together 'if everyone keeps to their religion in private'. They were less numerous in the Catholic private school (40%) than in the state school (48.5%). The Muslim respondents were divided (38% for; 27% against; and 34% without an opinion). However a similar question, but placed in the section on relations with peers, received noticeably different answers. The question was 'to what extent do you agree with the following statements your peers have made … religion belongs to private life'. A majority of pupils agreed (52%) with, as always, a difference between state schools and private Catholic schools (57% and 43% respectively), but the percentage is comparable between Catholic pupils (47%) and Muslims (48%). Here, the statement 'religion belongs to private life' took on a specific meaning in the context of the relations between young people. In the qualitative investigation, pupils expressed modesty in revealing their religious views straightaway, except with close friends, because they considered that this related to the sphere of friendship. Thus one pupil declared: 'I only talk about it with my three best friends' (Girl, 'Deist').

Criticism of the media through the prism of **laïcité**

Thus the pupils understood themselves to be in a *laïcité* of the every day, which favoured living together in community within a pluralist world. In the qualitative survey, the pupils also mentioned *laïcité* to criticise the role of the media. The media constitutes an important source of information about religion in society: the pupils talk about religion in reaction to the information received from the media more than in lessons. This fact shows the competition which exists between television and school, as means of socialisation, without for all that suggesting that there is a crisis in the role of the school as an institution for the acquisition of knowledge and the development of a critical spirit. In the qualitative enquiry, several pupils held the media at arms' length or were even suspicious of them. The pupils pointed out the media's responsibility when putting forward negative stereotypes of religions, notably Islam.

It is worth recalling that for the *Ligue d'enseignement* (League of teaching – an association devoted to permanent education since the late nineteenth century), between 1985 and 1995, the *laique* struggle was found to be above all against the 'new priesthoods': the power of money and the media. Some pupils were shocked when too much emphasis was placed on religion in the media and referred spontaneously to *laïcité* in the interviews:

> When the pope died, it was on all the networks. They showed everybody crying. I mean, I'm not against that but it was kind of over the top! (…) We aren't all

> Christian. If they talk about the pope all the time, France isn't a *laïque* country any more. I was shocked! You saw too many images. (Girl, no religion)

Does this criticism of the 'new priesthoods' include the 'old priesthoods', that is, religions themselves? The next point deals with this key question.

Laïcité *and a critical view of the role of religions in society*

In a socio-historical perspective, French *laïcité* was established against the monopoly of the Catholic church and could take on an anticlerical, even anti-religious, tone (Willaime 2004). For Jean-Paul Willaime, French *laïcité*, in comparison to other European countries, is characterised by a 'particular prejudice towards religion as such', notably concerning its presence in the public sphere.

This association between *laïcité* and criticism of religion can be explored amongst pupils in our qualitative investigation although the quantitative study balanced this finding by showing that it was statistically negligible. In the qualitative survey, numerous pupils expressed a negative view of religion in general and particularly the social role of religion, with the notable exception of the Alsace-Moselle region, in which pupils receive denominational religious education (Williame 2007). During the interviews, some pupils responded negatively to the question 'what is your religion?', some by the self-definition 'I am anticlerical.' One pupil responded to the question 'do you think that people from different religions can live together?' with 'by stopping believing in their religion. What would help would be to point out the disasters caused by different religions' (Girl, atheist).

However, these pupils represented an extreme and very minority point of view in the quantitative survey. Only a small minority of pupils agreed with the negative claims about religion: religion is associated with intolerance (agree: 18%; disagree: 52%), with aggression (agree: 21%; disagree: 47%), with stupidity and cruelty (agree: 24%; disagree: 49%); or as a general obstacle to peace in the world, 'without religion the world would be a better place,' with which 27% agreed against 40% who disagreed, and 23% who were not sure. The great majority of pupils witnessed to a respect for those who believed (85%), and amongst them a majority did not see a strong religious commitment as an obstacle to living together in community (58%; 25% not sure; and 16% disagreed). They rejected the proposition 'religion is nonsense' (disagree: 62%; agree: 17%).

Thus, a large proportion of the respondents rejected general criticisms of religion, that is, did not adopt an antireligious discourse. However, a majority of them feared that religion could lead to conflict in their dealings with friends who had different religious or non-religious points of view: 72% of the pupils asked thought that 'in my view talking about religion only leads to disagreement.' This figure seems to show reluctance in dealing with religious issues, rather than a general suspicion of religion.

To conclude, *laïcité* is associated by the pupils with a collection of values such as pluralism, tolerance and an ethos of discussion. These are correlated to be attitudes that favour the ability to live together in community, rather than the existence of a judge-like state that hangs over society and lays down strongly *laïque* laws. The pupils therefore set out a *laïcité* of proximity, lived out in everyday life. They also drew on the principle of *laïcité* to criticise the role of the media. Finally, attachment to *laïcité* is associated only with antireligious attitudes in a minority of cases, but pupils were wary that there was the risk of a negative impact in dealing with religion at a social level. How do these general points of view on *laïcité* translate into the school setting?

Laïcité in school as seen by the pupils

In France, *laïcité* is first and foremost affirmed in the school system in the Ferry and Goblet laws (1881, 1882, 1886), which were adopted even before the Law on the Separation of Churches and State, in 1905. The dispute over the public financing of private confessional schools has stayed as the most active and visible part of the dispute between the 'two France[s]' in the second half of the twentieth century. Thus, *laïcité* is primarily played out in schools.

Today, the role of *laïcité* in school is discussed in relation to new challenges. The issue of the acculturation of Muslims in France has crystallised through the numerous crises and legal battles over the wearing of the *hijab*, since the original dispute in Creil in 1989. This question was one of the most debated by the Stasi parliamentary commission which prepared the law of 2004 forbidding ostentatious religious symbols in school. The place of religion in the school syllabuses has not been a stranger to these debates, even if it is less emotional. What therefore are the views of the pupils interviewed on the role of religion in school, whether in school life generally, or in learning about religions (often expressed in France as the study of religious facts)?

Laïcité *and school life*

The qualitative questionnaire allows the evaluation of pupils' views concerning the forms of appropriate expressions of religion in the school setting. The responses are differentiated according to the statements put forward, which suggests a grading from that which is perceived as being acceptable to the respondents (majority in agreement), tolerated (opinion divided between agreement, disagreement and no comment) and unacceptable (majority disagree), that is to say *a scale of* laïcité *in school from the pupils' point of view*. The results from the qualitative survey illustrate and make explicit these different points (Table 2).

Pupils overwhelmingly accepted the wearing of discreet religious symbols: 78%, as authorised by the 2004 law, but the majority are opposed to the wearing of visible symbols – 58% (only 17% in agreement, being 21% of the pupils

Table 2. *Laïcité* in school and pupils' displays of religion.

Items	Yes (%)	No (%)	Without opinion
Students should be able to wear religious symbols at school, discreet ones (e.g. small crosses, etc. on necklaces).	78	7	15
At school meals, religious dietary requirements should be taken into account.	61	24	15
Students can be absent from school for religious festivals.	52	26	22
Voluntary religious services (e.g. school worship, payers) could be part of school life.	27	35	37
Students should be able to wear visible religious symbols at school (e.g. headscarves, *kippah*, etc.).	17	58	25
Students should be excused from taking some lessons for religious reasons.	17	61	22
Schools should provide facilities for students to pray in school.	13	62	25

who had a religious belief against 13% of those without). One can compare these findings, obtained during the French elements of the REDCo project, with those of other national surveys. From a compilation of surveys by the French poll institute CSA on samples of people over 18 years old, Pierre Tévanian shows that opinion has shifted from 43% in favour of banning the *hijab* in school, in April 2003, with 45% against, to 76% in favour and 20% against in September 2004 (Tévanian 2005). According to an official report on French policy on immigration (Brouard and Tiberj 2005), focusing on people of Turkish and African origin, and aged over 18 years, 52% of French people with Turkish origins agreed with the banning of *hijab* in school, and 57% of French people of African origin (principally from the Maghreb), against 80% of a sample of the entirety of the French population aged over 18 years old.

It should be remembered that the policy guidance of 18 May 2004 states that ostentatious religious symbols are those 'the wearing of which leads immediately to identification of a religious affiliation, such as the Muslim *hijab*, the *kippah*, or a cross of manifestly excessive dimensions'. While being somewhat hesitant in their responses, Muslim respondents in the REDCo research were clearly more numerous (35%) than the Catholic pupils (15%) in approving of the wearing of visible religious symbols in school. But the Muslim pupils were much more hesitant in their responses than Catholic pupils: 31% of the Muslim pupils disapproved of the wearing of visible symbols (against 58% of Catholic pupils), and 34% were undecided (compared with 21% of Catholics). The opinions of Muslim pupils were manifestly very divided on the subject, which is illustrated in an exchange during the qualitative research between Muslim pupils, both boys and girls, from a school in which they would have known each other's religion. Here, the adolescents drew on arguments relating to the protection of women and linked them to unsubstantiated stereotypes:

> That law doesn't help them at all; it's not a good law. I don't wear the headscarf that often myself. It's mostly when I pray. (Girl, Muslim)
>
> That law is a bad law. If girls dress too indecently, they end up in basements.[1] If they dress badly, they get mistreated by boys. The headscarf protects them. So it's not right to prohibit it. My mother wears a headscarf, and my wife will have to wear it. (Boy, Muslim)
>
> My mother wears a headscarf, but not my sisters. My wife will wear the headscarf, that law is no good. (Boy, Muslim)
>
> Women's hair excites men; it must be hidden. (Boy, Muslim)
>
> When I have children, I'll wear a headscarf. (Girl, Muslim)
>
> Usually the headscarf just covers the hair (demonstrating with a gesture). When you hide everything, that's not good. Pregnant women must wear the headscarf. Otherwise if a man looks at her, her baby will become like him, it would have that bad nature. (Boy, Muslim)

By contrast, an exchange between Jewish, Catholic and non-religious pupils can be quoted. The pupils were divided concerning the advisability of the 2004 law, even if they all underlined their attachment to *laïcité* in school:

> I agree with this law because the school is *laïque*. Ostentatious signs of belief, that's a personal thing. You can wear them at home and in the street, but not at school. At school there is no reason to wear those huge things, you are just being provocative. But a little cross for instance doesn't pose any problem and besides, it's allowed. (Girl, Jewish)
>
> I'm not so sure as you. Prohibiting it like that, I don't know if that will change anything. Still, the school has to stay *laïque*. (Girl, Jewish)
>
> A lot of people said that it was meant to protect young girls forced to wear the headscarf by their family, but if the girl's family is forcing her to wear it, the law won't change anything, if she's still forced to wear it outside school. (Girl, Jewish)
>
> Me, I'm split down the middle. A girl can wear the scarf, even at school. You don't need a law for that; at the same time, school is *laïque*. (Boy, Catholic)
>
> Me too, I'm split because it's true that school is *laïque*. All religions are represented at school and so you don't have to make sure they are viewed in front of everyone. But I wouldn't have made a law about that. (Girl, no religion)

Overall, 61% of students approved of the suggestion that school canteens should take into account religious food requirements when planning their menus. On this point, pupils differed according to whether they were in state school, marked by mixed religiosity, or at a more homogeneous private Catholic school: 66% in the former and 47% in the latter agreed that religious food requirements should be taken into account at school; there are no official rules on this point for schools, but there is in practice a policy of reasonable accommodation. In school canteens, religion is a factor, since some Muslim pupils do not wish to eat pork, a substitute meal is generally available at the self-service stand:

> At the self-service stand, for instance, before eating ... because Muslims can't eat pork. At the self-service stand, religion is always there, it always comes up. In the ways they eat, the ways they talk ... kind of everywhere. Because the Muslims say that they can't eat pork, they ask if there's pork inside, so at the self-service stand sometimes they make stuff without pork. At the self-service stand there is stuff with pork but every day there's some stuff without. (Boy, Catholic)

Amongst the statements received from the pupils, a split between Jewish and Muslim pupils can be discerned. The latter are more likely to demand a *halal* meal in the canteen, while the Jewish pupils who go to a state school are generally content to eat *kosher* food at home.

About half of the students interviewed thought that pupils ought to be allowed to be absent from school for a regular religious event. Respondents who had a religion were more favourable (63%) than pupils who did not (40%). For religious festivals (non-Catholic ones, for the majority of these are public holidays anyway), the official national bulletin of education authorises absences for the principal Jewish, Muslim, Orthodox, Armenian and Buddhist festivals (Massignon 2000, 363). The interviewees fully recognised the rights of their Muslim peers not to come to school over Eid-al-Fitr, and these absences even provoked curiosity and the desire to learn more about the other's religion:

> There was Eid before the holidays, my friends were celebrating the end of Ramadan, they didn't come to school, and we talked about it, why they didn't come, what it means, but not much more really. (Boy, no religion)

Even though there was a large difference between the respondents who had a religion and those who did not, the great majority of adolescents interviewed (61% in total, 55% of pupils with a religious conviction, against 70% of those without) disapproved of the refusal to take part in certain lessons for religious reasons, for example, as reported in the press between 1989 and 2004: philosophy or literature when they studied authors who were considered by some pupils to be 'godless' such as Voltaire; biology concerning the theory of evolution or reproductive processes; sports, for reasons of modesty or because of mixed classes. Official guidance from the Conseil d'Etat (State Council) on 14 April 1995 and various disputes have led to some reasons for pupils' absences being rejected as contrary to the requirement that pupils should attend school regularly (Ferry law on school obligation 1882). The official guidance was formulated as a result of a referral from the Central Israelite Consistory of France, and forbade repeated absences for religious reasons (e.g. Saturdays for Jews and Seventh Day Adventists, or Fridays for Muslims). However, some schools have put in place plans to avoid examinations on Saturdays. In order to secure the respect of school obligation while partially giving the right to religious believers not to work on the Shabat, observing Jewish and Adventist students are allowed not to take notes during Saturday courses, but must be present (Massignon 2000, 357).

Roughly six out of every 10 respondents disapproved of the statement: 'schools should provide facilities for students to pray at school' (53% of the pupils with a religious conviction, against 73% of the pupils without one). As to the statement 'voluntary religious services (e.g. school worship, prayer) should be part of school life,' it was remarkable that only 35% of the pupils disagreed and 27% agreed (37% were undecided). More interviewees with a religious conviction agreed with this proposition (32%) than pupils without one (22%).

Thus pupils in the interviews agreed with permitting discreet religious symbols to be worn, recognising religious dietary regulations in the canteen, and absences for festivals during term time. By contrast, they were divided over the suggestion that there should be religious services as part of school life. They rejected the wearing of visible symbols, exemptions from particular subjects and the presence of places of prayer within colleges and *lycées*. Their opinions on the place of religion in the school life included both some things which are permitted and some things which are forbidden under the law and current educational practice. Pupils had assimilated the norms relating to *laïcité* in school, solidly grasping the principles, but open to particular reasonable accommodation, which would allow the increasing liberalisation of the French religious landscape to be taken into account in state education. The same can be said, as we will see, when they commented on teaching of religious facts.

Laïcité ***and teaching of religious facts***

The responsibility for establishing *laïcité* in school falls on the teachers, since pupils are not subject to the same rules concerning the expression of their religious or non-religious convictions. Pupils expected neutrality and objectivity from their teachers which, moreover, is in line with the legal duty of reserve on state employees.

In France, there is no religious education as such in public schools, but religion is mentioned through various subjects, mostly in history and, to some extent, in French lessons. The commonly used expression 'teaching of religious facts' implies that teaching about religion must be achieved in a neutral and pluralist way (Willaime 2007).

The state school is perceived by pupils as a place where one learns about different religions in a neutral manner unconnected with a confessional approach, in contrast with religious private schools. This principle for the teaching of religious facts was accepted by pupils as this extract from the qualitative study shows:

> If you want to (study) just one religion, there are private schools. In public school you have to take religion in its entirety. You need a presentation of different religions. For those who want to know more, there are private schools. Religion has its place in a secular school but not in the form of a catechism. (Boy, no religion)

Thus pupils had assimilated the principles of *laïcité* in school in as much as it sets out the principle of absolute neutrality of teachers. They are also in favour of a non-confessional teaching of religious facts, which is both pluralistic and neutral, as set out in the national education syllabuses.

To conclude, our research data show that the principle of *laïcité* in relation to school life and the teaching of religious facts seem to have been assimilated well by the pupils interviewed. However, one can note a tension between what is said and done: derogatory comments and discriminatory behaviour were sometimes revealed in the research: racism, anti-Semitism/anti-Zionism, Islamophobia, and sexism (see Dhume-Sonzogni 2007; Wieviorka 2005). Nevertheless, the school institution transmits the norms, understandings and rules of behaviour that are appropriate for *laïcité*.

However, can this school socialisation deeply modify the values that are transmitted to young people from their families or their peer group? The pupils interviewed noted themselves an inconsistency between their attitudes inside and outside school. It seems that the rule of *laïcité* neutralises conflicts between religions and ethnic groups more than it allows them to be resolved: the *laïque* school is a sanctuary, but outside the school setting a particular set of internal group relationships may exist, as witnessed by the statement from a pupil during the qualitative survey:

> At school when you walk through the front door of the lycée, you aren't Christian or Muslim anymore, everyone is the same … there aren't too many religious conflicts … because when you are inside the lycée you aren't with the same people that you would when you're outside. For instance, when I'm outside, I'm almost always with my cousins, all my friends, they're Black like me. (Boy, Catholic)

Conclusion: deconstructing *laïcité*

Pupils are attached to a *laïcité* of proximity, based on mutual understanding and communal activities between pupils of different religions. This *laïcité* of every day fully integrates the civic objectives of the teaching of religious facts which can contribute to a peaceful co-existence between religions with different convictions.

The role of the media, an important source of information about religion for young people, can compete with academic learning. However, the majority of the pupils involved exercised a critical distance in relation to the negative stereotypes of religion that these sometimes conveyed. The values of pluralism and of a respect for religions transmitted through teaching about religious facts, as well as the genuine experience of religious diversity in state schools, form an effective counterweight to the world of television. This last fact throws into question discussions about the crisis in the institution of the school and shows its ability to pass on a *laïcité* of intelligence. This civic dimension to the teaching of religious facts accompanies recognition of its cognitive nature. Knowledge of the religion of the other is an important aspect of living together in community, which does not signify that the role of the state school is blurred when it passes on such knowledge.

A majority of the pupils had internalised the rules of *laïcité* at school, notably the distinction introduced by the 2004 law between visible religious symbols in the school setting, which were forbidden, and discreet religious symbols, which were permitted.

The French adolescents who were interviewed identified with a *laïcité* associated with the principles of tolerance, pluralism and dialogue. They discarded negative assertions about religion. Their perception of *laïcité* seems then mostly disconnected from antireligious attitudes. Therefore the findings of REDCo surveys lead us to deconstruct the link between *laïcité* and antireligious attitudes, a link presumed abroad amongst those who focus on French history rather than on the current situation.

Acknowledgement

The author expresses her gratitude to Dr Nigel Fancourt for translating this text from French into English.

Note

1. This refers to the notorious *tournantes*: the collective rape of a woman if she behaved in 'shameful' ways, typically in the basements of abandoned blocks.

References

Barbier, M. 1995. *La laïcité*. Paris: l'Harmattan.

Barthélémy, M., and G. Michelat. 2007. Dimensions de la *laïcité* dans la France d'aujourd'hui [The dimensions of *laïcité* in France today]. *Revue Française de Sciences Politiques*, 57, no. 5: 649–91.

Baubérot, J. 2004. *Laïcité (1905–2005), entre passion et raison* [Laïcité (1905–2005), between passion and reason]. Paris: Seuil.

Béraud, C., B. Massignon, and S. Mathieu. 2008. French pupils, religion and school: The ideal of *laïcité* at stake with religious diversity. In *Encountering religious pluralism in school and society – A qualitative study of teenage perspectives in Europe,* ed. T. Knauth, D.-P. Jozsa, G. Bertram-Troost, and J. Ipgrave, 51–80. Münster: Waxmann.

Béraud, C., B. Massignon, S. Séverine, and J.-P. Willaime. 2009. The school – An appropriate institution in France for acquiring knowledge on religious diversity and experiencing it firsthand. In *Teenagers' perspectives on the role of religion in their lives, schools and societies. A European quantitative study,* ed. P. Valk, G. Bertram-Troost, M. Friederici, and C. Béraud, 131–63. Münster: Waxmann.

Brouard, S., and V. Tiberj. 2005. *Français comme les autres? Les citogens d'origine maghrébine, africaine et turque* [French like others? Citizens from the Maghreb, African and Turkish origin]. Paris: Presses de Science-Po.

Chérifi, H. 2005. L'application de la loi du 15 mars 2004 sur le port des signes religieux ostensibles dans les établissements d'enseignement publics [The application of the law of 15 March 2004 on the wearing of ostentatious religious symbols in state educational establishments]. ftp://trf.education.gouv.fr/pub/edutel/rapport/rapport_cherifi.pdf

Debray, R. 2002. *L'enseignement du fait religieux dans l'école laïque. Rapport au ministre de l'Éducation nationale* [The teaching of religious facts in the *laïque* school. Report to the Minister of Education]. Paris: Odile Jacob, Scéren.

Dhume-Sonzogni, F. 2007. *Racisme, antisémitisme et 'communautarisme'? L'école à l'épreuve des faits* [Racism, antisemitism and 'communautarisme'? The school in the test of events]. Paris: l'Harmattan.

Massignon, B. 2000. Laïcité et gestion de la diversité religieuse à l'école publique en France. [Laïcité and the management of religious diversity in French state schools]. *Social Compass* 47, no. 3: 353–66.

Massignon, B. 2009. Les élèves et la laïcité, Chapter 6. In *Les Jeunes, l'Ecole et la Religion* [Youth, school and religion], ed. C. Béraud and J.-P. Willaime, 103–22. Paris: Bayard.

Tévanian, P. 2005. *Le voile médiatique. Un faux débat: l'affaire du foulard islamique* [The media veil. A false debate: the affair of the Muslim headscarf]. Paris: éditions Raison d'Agir.

Wieviorka, M., ed. 2005. *La tentation antisémite. Haine des juifs dans la France d'aujourd'hui* [The anti-Semitic temptation. Hatred of Jews in France today]. Paris: Robert Laffont.

Willaime, J.-P. 2004. *Europe et religions. Les enjeux du XXIe siècle* [Europe and religions. The stakes in the 21st century]. Paris: Fayard.

Williame, J.-P. 2007. Teaching religious issues in French public schools. From abstentionist *laïcité* to a return of religion to public education. In *Religion and education in Europe. Developments, contexts and debates,* ed. R. Jackson, S. Miedema, W. Weisse, and J.-P. Willaime, 87–101. Münster: Waxman.

Religion and religious education: comparing and contrasting pupils' and teachers' views in an English school

Joyce Miller and Ursula McKenna

Warwick Religions and Education Research Unit (WRERU), Institute of Education, University of Warwick, UK

This paper builds on and develops the English findings of the qualitative study of European teenagers' perspectives on religion and religious education (RE), part of 'Religion in Education: a Contribution to Dialogue or a Factor of Conflict in Transforming Societies of European Countries?' (REDCo) project. It uses data gathered from 27 pupils, aged 15–16, from a school in a multicultural northern town in England and compares those findings with data gathered from 10 teachers in the humanities faculty of the same school, collected during research for the Warwick REDCo Community of Practice. Comparisons are drawn between the teachers' and their pupils' attitudes and values using the same structure as the European study: personal views and experiences of religion, the social dimension of religion, and RE in school. The discussion offers an analysis of the similarities and differences in worldviews and beliefs which emerged. These include religious commitment/observance differences between the mainly Muslim-heritage pupils and their mainly non-practising Christian-heritage teachers. The research should inform the ways in which the statutory duties to promote community cohesion and equalities can be implemented in schools. It should also facilitate intercultural and interreligious understanding between teachers and the pupils from different ethnic and religious backgrounds.

Introduction

This study arose from two separate but linked research projects which were part of the REDCo project. The first was a European-wide qualitative study of teenage perspectives on religion (Knauth et al. 2008) in which the English study was conducted by Ipgrave and McKenna (2008). This was carried out in four schools, one of which, 'School C', was also where the second research project was based (Miller 2009) which investigated the transferability of the interpretive approach (Jackson 1997, 2000, 2005, 2008) to teachers' continuing professional development (CPD). Thus, an opportunity was created to combine data from both projects in order to undertake a comparison between teachers' and pupils' views on religion, including its social dimensions, and religious education (RE).

There were two main reasons for making the comparison. The first is that it could provide a detailed case study which could add further insights into the findings of the REDCo qualitative study and thus add to the evidence base on religion, dialogue and conflict in schools. The second was to investigate further a statement from the school, contained in its self-evaluation form (SEF),[1] that 'the community of the students is distant from the school in terms of distance and culture'. This 'distance' includes ethnicity, religion, language, social class and economic status. It is worth noting that the use of the singular 'community' could imply a homogenisation of the several minority communities in which the students' families are based. There was a strong desire expressed by the teachers that the distance between the pupils' families and the school should be overcome, including the lack of direct parental involvement. They wanted to 'bridge' the distance between them and their communities (Putnam 2000) not least because there is a statutory duty on schools to promote community cohesion. This is conducted by Ofsted[2] within a four-fold understanding of 'community', including the school as a community.

School C is set in one of the northern towns (it will be anonymised as 'Northtown') where riots took place in 2001 and where the minority ethnic population, mainly of Pakistani heritage, was just over 21% at the 2001 census. In 2007 the school had 1063 pupils: 76.5% were from a South Asian background with 71.4% of Pakistani heritage;[3] 738 students did not have English as a first language; and 37.5% of pupils were entitled to free school meals (13.1% nationally).[4]

Completed questionnaires were received from 27 pupils in the school and 10 teachers in the humanities faculty. The pupils were in Year 11 (mainly 15-year-olds), 22 from a Pakistani-heritage, Muslim background and the majority (18) were boys. Of the 10 teachers, one was from a Pakistani-heritage background and the rest were white. They were split equally in terms of gender; 70% were aged between 45 and 60; five self-identified as Christian, four said 'no religion' and one was a Muslim. All the teachers – who were spread across the school's hierarchy – had taught RE.[5] On average, the teachers lived 15 miles away from the school compared with the pupils' three miles. The wards – local political districts – from which the pupils primarily come are among the 20% most deprived areas in England.

Given these considerable differences between pupils and teachers, it might have been expected that the mainly Muslim-heritage, working-class pupils would hold different views from those of their mainly non-practising, Christian-heritage, middle-class teachers. Whilst within educational literature there is research on pupil sub-cultures (Gillborn and Mirza 2000; Mirza 1992; Sewell

1996) and research which looks at their views on various topics (Francis et al. 2008; McKenna, Ipgrave, and Jackson 2008), most analyse the separately held views of teachers and pupils rather than comparing and contrasting them. This publication attempts to address this gap.

Methodology

Data collection

Using broadly the same instrument – the REDCo qualitative questionnaire (see Knauth et al. 2008) – two separate sets of data were collected within the school. Additionally, data were gathered during the CPD research study, using qualitative methods: participant observation, semi-structured interviews, written submissions (in a variety of forms) and relevant published documentation (Burgess 1984; Cheetham 2001; Cohen, Manion, and Morrison 2007; Nesbitt 2001). These are used to supplement and illustrate the comparative analysis of the data gathered from the questionnaire.

Analysis of data

The first data analysed were the pupils' qualitative questionnaires. There was a reading of the responses to gain familiarity, looking for patterns, consistencies and exceptions. The categories, terms and ideas extracted from the data were those specifically referred to by the pupils. The data from the teachers' questionnaires were analysed independently in the first instance, using broadly the same processes, and again, using their responses as the basis for analysis and the creation of categories. In this way the respondents' authentic voices are heard; the analysis was 'inductive' (Hitchcock and Hughes 1995, 296). Perhaps unusually for a qualitative study, numerical analysis was also used to ascertain the proportions of respondents expressing particular views and hence how far they were representative of the total sample (Silverman 1993).

Because this paper provides comparison and contrast between pupils and teachers in one faculty in one community school in a northern English city, there is no suggestion that the conclusions will be immediately generalisable. It is recognised that this is a very small sample, from an untypical school. However, nonetheless, the evidence presented here can shed light on issues that teachers and pupils face in their understanding of and their relationships with each other, and their wider communities. It is worth noting that the conclusions drawn from the qualitative pupil study are confirmed by the larger quantitative survey (McKenna, Neill, and Jackson 2009) and while the findings reported in this publication may not be representative, they are illustrative (Scott 1996).

The reporting of the data follows the structure of the qualitative questionnaire: personal views and experiences of religion, the social dimensions of religion, and RE in schools.

Personal views and experiences of religion

'Religion' and 'God'

The first questions asked about the words 'religion' and 'God' and what comes to mind. The commonest answers from pupils were 'belief' (35) followed by the names of religions – Islam (19) and Christianity (13). The pupils used theological words and phrases, some consistently: for example, 'almighty' and 'merciful' were used 10 and 9 times, respectively, about 'God'. Other words about 'religion' included 'peace' 'Allah and life', 'judgement day', 'commitment' and 'imaan' [*sic*]. It could be assumed that the pupils' religious background was the key reason for this, but it should be borne in mind that they were 15 and in the second year of their full course GCSE Religious Studies examination, were studying Islam and Christianity, and so one would expect a reasonable grasp of key religious terminology.

The teachers provided 27 responses to 'religion', 19 of which were factual: 'church' (four) and 'faith' (three); or general, such as 'life'. Some (four) were positive in tone: 'good works' (two) while an equal number (four) were negative: war/conflict (two), 'inflexible' (one) and 'extremism (present in all religions)' in which the writer, though perhaps making a negative judgement, is trying not to be partisan. This can be compared to the very few pupils who gave negative answers in the whole study (10/167).

The teachers' answers to 'What comes to mind when you hear the word "God"?' followed a similar pattern to their pupils'. Out of a total of 29 responses, 17 were words associated with belief or practice: 'faith' (three), 'power' (two) and 'creator' (two). There was also use of theological terms: 'almighty', 'omnipotent', 'deity' and 'Father, Son, Holy Spirit'. There were six positive associations, including 'compassion' and 'forgiveness' and four responses that could be construed as negative. Four others were largely agnostic in tone: 'Whose God?' and 'questioning'.

In this first set of answers, then, there are no major differences between the teachers and their pupils, with the exception of a number of negative responses from some of the teachers.

The importance of religion in life

The questionnaire then asked how important religion/God was in their lives to which the pupils gave a strongly affirmative response – 19 out of 24 who answered the question said 'very important'. The only pupils who said that religion was not important to them were the two non-Muslim pupils. This is similar to other research findings (e.g. McKenna, Neill, and Jackson 2009; Smith 2005). The pupils' answers were very different from their teachers' – only three of whom said that religion was important in their lives. This is striking contrast.

The pupils were able to give detailed explanations of why religion was important to them, referring to their lifestyle and their religious practices. For example:

> Islam and God to me is very, very important. I base my whole lifestyle around Islam and try to be the best person that I can be. (Male, Muslim)

Of the three teachers who said their religion was important to them, one included the importance of daily prayer (from the female Muslim teacher), a male Roman Catholic who wrote: 'My faith … is the cornerstone of my life and provides me with a moral framework,' while the third writer echoed those views:

> …provides core moral values, a guide to life and a refuge…; provides the strength to cope with hard times; a reason to be. (Male, CE)

Some of the teachers gave evidence of religious influence in the past: 'brought up in a family who were regular attenders', adding: 'living a good life more important than the trappings of religion' (female, Methodist). Only two of the teachers gave unqualified negative responses to the importance of religion. Others added a variety of comments to their statement that religion was not important:

- … other than respect for others' views
- … but as I am teaching RE for the first time in several years I am very interested.

Personal connections with religion

The last question in this section on personal views and experiences of religion asked how respondents came to know about religions. Of the pupils 26 said 'family', 22 said 'school', 19 said 'place of worship' (mosque) and 13 said 'friends'. The responses from the teachers showed a similar response to 'family', slightly lower to 'school', and considerably fewer for 'places of worship' (50% as opposed to 70%) and much lower for 'friends'.

Reflections on personal views and experiences of religion

There is thus a significant difference in the importance of religion for pupils and their teachers and yet one of the themes that came through strongly in the CPD study was the teachers' desire to respect 'religion'. They were keen not to offend their pupils and their communities, they wanted to avoid charges of racism and they wanted to be able to differentiate between 'religion' and 'culture'. The teachers wanted to give primacy to religion: if a matter was religious then they would respect it, but if it was 'only cultural' then they could challenge it. This raises complex questions, including the reification of both religions and cultures and a view of both as fixed and separable when they are not (Cush 1999; Jackson 1997, 2004).

Given that only three of the 10 teachers said that religion is important in their lives, their responses overall can be interpreted as respectful and open and not as different from their pupils' answers as one might anticipate. As one of the teachers wrote of 'religion':

> Extraordinarily powerful influence in the world – which cannot be ignored or dismissed. Needs to be understood and respected. (Male, CE)

Social dimensions of religion

The first questions in this section aimed to gather data about religion as a topic of conversation: whether or not it happened, when it occurred and whether it was interesting.

Peer group

A significant proportion of pupils (18/27) said that they talked about religion with their friends, discussed problems and moral issues, shared information on special times, were keen to compare ideas and found religious topics interesting. Their conversations appear to take place regularly, sometimes linked to RE lessons or to religious festivals, though many were also normal day-to-day interactions.

When the teachers were asked this question half of them said they did not talk about religion with their friends. However, one has to include the teachers' comments. One who wrote 'no' is a practising Catholic who explained: 'It is something personal to me.' A negative response does not necessarily equate with indifference or antipathy to religion. The content of teachers' conversations was also different from their pupils': several mentioned political issues, including Palestine, terrorism and debate about 'the news'.

Experiences of religion

The next question under the social dimension of religion asked about personal experiences of religion and asked for examples to which almost half the pupils listed good experiences but eight listed bad.

Many of the good experiences were associated with religious festivals, not only Eid but also Easter, Christmas and Diwali, reflecting the multi-faith character of Northtown:

> Good experiences – celebrating Eid, enjoying the Christmas spirit, the lights in town for Divali, etc. (Female, Muslim)

> Good – celebrating Eid, it's a fun time when you party as a family. Easter – enjoying all those chocolate eggs. (Female, Muslim)

It is a cause for concern that the majority of bad experiences that were listed by pupils were linked to racism, especially Islamophobia, and perceived discrimination:

> Bad experiences – other religions feel they are superior, being treated unequally, racism. (Male, Muslim)

Half of the teachers made positive responses to the question about their experience of religion, including religious involvement in charities, the removing of injustice, community involvement, inter-faith dialogue and 'good people'. There were a small number of references to personal good experience: 'brings calmness to life' (male, CE) and enjoyment in singing hymns (male, lapsed CE/atheist). For others, personal memories were negative:

> Choir boy – boredom! Holier than … (Male, Christian)
> … forced into religion at a young age. (Female, Christian)
> … mosque hours too long. (Female, Muslim)

What some teachers describe as negative experiences are, in fact, often opinions. For example:

> Religion can divide communities … people accept their lot without questions being asked. Many religions have an elitist system that only see men as being able to be religious leaders. (Female, none given)

Religious pluralism

In both surveys, the question about whether people of different religions could live together was one of the most frequently answered. Not only did 25 pupils respond to this affirmatively – they also gave detailed reasons.

> Yes I think that people from different religions can live together because it shouldn't matter what race/religion you are from. Everyone should learn to get on with each other. (Female, Muslim)

Some pupils added the necessary conditions for this to happen:

> … they should respect each other's views and beliefs and they should be allowed to practise their religion without any interference. (Female, Muslim)

Pupils' answers were grounded in theology, including reference to 'God's creation' and an appeal to the authority of scripture, and they stressed the term 'equality'. For example:

> Yes because, even though they are from different religions God created, both of them … In the Qur'an it says treat everyone equally and that's what you should do and it's good for both of them because they can understand each other's religion. (Female, Muslim)

This positive attitude to pluralism is entirely congruent with the messages given by the school, and Ofsted agreed that it is a 'racially harmonious, inclusive community'. In the (rather graphic) words of one of the pupils:

> … we are a mixture of religion and we don't ever argue about which religion is alright. We stick our nose to our own business. (Male, Christian)

The teachers also demonstrated their affirmation of the possibility of living in a harmonious multi-faith/multi-ethnic community. One of the faculty managers wrote:

> It happens all the time … in classrooms and in the wider school community. I have nothing but positive encounters with students I meet in communities outside school and on mixed faith, culture [trips]. (Male, CE)

Like the pupils, the teachers added their own conditions and reservations. Five of the seven comments focused on the need for respect and toleration. There was also a recognition that living harmoniously in society made demands on all participants:

> Yes of course, we should all respect each other's religion as well as culture … we live in a multicultural society and we *all* need to adapt to each other's needs. (Female, no religion, emphasis added)

She also added:

> However, we should all act outside our homes to comply with the law and not use religion as an excuse.

The word 'excuse' here is used in a pejorative sense and it reflects one of the issues that arose in the CPD study, where there was evidence of a negative critique of both the Muslim communities and of religion by some members of staff (and one of their community informants),[6] although it sat alongside their positive commitment to equality and fairness.

Reflections on the social dimensions of religion

The evidence gathered in this section shows that the majority of pupils, who are Muslims, are much more likely to discuss religion with their peers than the teachers. Where teachers do, it is usually in the context of politics and the role of religion in conflicts. The experiences of the two groups also differ, with some pupils reporting negative 'religious racism' while some teachers experienced boredom in childhood. The teachers offered negative opinions when asked for experience. These comparisons will be explored further below. What emerges that is strongly positive from this section is the shared commitment to equality and the possibility of inter-community harmony. Both pupils and teachers recognise that certain conditions must be fulfilled, and none underestimates the complexity of the process, but the shared vision of society is significant, not least in its contribution to the ethos and well-being of the school community, and therefore to community cohesion. It is tempting to use the current political rhetoric of 'shared values' but it is important to exercise caution. Modood (2006) and Parekh (2006) warn of the dangers that lie within such terminology, and Jackson (2004) speaks in a more nuanced way of 'overlapping values'.

RE in school

General attitudes to RE

There was a strong affirmation by pupils of RE in the school curriculum. To the question 'Should there be a place for religion at school?', 22 of the pupils said yes and three said no. None thought that it should be an optional subject.

The teachers, like their pupils, affirmed the place of RE 'but not to inculcate faith' or to 'preach one form is better than another'. Their reasons for including RE in the curriculum fell into a number of categories: knowledge of world religions (five), respect/understanding for others (four), educate and inspire reflection (two) and one about pupils making choices. Thus, there is similarity of views on this topic.

Content of RE

Pupils' answers to the question about the content of RE were given in considerable depth. Six pupils, for example, wanted to know about the similarities and differences between religions and three emphasised the need for opportunities to ask questions and engage in discussions. They wanted to learn about beliefs, why they were believed and the impact they had on people's lives. Six thought that RE should include general life issues such as marriage, death, bullying and crime and punishment. Evidence from the two European-wide REDCo surveys supports these findings: pupils like the 'safe forum' of RE in which respect can develop (Fancourt 2009, 206).

The teachers' ideas on content were largely similar, their answers falling into four main categories. The first was 'learning about religions', emphasising the need for a broad range of religions to be included, and providing learning experiences in places of worship. There was an affirmation of knowledge without the requirement of personal religious conviction. Another group of answers was about morality and religious teachings on questions such as war and right to life issues. A third group of answers focused on community cohesion and Britain as a 'multi-faith society', offering 'compromise where conflict exists' and comparing similarities between faiths which can promote cohesion. The final group was 'learning from religion', enabling 'reflections to fundamental religious questions' and promoting 'respect for other beliefs and non-belief'. The 'learning about and learning from' formula has its basis in the work of Michael Grimmitt (1987) (compare 'learning from religion' with Jackson's concept of edification: Jackson 1997), and has been widely adopted as the attainment targets for RE in England, in both national documentation (e.g. QCA 2004) and Northtown's local agreed syllabus. There is also evidence of adult concerns and language in the teachers' responses, such as community cohesion, but in general there is agreement between teachers and pupils.

Religiousness of teachers

The question 'Should teachers have a religious faith?' was given a positive answer by 21 pupils though the majority gave answers that teachers *could*, rather than *should*, have a faith and that it should not affect their right to their chosen occupation. One thought it would be helpful because they could then get the teacher's views about religion while another added that religious faith should not affect their teaching:

> ... they should put this to one side and be friendly and acceptable to all religions. (Male, Muslim)

At first sight, the teachers' answers would appear to be opposite to their pupils' since seven of them said no, adding comments such as 'it doesn't make them a better person or teacher' but perhaps the teachers are simply being more precise in their use of language, understanding 'should' as implying desirability.

RE – integration or separation

Most of the pupils thought that they should be taught RE together, a view held by 20 of the 21 who answered this question. They were able to give positive views about why this should be, saying that understanding would increase while 'religious racism' could be reduced.

The teachers were also convinced of the importance of integrated teaching. Seven of them gave reasons which were broadly similar to their pupils': 'the only chance of having insight into other faiths', 'encourage dialogue and mutual respect' with one asking 'why separate?' Another pointed out the potential negative impact of separation which would lead to 'misunderstanding and prejudice'.

Reflections on RE

Despite some differences in the interpretation of the questions, the data reveal broad agreement between pupils and teachers on RE in schools, its aims, content and the role of the teacher. This is congruent with findings in both the qualitative and quantitative REDCo surveys across Europe: pupils are largely conformist in their views of RE, showing preference for the model of which they have had personal experience (Bertram-Troost and O'Grady 2008, 350; McKenna, Neill, and Jackson 2009, 61). The English and Welsh model of RE sets out to inform pupils about religious diversity and encourage them to relate their studies to their own personal development (e.g. Grimmitt 1987; QCA 2004; Schools Council 1971). Teachers and pupils in School C demonstrated their acceptance of one of the values for RE in the non-statutory National Framework: 'the celebration of diversity in society through understanding similarities and differences' (QCA 2004, 8).

Reflections and conclusions on the comparative data

The first major conclusion from the data gathered from these teachers and pupils is the notable extent of agreement between them, despite their many differences, including personal religious commitment. One of the most significant is their shared commitment to pluralism and to respect for religion. In RE, pupils found a 'safe space' in which such issues could be discussed with others from different or no religious tradition. This accords with evidence from the REDCo studies that pupils with religious commitment, particularly Muslims, were more open to dialogue than others (McKenna, Neill, and Jackson 2009, 64).

One of the main areas of difference between them is that teachers made some negative comments about religion and there was incidental use of pejorative terms like 'trappings of religion' and religion as an 'excuse'. In answer to the question about bad experience of religion, three gave personal examples and two expressed negative opinions about religions as dividing communities and being patriarchal, dogmatic and elitist. This is not at all surprising since a good deal of public discourse is negative, in relation to Islam. One study found that two-thirds of newspaper articles published in the UK about Muslims between 2000 and 2008 were negative and stereotypical, showing Muslims as a 'problem' (Moore, Mason, and Lewis 2008).

During the CPD study, evidence that emerged from other data gave further insight into the teachers' views, with quite frequent criticism of the Pakistani-heritage communities. There was a view that the 'community' (as if it were a homogeneous community) is living in a 'time warp' and that, while life in Pakistan has 'moved on', the community here remains 'traditional'. When teachers were given a free hand to write in their reflective diaries, a number of negative comments and anxieties emerged, more so than, say, in interviews. One of the women teachers wrote:

> I find it really frustrating that there is a lack of any move towards integration which I feel is at the centre of the problem – my prejudice I'm afraid! … Hindus are more likely to integrate with and succeed in British society … I did not find it threatening as I sometimes do with aspects of Islam. (Female, Methodist)

The youngest member of the faculty became 'annoyed' and 'sad' about the separate sections in the mosque for women which she found 'demeaning':

> … I am sure I am imposing my western liberal values on them, but it left me feeling angry that if we segregated by race it would cause an outcry, and yet to segregate by gender was somehow acceptable and justifiable. (Female, no religion)

The teachers demonstrated strongly positive attitudes towards pluralism and racial and religious tolerance in the questionnaire and in their conversation. They wanted to improve relationships and deepen their understanding of their communities (like the teachers in the *Building E-Bridges Project* (McKenna, Ipgrave, and Jackson 2008, 104),[7] but there is some dissonance between this and the negative views that were also expressed. There was, to use Ricoeur's terminology, both a hermeneutic of suspicion and of faith: 'willingness to suspect, willingness to listen' (cited in Wright 2003, 281).

Alam and Husband suggest that the Pakistani community of Northtown is often portrayed as 'fundamentally flawed' and in need of reform (2006, 17). There is a tendency towards pathological definitions in which the victims are blamed for their circumstances. This is further embedded in public consciousness by literature emanating from Muslims which is deeply critical of aspects of Islamic society (e.g. Manji 2005).The title of Ahmed's (2003) book *Islam under siege* summarises the prevailing trend, which has been subject to critique by Said (1997).

Alam and Husband challenge this deficit model and argue that what is missing is a recognition of the strengths that exist within communities. They differentiate between social bonding and bridging (Putnam 2000) and argue that within communities there is 'a variety of social relations and solidarity … that sustains their economic resilience and provides a foundational basis for social cohesion' (2006, 55–6).

This is not to say that there are not issues and problems within the Pakistani-heritage communities in Northtown, for there are. But generalised, negative assumptions about whole communities, in which Muslim identity becomes 'reified and exaggerated' (Hussain 2008, 40), deny social and familial strengths and the rapid rate of change, and they risk pathologising communities when the focus could be on alleviating deprivation, increasing employment and raising standards in schools. An informed critique of negative public discourse is an increasingly urgent task if teachers are to promote community cohesion.

Such a critique would also inform the debate about the perception voiced in School C's SEF that the pupils are 'distant from the school in terms of distance and culture'. This publication has shown that there are many shared perceptions and attitudes between the teachers and their pupils, despite differences in personal commitment, towards religion, RE and a plural society. On this, the school can continue to build.

Notes

1. Each community school in England and Wales has completed a self-evaluation form providing evidence for Ofsted inspections. Since the change of government, this is no longer required.
2. Ofsted is the Office for Standards in Education, Children's Services and Skills for English schools. It inspects community cohesion under four headings: school/local/national/global.
3. According to the draft document published by Ofsted in its consultation on the duty to promote community cohesion, there are 63 secondary schools that have more than 50% of Black and Minority Ethnic pupils, of which this school is one.
4. These figures are from Ofsted data, 2006.
5. In Religious Studies examinations, the school has achieved consistently high results, out-performing predictions.
6. This stands in contrast to 'constructive critique' – one aspect of Jackson's reflexivity within his Interpretive Approach (IA) (Jackson 2008, 195). The IA was the theoretical stimulus for the REDCo project, including both research projects from which these data are drawn.
7. The E-Bridges project explores children's religious understanding and inter faith encounter through email dialogue, linking children living in different parts of England, and from various religious and non-religious backgrounds.

References

Ahmed, A.S. 2003. *Islam under siege.* Cambridge: Polity Press.

Alam, M.Y., and C. Husband. 2006 *British-Pakistani men from Bradford.* York: Joseph Rowntree Foundation.

Bertram-Troost, G., and K. O'Grady. 2008. Religion and education in England and the Netherlands. In *Encountering religious pluralism in school and society: A qualitative study of teenage perspectives in Europe*, ed. T. Knauth, D.-P. Jozsa, G. Bertram-Troost, and J. Ipgrave, 339–56. Münster: Waxmann.

Burgess, R.G. 1984. *In the field: An introduction to field research.* London: Unwin Hyman.

Cheetham, R. 2001. How on earth do we find out what is going on in collective worship? An account of a grounded theory approach. *British Journal of Religious Education* 23, no. 3: 165–76.

Cohen, L., L. Manion, and K. Morrison. 2007. *Research methods in education.* London: Routledge.

Cush, D. 1999. Potential pioneers of pluralism: The contribution of religious education to intercultural education in multicultural societies. *Diskus* 5, no. 1. http://web.uni-marburg.de/religionswissenschaft/journal/diskus/cush.html (accessed October 15, 2009).

Fancourt, N. 2009. 'The safe forum': Difference, dialogue and conflict. In *Religious education research through a community of practice*, ed. J. Ipgrave, R. Jackson, and K. O'Grady, 201–15. Münster: Waxmann.

Francis, B., C. Skelton, B. Carrington, M. Hutchings, B. Read, and I. Hall. 2008. A perfect match? Pupils' and teachers' views of the impact of matching educators and learners by gender. *Research Papers in Education* 23, no. 1: 21–36.

Gillborn, D., and H.S. Mirza. 2000. *Educational inequality: Mapping race, class and gender – A synthesis of research evidence.* London: Ofsted.

Grimmitt, M.H. 1987. *Religious education and human development.* Great Wakering: McCrimmons.

Hitchcock, G., and D. Hughes. 1995. *Research and the teacher: A qualitative introduction to school based research.* London: Routledge.

Hussain, D. 2008. Islam. In *Faith in the nation*, ed. Z. Cooper and G. Lodge, 39–46. London: IPPR.

Ipgrave, J., and U. McKenna. 2008. Diverse experiences and common vision: English students' perspectives on religion and religious education. In *Encountering religious pluralism in school and society: A qualitative study of teenage perspectives in Europe*, ed. T. Knauth, D.-P. Jozsa, G. Bertram-Troost, and J. Ipgrave, 113–48. Münster: Waxmann.

Jackson, R. 1997. *Religious education: An interpretive approach.* London: Hodder & Stoughton.

Jackson, R. 2000. The Warwick religious education project: The interpretive approach to religious education. In *Pedagogies of religious education: Case studies in the research and development of good pedagogic practice in RE*, ed. M. Grimmitt, 130–52. Great Wakering: McCrimmons.

Jackson, R. 2004. *Rethinking religious education and plurality: Issues in diversity and pedagogy.* London: RoutledgeFalmer.

Jackson, R. 2005. Intercultural education, religious plurality and teaching for tolerance: Interpretive and dialogical approaches. In *Intercultural education and religious plurality* (Oslo Coalition Occasional Papers), ed. R. Jackson and U. McKenna, 5–13. Oslo: The Oslo Coalition on Freedom of Religion and Belief.

Jackson, R. 2008. The emergence and development of the interpretive approach. In *Lived religion: Conceptual, empirical and practical-theological approaches – Essays in honour of Hans-Günter Heimbrock*, ed. H. Streib, A. Dinter, and K. Soderblom, 309–22. Leiden/Boston: Brill.

Knauth, T., P. Jozsa, G. Bertram-Troost, and J. Ipgrave, eds. 2008. *Encountering religious pluralism in school and society: A qualitative study of teenage perspectives in Europe.* Münster: Waxmann.

Manji, I. 2005. *The trouble with Islam today: A Muslim's call for reform in her faith.* New York: St Martin's Press.

McKenna, U., J. Ipgrave, and R. Jackson. 2008. *Inter faith dialogue by email in primary schools: An evaluation of the Building E-Bridges Project.* Münster: Waxmann.

McKenna, U., S. Neill, and R. Jackson. 2009. *Personal worldviews, dialogue and tolerance – Students' views on religious education in England.* In *Teenagers' perspectives on the role of religion in their lives, schools and societies: A European quantitative study*, ed. P. Valk, G. Bertram-Troost, M. Friederici, and C. Beraud, 49–70. Münster: Waxmann.

Miller, J. 2009. Raising humanities teachers' understanding of their pupils' religious and cultural backgrounds. In *Religious education research through a community of practice*, ed. J. Ipgrave, R. Jackson, and K. O'Grady, 119–38. Münster: Waxmann.

Mirza, H.S. 1992. *Young, female and black.* London: Routledge.

Modood, T. 2006. British Muslims and the politics of multiculturalism. In *Multiculturalism, Muslims and citizenship: A European approach*, ed. T. Modood, A. Triandafyllidou, and R. Zapata-Barrero, 37–56. London: Routledge.

Moore, K., P. Mason, and J. Lewis. 2008. Images of Islam in the UK: The representation of British Muslims in the national print news media, 2000–2008. Cardiff: Cardiff School of Journalism, Media and Cultural Studies. http://www.cardiff.ac.uk/jomec/resources/08channel4-dispatches.pdf (accessed August 30, 2010).

Nesbitt, E. 2001. Ethnographic research at Warwick: Some methodological issues. *British Journal of Religious Education* 23, no. 3: 144–55.

Parekh, B. 2006. *Rethinking multiculturalism: Cultural diversity and political theory.* Basingstoke: Palgrave Macmillan.

Putnam, R.D. 2000. *Bowling alone: The collapse and revival of American community.* New York: Simon and Schuster.

QCA (Qualifications and Curriculum Authority). 2004. *Religious education: The non-statutory national framework.* London: QCA.

Said, E. 1997. *Covering Islam.* London: Vintage.

Schools Council. 1971. *Religious education in secondary schools.* London: Evans/Methuen Educational.

Scott, D. 1996. Ethnography and education. In *Understanding educational research*, ed. D. Scott and R. Usher, 143–58. London: Routledge.

Sewell, T. 1996. *Black masculinities and schooling: How black boys survive modern schooling.* Stoke-on-Trent: Trentham Books.

Silverman, D. 1993. *Interpreting qualitative data.* London: Sage.

Smith, G. 2005. *Children's perspectives on believing and belonging.* York: Joseph Rowntree Foundation.

Wright, A. 2003. The contours of critical religious education: Knowledge, wisdom, truth. *British Journal of Religious Education* 25, no. 4: 279–91.

The interpretive approach as a research tool: inside the REDCo project

Robert Jackson

Warwick Religions and Education Research Unit, Institute of Education, University of Warwick, UK

This contribution shows how the author's interpretive approach to religious education was used as a theoretical and pedagogical stimulus and an empirical research tool by researchers in the European Commission Framework 6 REDCo (religion, education, dialogue, conflict) project. The origins and development of the interpretive approach, from its roots in the ethnographic study of children from religious backgrounds, are summarised, and an account is given about how its key concepts were used to frame a checklist of questions for REDCo researchers dealing with both empirical research methodology and pedagogy. Examples and case studies are presented illustrating how the approach was used by REDCo researchers as a methodological tool for empirical research, a pedagogical tool or stimulus to pedagogical clarification and a tool for meta-analysis and theory development.

Introduction

The interpretive approach to religious education (Jackson 1997, 2004, 2006, 2008a, 2008c) was developed originally for use in publicly funded community schools in England and Wales, where the subject is concerned with helping students to gain a critical and reflective understanding of religions. Subsequently, the approach has been developed further in the UK, and has also been used and discussed in various countries, including Turkey (Jackson 2005a), Canada (Jackson 2005b) and Japan (Fujiwara 2008), as well as being utilised in a Council of Europe project on the contribution of studies of religions to intercultural education across Europe (Council of Europe 2004; Keast 2007).

The interpretive approach continues to be used and developed in a variety of contexts. It is advanced as a pedagogical and research tool and a contribution to various debates and has never been intended to be seen as *the* pedagogical approach to the subject (Jackson 1997, 6); it is complementary to various other approaches and lends itself particularly to the study of contemporary religious practice (Jackson 2004, 2006). Some ontological and epistemological issues relating to the approach have been debated (Eriksen 2010; Jackson 2008b; Wright 2008). The present discussion illustrates how the interpretive approach was used and developed as a tool during the European Commission REDCo project (Jackson et al. 2007; Weisse 2007).

The interpretive approach was originally developed during ethnographic studies of children (e.g. Jackson and Nesbitt 1993). Studies of children from different religious backgrounds in Britain stimulated methodological reflection and were used as a primary source for pedagogical thinking and curriculum development. A close link was seen between the activity of the ethnographic researcher, working on field research, and the activity of the learner in the classroom, attempting to understand religions in the contemporary world. At their own level, each faces similar theoretical, methodological and analytical questions (Jackson 1989, 1997; Jackson and Killingley 1988, 23–39; Jackson and Nesbitt 1990). Ideas developed during ethnographic research were applied to religious education pedagogy and were used in the development of curriculum texts (the Warwick RE Project) written for children of different ages (e.g. Barratt 1994; Barratt and Price 1996; Everington 1996; Jackson, Barratt, and Everington 1994; Wayne et al. 1996). The books aimed to help learners and teachers to use interpretive methods in engaging with ethnographic data on children from religious backgrounds, portrayed in the context of the communities in which they lived and the wider religious tradition to which they related.

Subsequently, the broad approach was employed in various pedagogical studies which were sensitive to pupils' self-identity and to the representation of their life-worlds in the classroom (e.g. O'Grady 2003, 2005), and as a tool in developing a methodology for pupil-to-pupil dialogue, in which children from different religious and cultural backgrounds were encouraged to communicate with and learn from one another (e.g. McKenna, Ipgrave, and Jackson 2008). The design and implementation of a European Commission Framework 6 project (REDCo) on religion, education, dialogue and conflict provided an opportunity for further international developments.

The interpretive approach in summary

The following summary of the key concepts of the interpretive approach, used also in the ethnographic methodology associated with it, gives attention both to pedagogy and to field research.

Representation

The interpretive approach is concerned with how religions are represented – for example, by practitioners, the media, and by resources for religious education. It takes a critical stance towards Western, post-Enlightenment models of representing 'world religions' as homogeneous belief systems, whose essence is expressed through set structures and whose membership is seen in terms of necessary and sufficient conditions (Jackson 1997). This does not entail abandoning the use of the language of 'religions' or claiming that 'religions' as 'wholes' are incapable of description or that they are not in some sense 'real'. However, the approach is critical of stances which essentialise or stereotype religions and is equally critical of simplistic representations of cultures and of the religion/culture relationship. Debates in social/cultural anthropology and other social sciences are used to develop more sophisticated models of the representation of cultures, cultural processes and ethnicity (e.g. Barth 1981; Baumann 1996; Clifford 1988; Eriksen 1993; Geertz 1973; Said 1978).

A model for representing religious material was developed which encourages an exploration of the relationship between individuals, in the context of religio-cultural groups with which they are associated, and the wider religious tradition. It neither privileges the individual nor the religion, but is concerned with the hermeneutical relationship between the two, taking account of the strong influence of different kinds of groups (such as denominations, sects and movements). The tradition is seen as a contested 'whole', with power acknowledged as a factor in the representation of religions (Jackson 1997, 55–7), and it is recognised that different insiders (and outsiders) might have varying understandings of the nature and scope of particular religious traditions. The model offers a view of religions which acknowledges their complexity and internal diversity, including their varying interactions with 'culture'. The personal element in religions is emphasised, with religion being presented as part of lived human experience, but the idea of religions as 'wholes' (albeit contested wholes) is not rejected. The approach is not relativistic in relation to truth, acknowledging varying and often competing truth claims (e.g. Jackson 1997, 122–6). The interpretive approach also recognises that some individuals draw eclectically on religious and other sources in expressing a 'postmodern' worldview. Such individuals might have a tenuous, or no formal, connection with religious groups (Jackson 2004).

Interpretation

In contrast to the phenomenology of religion, in which researchers or learners are expected to leave their presuppositions to one side, the interpretive method requires a comparison and contrast between the religious symbols, concepts and experiences of those being studied and the nearest equivalent concepts, symbols and experiences of the researcher or learner (whether religious or not). The student's or the researcher's *sensitivity* is a necessary condition, with genuine empathy being possible once the concepts of the other's discourse have been understood. Thus, the approach is very much concerned with understanding religious language and discourse and therefore with religious literacy, including issues of translation. As I have remarked elsewhere, '... a basic aim of RE is to develop a knowledge and understanding of the grammar – the language and wider symbolic patterns – used by people within religious traditions, so one might understand better their beliefs, feelings and attitudes' (Jackson 1984, 142, 1997, 123).

The application of the model of representation outlined above requires moving between individuals in the context of their groups and the wider religious tradition – the consideration of one informs the other. This is a second feature of the process of interpretation. The work of the American cultural anthropologist Clifford Geertz (1973, 1983) influences the method as does the discussion of 'religion' by the Canadian scholar Wilfred Cantwell Smith (1978), although some aspects of their work are criticised or not adopted in the interpretive approach (e.g. Smith's theology: the interpretive approach is not derived from theology). Both scholars essentially use a hermeneutical methodology, Geertz's developed consciously from the work of the French philosopher Paul Ricoeur (Geertz 1973, 19). The interpretive approach utilises other aspects of Ricoeur's hermeneutics, including the concepts of participation and distanciation (Jackson 1997, 129; Ricoeur 1973).

Reflexivity

Reflexivity is understood as the relationship between the experience of researchers/students and the experience of those whose way of life they are attempting to interpret. Three aspects of reflexivity are identified as applicable to religious education. Researchers/learners are encouraged to review their understanding of their *own* worldview in relation to what they have studied (edification). They are helped to make a constructive and informed critique of the material studied at a distance, and they are involved in reviewing their own methods of research/study.

One of the key aims of religious education, as understood in several European countries, is to help students to reflect on their studies of ways of life that are different from their own in some ways. Interestingly, from a social science perspective, some anthropologists have written about how their studies of others have prompted a re-assessment of their understanding of their *own* worldviews or ways of life (e.g. Leach 1982, 127). In the interpretive approach, the term 'edification' is used to describe this form of learning.[1] In practice, such reflexive activity is not easily separable from the process of interpretation. Interpretation might start from the other's language and experience, then move to that of the student, and then move between the two. Thus, the process of understanding another's way of life is inseparable, practically, from considering issues and questions raised by it. Teachers cannot guarantee that such reflexive activity will happen, but they can facilitate opportunities for reflection. Moreover, reflexive activity often helps to motivate students to participate more fully in religious education (O'Grady 2003). Whatever differences there might appear to be between the student's way of life and the one being studied, there may also be common features or points of contact. What might appear to be entirely 'other' might link with one's own experience in such a way that new perspectives are created or unquestioned presuppositions are challenged. Edification need not only results from studying religions or cultures other than one's own. The study of *one's own* ancestral tradition, in religious or cultural terms, can also give new insights in re-examining one's sense of identity. In the case of religious education, young people might see religions, including the one of their own history, from a new perspective (Meijer 2004).

Edification does not imply the *adoption* of the beliefs of followers of a religion being studied, but does recognise similarities and differences between all humans and of the relationship between the identity of each person and the manifestation of differences. Moreover, it builds upon a positive attitude towards diversity, recognising the encounter of people with different beliefs and cultural practices as enriching in principle, and seeing individual identity as potentially developing through meeting the 'other'. 'Recognition' of the 'other' can lead to a more positive approach to plural societies, leading to an active accommodation of differences, while upholding and strengthening shared values and a common human identity.

Reflexivity also involves the learner (or researcher) being able to engage critically with material studied. The management of such critical work is a sensitive pedagogical issue, especially in pluralistic classrooms. Criticism can also be applied to method. Just as researchers should spend time reflecting on the effectiveness and the ethics of the methods they have used, so a critique ofmethods used in religious education can be a fruitful part of its content. Methodological reflection can reveal issues of representation and can also stimulate creative ideas for improvement, in the presentation of findings to others, for example.

Adapting the interpretive approach to the REDCo project

The co-ordinator of the REDCo project, Professor Wolfram Weisse, incorporated the interpretive approach into the project proposal (Weisse 2007). Weisse was conscious that his multinational project would draw on a range of different disciplinary, methodological and theoretical traditions and used the interpretive approach to provide theoretical stimulus for research and pedagogical development within the project. The research was conducted by a consortium of scholars from nine European universities, from England (Warwick), Estonia (Tartu), France (Paris, Sorbonne), Germany (Hamburg and Münster), the Netherlands (Amsterdam, VU), Norway (Stavanger), the

Russian Federation (St Petersburg) and Spain (Granada). In a project including researchers steeped in a range of epistemological and theoretical positions and methodological approaches, it was considered appropriate to use the interpretive approach not to impose any uniformity in theory, epistemology or method, but as a *stimulus* to theoretical thinking in relation to field research methods and to pedagogy (Weisse 2007).

The REDCo project included generic qualitative and quantitative studies across all the participating countries (e.g. Knauth et al. 2008; ter Avest et al. 2009; Valk et al. 2009), plus nationally based studies (e.g. Ipgrave, Jackson, and O'Grady 2009; Schihalejev 2010; van der Want et al. 2009), some of which included partners from project teams from the other countries. In successive discussions by the REDCo project team, the interpretive approach was summarised as a series of *questions* to be reviewed as research and pedagogical development proceeded (Jackson 2008d). The questions apply equally to the research process (in which the interpretive approach was itself rooted) and to the development and review of pedagogical processes. Each group of questions corresponds to one of the three key concepts of the approach.

Representation

As researchers and developers of pedagogies:

- How well are we portraying the way of life of those we are studying so that we avoid misrepresentation and stereotyping?
- Are we presenting 'religions' in too monolithic a way?
- Are we giving sufficient attention to diversity within religions?
- Are we considering whether individuals might be drawing on a wider range of spiritual or ethical resources than are reflected in traditional portrayals of religions?
- Are we showing awareness that individuals might be combining elements from a religion seen in traditional terms with values and assumptions derived from a more post-modern outlook?
- How far are we aware of the perceived relationship (or lack of relationship) of individuals studied to background religious and cultural traditions?
- How far does the use of power by relevant authorities/actors (national, regional, local) affect the representation of 'others' and 'self'/'own group/tradition'?

Interpretation

As researchers and developers of pedagogies:

- How far are we giving attention to the religious language/concepts/symbols used by those whom we are studying/representing?

- How well are we 'translating' the other person's concepts and ideas (or comparing the other person's language/concepts with our own nearest equivalent language/concepts) so we have a clear understanding of them?
- How far are we able to empathise with the experience of others after we have grasped their language/concepts/symbols?
- Have we considered the relationship of individuals to groups to which they belong (e.g. sub-tradition, sect, denomination, movement, caste, ethnic group) and of these groups to their background religious and cultural traditions?
- Have we considered the impact of power relations on processes of interpretation?
- How far have we considered issues of 'translation' (linguistic and cultural) in relation our use of religious language?

Reflexivity

In relation to research:

- How far are we aware of the impact of our own cultural background/ values and beliefs/gender/research role/power, etc., on the research process or development of pedagogical ideas?
- How far are we relating the data of our research to our own current understandings of difference?
- How far are we giving attention to the evaluation of our research methods?

In relation to pedagogy:

- How far are we enabling students and teachers to reflect on their own assumptions/presuppositions/prejudices in relation to studying those with different religious/cultural beliefs/practices?
- How far are we giving attention to issues of enabling students and teachers to relate material studied to their own ideas and values?
- How far are we giving attention to issues of motivation in relation to reflexivity?
- How far have we enabled students and teachers to make a careful, sensitive and distanced critique of new ideas studied?

Individual project members were free to use these questions (and other literature on the interpretive approach) as they wished, but were required to report on how they had used the approach in a progress report (milestone M2.1) and as part of a report written near the end of the project (Jackson 2008d). The following accounts of uses and developments of the interpretive approach refer to examples from the texts submitted for the final report[2] and also various publications from members of the REDCo project team.

Reviewing the internal and public outputs of the REDCo project, it is clear that the interpretive approach was utilised in a number of ways, with researchers often using it in at least two ways. In summary, these uses of the interpretive approach can be classified as:

- A methodological tool for empirical research
- A pedagogical tool or stimulus to pedagogical clarification
- A tool for meta-analysis and theory development

Under each heading, I will make some brief general remarks, with reference to various studies within the project. I will then take a specific example to discuss in more detail as a case study.

A methodological tool for empirical research

Methodologically, the checklist of questions based on the interpretive approach was used as a tool in formulating research questions, developing interview schedules and designing the quantitative questionnaire used across all eight countries participating in the project. In relation to the quantitative questionnaire, the interpretive approach was used as a device to ensure that questions reflected religious traditions in their variety, and addressed issues of 'translation' and interpretation (Valk et al. 2009). In particular, different understandings of the term religion, or its equivalent in the languages of the project partners, were teased out and discussed in relation to the formulation of questions to be used across all eight countries.

The Hamburg team used the interpretive approach to analyse religious diversity among the student population (Jackson 2008d). In relation to data analysis, the team from the Netherlands employed the interpretive approach to analyse student discourse on religion and values, with particular reference to gender in the relationship between researcher and interviewees (Jackson 2008d). As well as being employed in the design of interview schedules, the key concepts of the interpretive approach were used by the Warwick team to shape school- and university-based action research studies, while the comparison of findings within the Warwick community of practice suggested generic ideas that could be applied to further studies (Ipgrave, Jackson, and O'Grady 2009; O'Grady 2009; Skeie 2009a).

Case study: Estonia

In her qualitative studies of young people in Estonian schools, Olga Schihalejev used the three key concepts of the interpretive approach as methodological tools. Rather than applying the concepts specifically to people from religious backgrounds, she used the checklist of questions as an instrument to reconstruct the meanings of young people in schools, and to uncover her own understandings and presuppositions as a researcher.

In her qualitative study of young people, she initially conducted extended semi-structured interviews with individual students. The analysis of these revealed not only information about the ways students think about religion in school life and relationships with others, but also much about how students understood her questions. In the following phase she included open questions in order to give space for students to prioritise their own concerns (Schihalejev 2010, 69–106). In her classroom interaction study, in which examples of videoed lessons in two contrasting schools were analysed, she aimed to identify potentials and limitations for dialogue in students' engagement with each other and with teachers. In data analysis, in order to apply questions related to the *representation* element of the interpretive approach, group interviews with students by means of stimulated recall and semi-structured interviews with teachers were used. Interviews enabled the reconstruction of students' personal views on religion. Classroom interaction was also studied from the perspective of the learners and teachers. Stimulated recall was used in the analysis of videoed lessons, allowing participants to express their own interpretations of classroom interactions. With regard to representation, respondents were viewed as unique individuals. Schihalejev highlights not only each individual's social context, but also his or her relation to time; she recognises that in another temporal context interviewees might have answered differently (2010, 157–78).

Drawing on the questions derived from the interpretive approach, Schihalejev used the principle of *interpretation* reflexively in order to uncover her own presuppositions, and to compare them with new concepts emerging from fieldwork. The checklist had a central role in influencing her data collection and analytical methods. Her interview techniques required explanations from respondents, during data collection and through their feedback during data analysis. The main focus was on students' use of religious language. In the first phase of the fieldwork, the key term 'religion' was not imposed on respondents; instead, they were asked about their views and understandings. During interviews, possible interpretations of religious terminology were requested from each interviewee ('Did I understand correctly that you meant …?').

The principle of reflexivity was used to maintain the researcher's self-awareness in relation to the data, requiring sensitivity to the meanings expressed by others as well as critical distance from her own thinking and the material under study (Schihalejev 2010, 37–9). A combination of ethnographic and hermeneutical methods, starting from the qualitative study of views about religious diversity, enabled a reflexive analysis of data and methods used. Schihalejev introduced the idea of 'self-interview', in order to raise her awareness of her own presuppositions and ideas. She first 'interviewed' herself on the topics to be covered in interviews with students and teachers, and then distanced herself from her responses in order to compare and contrast them with the interviewees' responses. The students who were videoed and the teachers who were interviewed, in turn, were asked to distance themselves and to reflect upon their own views, ideas and values as expressed in the video or experienced in their lessons (Schihalejev 2010, 35–9).

A pedagogical tool or stimulus to pedagogical clarification

Pedagogically, researchers from Granada and Münster used the interpretive approach as a *response* to research findings. As a strategy to improve pedagogy, the Granada team, in collaboration with a Muslim religion teacher, encouraged the development of new approaches to teaching and learning in order to facilitate inter-religious and inter-cultural dialogue (Jackson 2008d). In the case of Münster, the interpretive approach was seen a source for pedagogical principles aimed at minimising the tension between students' positive ideals about society and their fears of the conflict they felt would result from learning together about different religions and worldviews. It was suggested that the interpretive approach could be adapted for use in a confessional (e.g. Islamic) context in developing intra-religious as well as inter-religious understanding (Jackson 2008d; Jozsa 2008). In St Petersburg, the researcher used the concepts of the interpretive approach as a tool to structure teaching and learning methods in order to maximise student participation and utilise students' own knowledge and experience (Kozyrev 2008, 2009; Jackson 2008d). The resultant lessons were the object of research observation and analysis. The range of studies from within the Warwick community of practice used the interpretive approach to develop pedagogical principles and strategies in a variety of teaching and learning situations in schools and teacher training courses (Ipgrave, Jackson, and O'Grady 2009; O'Grady 2009).

Case study: Norway

From the Stavanger team, Marie von der Lippe studied identity construction and intercultural dialogue in relation to educational policy and classroom practice in Norwegian religious education. She used the interpretive approach in formulating research questions during ethnographic fieldwork (von der Lippe 2010a). However, of particular interest are her analyses and reflections upon fieldwork, which provide insights for developing the interpretive approach pedagogically.

With regard to representation, von der Lippe's classroom interaction study showed how much students made use of various discourses available to them, including politics, media and religion; they were especially affected by representations of religions in the media, particularly Islam. Students tended to be more negative about Islam and Muslims in the classroom than in interviews (von der Lippe 2009). They drew on dominant – especially media – discourses

(Baumann 1996). However, they also had more personal discourse arenas relating to family, friends, school and activities. Young people were found to have a repertoire of such discourse arenas which tended to change contextually. These repertoires provided resources with friends, at home, at school, during activities, at church or mosque and beyond the local level in relation to the media, politics and national and international events. The young people's use of different repertoires of discourse was seen to affect how they understood themselves and others and how they viewed and are shaped by society.

Several points emerge that might help in clarifying and developing the interpretive approach. With regard to representation, insight is shown into the relationship between individuals and wider groupings from a linguistic point of view. The powerful effect of various discourses is clear, but so is the potential for individual agency. Students were seen to be capable of formulating their own more independent positions. However, von der Lippe observes that students need more assistance in doing this in order to deconstruct stereotypical representations of religion and culture (von der Lippe 2011). This is an important pedagogical point.

A second point relating to 'representation' is the finding that some religiously committed students, especially those of a Muslim and charismatic Christian background, were anxious that conversations about religion might lead to conflict, especially fearing that their own beliefs might be criticised or that they personally would have to respond to stereotypical representations of their faith. The finding reinforces the need for a high degree of sensitivity in developing approaches in which students reveal their own personal positions.

With regard to interpretation, it was evident that the majority of students had no personal experience of religion and had a very limited understanding of religious concepts. A much smaller student group participated in religious life, and these students found it much easier than their more secular classmates to comprehend the religious discourse of others. For the 'secular' majority, the question is raised about how effectively religious concepts can be compared and contrasted with the closest possible non-religious concepts in order to deepen students' understanding of religious language. There is also a question of motivation in relation to those students who have had no experience of religion (compare O'Grady 2003). Data from various REDCo studies, including those from Estonia, England, Norway, France and the Netherlands, show that there is a low level of motivation for many 'secular' students to engage directly with religious vocabulary. However, tolerance *did* emerge as an important value to the majority of students, both in Norway and across the project as a whole. Since most young people felt that learning about religions in schools was necessary to promote tolerance in plural societies, one might look to developing discussions of tolerance of religious difference as a bridge to engaging with others' religious language (von der Lippe 2008). Von der Lippe's finding was mirrored by the Dutch research team who found that students in vocational secondary schools used very little overtly religious vocabulary and, even then, used it in a fragmented way. However, Turkish and Moroccan students had a stronger awareness of concepts from their Islamic background than their Dutch/Christian counterparts. Generally, students' language reflected common values of Dutch society, such as 'tolerance' and 'respecting each other'. Thus, in interpreting religious vocabulary, many students needed to draw on their understanding of concepts outside formal religion – of values for example (Jackson 2008d; ter Avest et al. 2008).

In relation to reflexivity, von der Lippe's analysis shows links between edification at an individual level, and broader social values and actions. An individual's personal insights are connected to wider social attitudes relating, for example, to citizenship. Finding pedagogical ways to explore this connection would enhance and show the inter-relatedness of religious and values education and a broadly understood citizenship education, such as that promoted by the Council of Europe (Jackson 2007, 2008e, 2010).

von der Lippe's case study research with young people from Christian, Muslim and non-religious backgrounds showed the contextual nature of their views of the importance of religion in dealing with questions of personal identity (see Jackson 2004). Her case studies showed various ways in which religion was included in reflections on identity by students from religious backgrounds. However, in the case of a student who would not have self-ascribed as religious, his interview illustrated how ideas from various religious traditions could be used in constructing a personal view of religion. Another case study student stated the lack of importance of religion in her existential thinking, yet nevertheless used religious claims as a foil for her atheistic choices. Everyday discourses, related to personal experiences, were seen to assist students in formulating their own views. These more personal micro-discourses related to dominant discourses from the media, public debate, the school and religious institutions.

A tool for meta-analysis and theory development

From a theoretical point of view, several teams formulated developments to the interpretive approach. The Hamburg team's combination of the interpretive approach with Levinas' idea of 'neighbour religions', including taking account of contextual social and economic factors in understanding religion in the life of a city, is an innovation (Jackson 2008d). From the Granada team, Gunther Dietz developed the reflexive side of the interpretive approach with reference to the Spanish data. Focusing on the inter-subjective, dialectical relationship between the researcher and the subject being researched he analysed the reciprocal process of criticism and self-criticism between both parties (Dietz, forthcoming; see also Álvarez Veinguer and Rosón 2009). For the case study I will outline and discuss Skeie's use of the interpretive approach in providing a meta-analysis of the classroom interaction studies in the REDCo project.

Case study: Geir Skeie

In his analysis of classroom interaction studies, Geir Skeie developed a form of conceptual hermeneutics inspired by the interpretive approach, with the goal of explaining understandings of dialogue and conflict in religious education contextually and then comparatively (Skeie 2009b). He traced how the concepts of dialogue and conflict were represented and interpreted initially by different contributors to the project proposal, and then in the classroom interaction studies conducted by each national partner, giving attention to the wider national (or sub-national) context, dominant theoretical assumptions and predominant styles of teaching and learning in the different countries. He proceeded to make some comparative points, and then to make some cautious generic points on the basis of the combined studies. Finally, he asked what all these processes contribute to the understanding of the researchers' initial presuppositions, thus completing the hermeneutic circle.

To flesh this out in relation to comparative issues, Skeie points out that in Hamburg there is a well-established local dialogical religious education model. The Spanish confessional model is very different, showing a marked distinction between policy discourse, which supports dialogical approaches, and actual practice, where dialogue hardly appears. The French example shows the impact of the idea of laïcité, but also shows France as less different from the other countries than one might expect, at least at the level of classroom interaction. The English study focuses on the potential of utilising conflict situations in order to promote learning through dialogue, the Estonian study reveals historical and structural reasons why dialogue in class is uncommon, while the Dutch study emphasises the personal dimension of dialogue in classroom interaction. All of Skeie's examples show how context influences the representation and interpretation of dialogue and conflict.

Skeie goes on to make some generic points about *students* from the eight countries. He notes that there is a general awareness of religious diversity and that knowledge about religions is seen as important to general education and citizenship. Students prefer to focus on present-day issues in relation to religions. In general, students are tolerant of others' religions and worldviews, but there is also some expression of prejudice. Students are concerned that conflicts may arise in the wider community, and their attitudes to dialogue in school tend to reflect this.

With regard to *teaching styles*, Skeie points out that these range from academic, cognitive and teacher-led approaches (Russia, Estonia, France) to more conversational ways of teaching with a much higher degree of student involvement (England and Norway, for example). Some ways of teaching and acting in the classroom can bring about tension and insecurity among students, and thus can be seen as contributing to conflict. However, in other cases, students' expressed prejudices have been used as a tool for promoting dialogue, combining pedagogy and teacher skill to make individual students feel secure enough to voice their opinions. In certain cases a dialogical teaching style may privilege more able students, as in the Estonian example.

Generically, *student involvement and activity*, and therefore motivation, increased with the introduction of 'experience near' issues, whether from teachers or students. Many students appreciated open discussion about religious issues if the atmosphere was safe and the teacher was non-judgemental. This was so even for some countries (e.g. Estonia) where teaching styles tend to be formal.

Lesson content can range from textual analysis (e.g. France) to starting points being related to the life-world of students (e.g. the Netherlands). There is a common tendency to focus on Islam when issues of religion and conflict are raised, as examples from Norway, Germany (Münster), France, England and Spain show. Where lesson content is not strictly fixed, or student agency is more prominent, the qualifications of the teacher – in relation to both subject knowledge and pedagogical skill – are tested. Despite all the evidence from the research for the need for teachers to have facilitation and pedagogical skills, strong subject knowledge is also seen to be important.

With regard to the *role of teachers*, the studies largely confirm that teachers see themselves as mediators between cultural and religious groups – as these are represented by their students in class – and as contributing to the school's role in integration. However, there is sometimes a gap between teachers' discourse on dialogue and their actual teaching practice. There are various reasons for this which can be expressed in terms of power relations.

Students have their own agenda partly influenced by contextual factors and partly by their own intentions within classroom dynamics. Issues of social relations and identity are especially important to the age group studied. Conversations about religion in class are part of identity politics, including the dimension of gender.

In drawing on the range of studies in order to formulate a generic view of dialogue, Skeie utilises Olga Schihalejev's representation of dialogue as a 'shared inquiry', seen as a 'communicational act consisting of three components: exploration of own ideas, discovery of the ideas of another human being and examination of the subject under investigation' (Schihalejev 2009, 62–83, 2010, 29–33). Skeie relates this generic view to the concept of edification as used in the interpretive approach (2009b, 273).

Conclusion

The employment of the interpretive approach generally by project teams, as illustrated in particular by the three case studies, shows an imaginative use of the key concepts from the approach and of the checklist of questions formulated for use by project team members.

Schihalejev's use of interpretive approach as a methodological tool shows creativity, both in uncovering young people's meanings in relation to religious language and her own presuppositions as a researcher. The technique of self-interview by the researcher, followed by a distanced analysis, is an interesting application of the concepts of participation and distanciation, as is the reflexive use of extracts from videoed lessons as a stimulus for young people to explain their meanings during classroom interaction.

von der Lippe's research findings suggest a number of possibilities in relation to the development of the interpretive approach as a pedagogical method. Especially pertinent is her work on the relationship between the personal discourses of students and wider dominant discourses relating to religion and a range of other themes. Her work shows that giving students the opportunity to share their views and to criticise dominant discourses can enable them better to relate their knowledge and understanding of religions to their own personal and social development (von der Lippe 2010b). The connection of the personal and the social suggests ways in which the reflexive process at an individual level can be connected with themes of social morality and citizenship. From the perspective of a contextual form of religious education, Leganger-Krogstad (2001) similarly sets out to explore the relationship between what she calls the student's 'inner space' with the 'outer space' of family, school, locality and society. It is worth noting that Bruce Grelle also explores the relationship between the personal and the social in suggesting an adaptation of the interpretive approach for use in public schools in the USA. In the American context, it would be impossible, in the public school classroom, to give close attention to the ways in which individuals might be edified through reflecting on what they have learned about religions. Instead of concentrating on the personal, Grelle (2006) suggests applying insights from religious traditions to wider social issues related to citizenship, thereby distancing discussion of the issues from the personal views of individuals in the class. von der Lippe's findings could be used as a tool for such a development.

Skeie's meta-analysis of the various classroom interaction studies shows creativity in applying the methodology of the interpretive approach to the concepts of dialogue and conflict as understood by the various project teams and by participants in the research. He points out important contextual differences across the various national studies, revealing the issues in moving from individual cases to a generic overview relevant to policy development at the European level.

The case studies thus illustrate the relevance of the interpretive approach to research methodologies aiming to understand the worldviews of others. They also show opportunities for pedagogical developments linking reflexive processes in relation to religions to issues of social morality and citizenship, and in broadening the interpretive approach to deal with meta-analysis of themes relating to dialogue and conflict.

Notes

1. This concept resembles Michael Grimmitt's idea of 'learning from' religion but is not identical to it (see Grimmitt 1987, 225; Jackson 1997, 131–2).
2. The unpublished reports used as sources for Jackson (2008d) were prepared by Ina ter Avest (Amsterdam), Aurora Álvarez Veinguer (Granada), Wolfram Weisse (Hamburg), Dan-Paul Jozsa (Münster), Bérengere Massignon (Paris), Fedor Kozyrev (St Petersburg), Marie von der Lippe (Stavanger), Olga Schihalejev (Tartu) and myself (Warwick).

References

Álvarez Veinguer, A., and J. Rosón. 2009. Pupils, teachers and researchers: Thinking from double hermeneutics – An ethnographic approach to a triadic methodology. In *Dialogue and conflict on religion: Studies of classroom interaction in European countries,* ed. I. ter Avest, D.-P. Jozsa, T. Knauth, J. Rosón, and G. Skeie, 222–45. Münster: Waxmann.

Barratt, M. 1994. *Something to share* (Bridges to Religions – The Warwick RE Project). Oxford: Heinemann.

Barratt, M., and J. Price. 1996. *Meeting Christians: Book one* (Bridges to Religions – The Warwick RE Project). Oxford: Heinemann.

Barth, F. 1981. Ethnic groups and boundaries. In *Process and forms in social life: Selected essays,* ed. F. Barth, 198–227. London: Routledge & Kegan Paul.

Baumann, G. 1996. *Contesting culture: Discourses of identity in multi-ethnic London.* Cambridge: Cambridge University Press.

Clifford, J. 1988. *The predicament of culture.* Cambridge, MA: Harvard University Press.

Council of Europe, ed. 2004. *The religious dimension of intercultural education.* Strasbourg: Council of Europe.

Dietz, G. Forthcoming. A doubly reflexive ethnographic methodology for the study of religious diversity in education. *British Journal of Religious Education.*

Eriksen, L.L. 2010. Learning to be Norwegian: A case study of identity management in religious education in Norway. Unpublished PhD diss., University of Warwick.

Eriksen, T.H. 1993. In which sense do cultural islands exist? *Social Anthropology* 1: 133–47.

Everington, J. 1996. *Meeting Christians: Book two* (Bridges to Religions – The Warwick RE Project). Oxford: Heinemann.

Fujiwara, S. 2008. *Textbooks on religions from around the world.* Tokyo: Taisho University Press (DVD: text in Japanese).

Geertz, C. 1973. *The interpretation of cultures.* New York: Basic Books.

Geertz, C. 1983. *Local knowledge.* New York: Basic Books.

Grelle, B. 2006. Defining and promoting the study of religion in British and American schools. In *International handbook of the religious, moral and spiritual dimensions of education,* ed. M. de Souza, K. Engebretson, G. Durka, R. Jackson, and A. McGrady, 461–74. Dordrecht: Springer Academic.

Grimmitt, M. 1987. *Religious education and human development: The relationship between studying religions and personal, social and moral education.* Great Wakering: McCrimmons.

Ipgrave, J., R. Jackson, and K. O'Grady, eds. 2009. *Religious education research through a community of practice: Action research and the interpretive approach.* Münster: Waxmann.

Jackson, R. 1984. The concerns of religious education and the characterisation of Hinduism. *British Journal of Religious Education* 6, no. 3: 141–6.

Jackson, R. 1989. *Religions through festivals: Hinduism*. London: Longman.

Jackson, R. 1997. *Religious education: An interpretive approach*. London: Hodder and Stoughton.

Jackson, R. 2004. *Rethinking religious education and plurality: Issues in diversity and pedagogy*. London: RoutledgeFalmer.

Jackson, R. 2005a. *Din Egitimi: Yorumlay c Bir Yaklaþ m. Istanbul, Deðerler Eð itimi Merkezi Yay nlar* [Religious education: An interpretive approach]. Istanbul: DEM.

Jackson, R. 2005b. L'éducation interculturelle et la diversité religieuse: les approches interprétatives et dialogiques en Angleterre [Intercultural education and religious diversity: Interpretive and dialogical approaches in England]. In *Quelle formation pour l'education a la religion?* ed. F. Ouellet. Quebec: Les Presses de l'Universite Laval.

Jackson, R. 2006. Understanding religious diversity in a plural world: the interpretive approach. In *International handbook of the religious, moral and spiritual dimensions of education,* ed. M. de Souza, K. Engebretson, G. Durka, R. Jackson, and A. McGrady, 399–414. Dordrecht: Springer Academic.

Jackson, R. 2007. European institutions and the contribution of studies of religious diversity to education for democratic citizenship. In *Religion and education in Europe: Developments, contexts and debates,* ed. R. Jackson, S. Miedema, W. Weisse, and J.-P. Willaime, 27–55. Münster: Waxmann.

Jackson, R. 2008a. The emergence and development of the interpretive approach. In *Lived religion – Conceptual, empirical and practical-theological approaches: Essays in honour of Hans-Günter Heimbrock,* ed. H. Streib, A. Dinter, and K. Söderblom, 309–22. Leiden: Brill.

Jackson, R. 2008b. Contextual religious education and the interpretive approach. *British Journal of Religious Education* 30, no. 1: 13–24.

Jackson, R. 2008c. Hermeneutics and religious education: The interpretive approach in relation to the work of Jürgen Lott. In *Religion education: On the boundaries between study of religions, education and theologies – Jürgen Lott and the Bremen approach in international perspective,* ed. C. Dommel and G. Mitchell, 189–208. Bremen: Kleio Humanities.

Jackson, R. 2008d. *REDCo deliverable D.2.1: Report on the validity and changes of the interpretive approach – Findings on the basis of this theory and adaptation of the interpretive approach on the basis of the triangulation.* Brussels: European Commission.

Jackson, R. 2008e. Teaching about religions in the public sphere: European policy initiatives and the interpretive approach. *Numen: International Review for the History of Religions* 55, nos. 2–3: 151–82.

Jackson, R. 2010. Religious diversity and education for democratic citizenship: The contribution of the Council of Europe. In *International handbook of inter-religious education, Volume 4: Religion, citizenship and human rights,* ed. K. Engebretson, M. de Souza, G. Durka, and L. Gearon, 1121–51. Dordrecht: Springer Academic.

Jackson, R., M. Barratt, and J. Everington. 1994. *Teacher's resource book* (Bridges to Religions – The Warwick RE Project). Oxford: Heinemann.

Jackson, R., and D. Killingley. 1988. *Approaches to Hinduism.* London: John Murray.

Jackson, R., S. Miedema, W. Weisse, and J.-P. Willaime, eds. 2007. *Religion and education in Europe: Developments, contexts and debates.* Münster: Waxmann.

Jackson, R., and E. Nesbitt. 1990. *Listening to Hindus*. London: Unwin Hyman.
Jackson, R., and E. Nesbitt. 1993. *Hindu children in Britain*. Stoke-on-Trent: Trentham.
Jozsa, D.-P. 2008. Religious education in North-Rhine Westphalia: Views and experiences of students. In *Encountering Religious pluralism in school and society: A qualitative study of teenage perspectives in Europe,* ed. T. Knauth, D.-P. Jozsa, G. Bertram-Troost, and J. Ipgrave, 173–206. Münster: Waxmann.
Keast, J., ed. 2007. *Religious diversity and intercultural education: A reference book for schools*. Strasbourg: Council of Europe.
Knauth, T., D.-P. Jozsa, G. Bertram-Troost, and J. Ipgrave, eds. 2008. *Encountering religious pluralism in school and society: A qualitative study of teenage perspectives in Europe*. Münster: Waxmann.
Kozyrev, F. 2008. Religion and education through the eyes of students from St Petersburg. In *Encountering religious pluralism in school and society: A qualitative study of teenage perspectives in Europe,* ed. T. Knauth, D.-P. Jozsa, G. Bertram-Troost, and J. Ipgrave, 279–308. Münster: Waxmann.
Kozyrev, F. 2009. Dialogue about religion: Incident analysis of classroom interaction in St Petersburg. In *Dialogue and conflict on religion: Studies of classroom interaction in European countries,* ed. I. ter Avest, D.-P. Jozsa, T. Knauth, J. Rosón, and G. Skeie, 194–224. Münster: Waxmann.
Leach, E. 1982. *Social anthropology*. Glasgow: Collins (Fontana).
Leganger-Krogstad, H. 2001. Religious education in a global perspective: A contextual approach. In *Towards religious competence: Diversity as a challenge for education in Europe,* ed. H.-G. Heimbrock, P. Schreiner, and C. Sheilke, 53–73. Hamburg: Lit Verlag.
McKenna, U., J. Ipgrave, and R. Jackson. 2008. *Interfaith dialogue by email in primary schools: An evaluation of the building e-bridges project*. Münster: Waxmann.
Meijer, W. 2004. Tradition and reflexivity in religious education. In *Hermeneutics and religious education,* ed. H. Lombaerts and D. Pollefeyt, 121–38. Leuven: Leuven University Press/Uitgeveru Peeters.
O'Grady, K. 2003. Motivation in religious education: A collaborative investigation with year eight students. *British Journal of Religious Education* 25, no. 3: 214–25.
O'Grady, K. 2005. Pedagogy, dialogue and truth: Intercultural education in the religious education classroom. In *Intercultural education and religious plurality* (Oslo Coalition Occasional Papers 1), ed. R. Jackson and U. McKenna, 25–33. Oslo: Oslo Coalition on Freedom of Religion or Belief.
O'Grady, K. 2009. Researching religious education pedagogy through an action research community of practice. *British Journal of Religious Education* 32, no. 2: 89–102.
Ricoeur, P. 1973. Ethics and culture. *Philosophy Today* 17: 153–65.
Said, E. 1978. *Orientalism*. London: Routledge & Kegan Paul.
Schihalejev, O. 2009. Prospects for and obstacles to dialogue in religious education in Estonia. In *Dialogue and conflict on religion: Studies of classroom interaction in European countries,* ed. I. ter Avest, D.-P. Jozsa, T. Knauth, J. Rosón, and G. Skeie, 62–5. Münster: Waxmann.
Schihalejev, O. 2010. *From indifference to dialogue? Estonian young people, the school and religious diversity*. Münster: Waxmann.
Skeie, G. 2009a. A community of dialogue and conflict? Discussion of community of practice findings in a wider European context. In *Religious education research*

through a community of practice: Action research and the interpretive approach, ed. J. Ipgrave, R. Jackson, and K. O'Grady, 216–34. Münster: Waxmann.

Skeie, G. 2009b. Power to the people! Dialogue and conflict in the light of classroom interaction studies. In *Dialogue and conflict on religion: Studies of classroom interaction in European countries,* ed. I. ter Avest, D.-P. Jozsa, T. Knauth, J. Rosón, and G. Skeie, 249–75. Münster: Waxmann.

Smith, W.C. 1978. *The meaning and end of religion.* London: SPCK.

ter Avest, I., G. Bertram-Troost, A. van Laar, S. Miedema, and C. Bakker. 2008. Religion in the educational life world of students: Results of the Dutch qualitative study. In *Encountering religious pluralism in school and society: A qualitative study of teenage perspectives in Europe,* T. Knauth, D.-P. Jozsa, G. Bertram-Troost, and J. Ipgrave, 81–111. Münster: Waxmann.

ter Avest, I., D.-P. Jozsa, T. Knauth, J. Rosón, and G. Skeie, eds. 2009. *Dialogue and conflict on religion: Studies of classroom interaction in European countries.* Münster: Waxmann.

Valk, P., G. Bertram-Troost, M. Friederici, and C. Béraud, eds. 2009. *Teenagers' perspectives on the role of religion in their lives, schools and societies: A European quantitative study.* Münster: Waxmann.

van der Want, A., C. Bakker, I. ter Avest, and J. Everington. 2009. *Teachers responding to religious diversity in Europe: Researching biography and pedagogy.* Münster: Waxmann.

von der Lippe, M. 2008. To believe or not to believe: Young people's perceptions and experiences with religion and religious education in Norway. In *Encountering religious pluralism in school and society: A qualitative study of teenage perspectives in Europe,* ed. T. Knauth, D.-P. Jozsa, G. Bertram-Troost, and J. Ipgrave, 149–72. Münster: Waxmann.

von der Lippe, M. 2009. Scenes from a classroom: Video analysis of classroom interaction in religious education in Norway. In *Dialogue and conflict on religion: Studies of classroom interaction in European countries,* ed. I. ter Avest, D.-P. Jozsa, T. Knauth, J. Roson, and G. Skeie, 174–93. Münster: Waxmann.

von der Lippe, M. 2010a. Youth, religion and diversity: A qualitative study of young people's talk about religion in a secular and plural society – A Norwegian case. Unpublished PhD diss., University of Stavanger.

von der Lippe, M. 2010b. 'I have my own religion': A qualitative study of young people's constructions of religion and identity in a Norwegian context. In M. von der Lippe, *Youth, religion and diversity: A qualitative study of young people's talk about religion in a secular and plural society – A Norwegian case.* Unpublished PhD diss., University of Stavanger.

von der Lippe, M. 2011. Young peoples' talk about religion and diversity: A qualitative study of Norwegian students aged 13–15. *British Journal of Religious Education* 33, no. 2: 125–40.

Wayne, E., J. Everington, D. Kadodwala, and E. Nesbitt. 1996. *Hindus* (Interpreting Religions – The Warwick RE Project). Oxford: Heinemann.

Weisse, W. 2007. The European research project on religion and education 'REDCo': An introduction. In *Religion and education in Europe: Developments, contexts and debates,* ed. R. Jackson, S. Miedema, W. Weisse, and J.-P. Willaime, 9–25. Münster: Waxmann.

Wright, A. 2008. Contextual religious education and the actuality of religions. *British Journal of Religious Education* 30, no. 1: 3–12.

The 'contextual setting approach': a contribution to understanding how young people view and experience religion and education in Europe

Thorsten Knauth[a] and Anna Körs[b]

[a]*Institute of Evangelical Theology, Faculty of Humanities, University Duisburg-Essen, Universitätsstraße 12, 45141 Essen, Germany;* [b]*Institute of Sociology, Department of Humanities and Social Sciences, Helmut Schmidt University, University of the Federal Armed Forces, Holstenhofweg 85, 22043 Hamburg, Germany*

This publication focuses on pupils' attitudes towards religion in school, having specific regard to four key issues of the religious pedagogical debate: the role of religion in school, the content of learning, teachers' religiosity and learning models. It draws on the results of the qualitative study within the international research project REDCo: 'Religion in Education. A Contribution to Dialogue or a Factor of Conflict in Transforming Societies of European Countries?' carried out in eight European countries. Based on a European comparison, in terms of the four issues identified above, we aim to interpret the findings by introducing a 'contextual setting approach'. The assumption is that the similarities and differences among the pupils who contributed to a qualitative study (over 1000) are highly influenced by the particular contextual setting of religious education – that is the way in which religion/religious education is shaped according to national/regional traditions, structures, etc. – and that this is the case, especially in terms of their attitudes towards religion in the school environment.

Introduction: research design and methodology

The qualitative study conducted in the framework of the research project REDCo was dedicated to the subject of 'youth and religion'(Knauth et al. 2008), pursuing three main aspects that can be conceived of as concentric circles, expanding the horizon from the individual and the personal importance of religion for young people's life (Ipgrave and Bertram-Troost 2008), their experiences with religion and religions in their immediate environment and on a societal level (Jozsa and Friederici 2008) as well as their views on religion in the school environment. As yet, no direct precedents exist for a qualitative study on a similar scale. Therefore, we will mention some characteristic features of the research design.

The variety of countries and contexts which are involved in the survey

Initially, the difference and variety of the contexts involved in this study need to be mentioned. In Estonia and Russia, for example, religious education in schools is a very new and controversial topic; in Spain, religious education is entirely confessional with some first attempts being made at offering Islamic religious education alongside the traditional Catholic Christian variety; France dispenses with the subject religious education in schools altogether (except for Alsace-Lorraine and the Moselle region), addressing the issue in the context of other school subjects. In Norway, religious education is undergoing a phase of transition transforming itself from mono-perspective Christian approaches into an interreligious and intercultural learning environment.

English community schools promote multireligious learning and an integrated religious education. Germany and the Netherlands both combine settings with confessional and with non-confessional interreligious education. These different contexts shape the image and form of religion in school and public contexts, thereby having an impact on the views of students on the matter. Against this background, we have coined the term ‘contextual settings’ which shape students’ views on the issues of religion at stake.

The variety of perspectives

The sample in the study also mirrors the plurality of religious perspectives of young people in Europe as well as the variety of contexts. All participant research partners agreed to aim for a degree of religious plurality and gender balance in assembling their respective samples. They also let regionally specific research questions inform their selection of the regions and schools studied.

The overall sample (see Table 1) of the study consists of 1011 students. The national samples differ with regard to the number of students included in the survey, ranging from 71 students in the samples of Russia and the Netherlands to 154 students in Norway and 317 students in the overall German sample.

The methodological design of the qualitative study

The study was based on a qualitative questionnaire that was distributed to at least 70 students per country. In order to draw a comprehensive outline of the significance of religion in the overall life of young people, researchers addressed different domains of the individual, societal and scholastic significance of

Table 1. Overall sample table.

	Germany (317)	Estonia (73)	Russia (71)	Norway (154)	The Netherlands (71)	England (109)	Spain (113)	France (103)	Total (1011)
Sex									
Female	181	34	42	85	48	49	70	68	577
Male	136	39	29	69	23	60	43	35	434
Religion									
Christian	155	18	29	79	23	39	85	26	454
Specified: Protestant	87	2		74	13	–	–	5	181
Specified: Catholic	58	–	1	3	10	–	–	11	83
Specified: Orthodox	4	11	19	2	–	–	–	1	37
Muslim	120	–	2	5	3	25	19	23	197
Jewish	1	–	–	–	–	–	–	9	10
Buddhist	–	–	–	–	–	1	–	3	4
Hindu	–	–	–	2	–	–	–	–	2
Sikh	1	–	–	–	–	–	–	–	1
No religion/not specified	42	42	31	68	39	42	–	42	306
Atheist/agnostic/non-believer	–	6	9	–	–	–	5	–	20
Others	1	7	–	–	6	2	2	–	18
Migration background									
Migration background	183	20	5	40	10	48	7	38	351
No migration background	134	53	66	114	61	61	106	65	660

religion. Through these questions, the students were encouraged not only to describe their experiences and existing practices within their schools but to share their views of what might be possible and what should be aimed for in their educational context and wider society.

The survey was designed for what we have called a 'bottom-up' analysis consisting of three levels.

The *regional analyses* are conceptualised as contextual case studies. Depending on the sampling strategies used, it has been possible to draw conclusions that relate findings to typical features of the local, sometimes even regional or national, context. But, in general, the studies can be characterised more as snapshots of a specific contextual setting rather than as national surveys. They allow for a sharp analytical view of the features of particular cases. Analysis started with the individual meaning ascriptions and patterns of young people in specific national contexts. This analysis took into account both individual and school-specific variables.

At a second level, the data from pairs of countries were compared with each other. This comparison of salient results was carried out between those countries that seemed to be closest to each other with regard to features such as religious diversity and (religious) history. In all cases, the findings of the regional analyses were interpreted against the background of the legal framework but also taking account of topical debates in the relevant pedagogical, sociological and theological discussions. As these bilateral analyses are based on the findings of contextual case studies, it would be misleading to call them bi-national comparisons. The term 'bi-contextual analyses' is more accurate.

In the final analysis, which was at a European level, the common and divergent traits of individual perspectives, as well as those across countries, were taken into account in full awareness of contextual factors. It must be conceded that what is being compared are fundamentally not data on the student populations of European countries in the abstract but data generated by students from different religious, cultural, family and individual backgrounds, from settings that differ not only by country, but also by region and environment. Nonetheless, they show clear tendencies and afford us a glimpse of the diverse European perspectives on religion, religious plurality and religion in education.

So, what we finally were able to present as the overall survey can be regarded as an example of intercultural contextual comparative research. Coming from regional context analyses, the research proceeds through bi-national comparisons to a wider European level.

Our focus here is on religion in the school environment. The young people's views, positions and arguments on religion in school were studied using four central questions:

- Should there be a place for religion in school or not?
- If religion is taught at school, what do students think they should learn about it?

- Should the teacher have a religious faith or not?
- Should the students be taught together or in separate groups in relation to religion in school?

In the following, the results of this comparative survey will first be presented briefly. An interpretation based on the different *contextual settings* that define the place of religion in schools in the different participant countries will follow in order to aid reflection on the future place of religion in school in a Europe, defined by religious plurality. Our study is thus guided by the overarching question of how the views and positions of young people can be grasped at a pan-European level. What potential for coexistence and dialogue, and, also, what differences and tensions can be identified? The influence of the institutional and environmental context in different countries is taken into consideration when accounting for both similarities and differences. To explain this central concept, initially theoretically, we start with a short clarification.

Clarification of the 'contextual setting' concept in the realm of religious education

The term '*contextual setting*' takes account of the fact that institutional traditions in the school systems of different European regions predefine the place of religion in their schools to a great degree. They take concrete shape in administrative and curricular regulation and its implementation in the classroom, as well as in 'softer' aspects of pedagogical and political traditions that influence the choice of thinkable options. This interaction of structural and administrative facts at the macro-level and the traditions and patterns shaping the decisions and actions of individuals at the meso-level creates the contextual setting. To have an even more differentiated view of the term, conditions at the micro-level of schools and classes, such as the composition of the student body and the place of religion in the school curriculum, must be taken into consideration: these aspects altogether form a contextual framework which predetermines the boundaries of the possible position and rank of religion in school contexts. To put it more directly, the set of normative standards and cultural traditions shapes the way religion can be fitted into education and the school.[1]

This framework determines the fundamental importance that can be accorded to religion (is it to be treated openly or remain invisible in school?) as well as the forms in which it can legitimately appear (what religions are allowed to enter the school and how may they be expressed?); and it defines how and to what degree religion can be part of the curriculum and educational goals. These points affect the type of religious education offered (confessional versus non-confessional religious education; separate identity or integration within other subjects), the curricular content and the conceptual approaches (teaching about, introducing into, learning from).[2] All these, in turn, further shape the contextual setting.

We use this concept of '*contextual settings*' to acknowledge the fact that the different regional samples of the qualitative survey should not be mistaken as representations of the overall national situation. In any case, we want to avoid the misinterpretation of doing a multi-national comparison. For this reason, we relate to the findings of the regional studies as cases, speaking of the Spanish case, the English case, the Estonian case, etc.

Summary of empirical research results

In the following, the results will be briefly summarised with regard to the central questions named above. We will begin by describing the common structure of the given meanings to religion in school by the pupils and then proceed to elaborate on the differences.

Place for religion in school

There is a clear division between those respondents who think that religion should have a place in school and those who do not regard religion as a topic to be dealt with in school. The pros and cons given for the place of religion in school are dependent on pupils' previous experiences with this topic.

Looking at the responses to the question of whether religion should have a place in school, we found that a clear majority of respondents supported this view. A relationship between school and religion was viewed positively, though school was mainly understood here as a place of religious education, not a venue for religious practice. The place of religion, in the view of the respondents, is as a subject of study. However, the size of the majority varies between the countries. While most students in some places were in favour of this solution, in other cases the samples were almost evenly split, with arguments both in favour and against being defended forcefully. The arguments in favour can broadly be summarised as follows: young people favoured religion as a subject of study because they considered it important to learn about their own religion, which they understand as a vital part of their life, their education or their cultural and national roots or to learn about other religions, cultures and traditions. At a societal level, they also believed that religious education can instil religious and moral values and contribute to a peaceful coexistence of different religions.

However, some of the respondents argued against dealing with religion as a topic in school. A primary reason for this was that they were generally not interested since they regarded religion as boring, irrelevant, outdated or an unnecessary burden on an already overloaded curriculum. There seems to be a tension between religion and youth culture, which is the reason for religion being regarded as irrelevant. A further reason for the opposition to the inclusion of religion in school is the fear of religious propaganda and proselytising by teachers and fear of conflict between students being generated in the classroom, the broader school setting or society in general. Such fears underpin the position that religion is a purely private matter and should have no place in school.

The position of respondents is strongly influenced by previous experiences with religious issues being addressed in a school context. As long as students had not had bad experiences (some students in Spanish schools reported bad experiences of indoctrination in Catholic religious education), they were in favour of religion being addressed in school, while those students who had not experienced religion in school, were against it. Whether and how religious topics were addressed in school were, in turn, dependent on the educational policies and traditions of a given country that thus play an important role in shaping the positions of students.

Lesson contents

It is widely accepted that teaching *religion* in school means teaching *religions* (plural). The majority of answers regarding the content of religion lessons in school focus on acquiring knowledge. As the students wish to learn both about their own and other religions, the range of suggestions includes a dialogical exchange of personal experiences and attitudes. This plea for dialogical learning often relates to previous personal experience with mixed multi-faith education but can also emerge among students who only had confessional religious education.

The answers to the question whether religion has a place in school already showed that the respondents mostly regarded the school as a place for acquiring knowledge, rather than a venue to practise religion. This view became more explicit in the responses to the question asking what they should learn in school about religion. Across all regional settings and cases, the majority of students were in favour of gaining information about religions in school. School and the classroom were widely conceived of as places of knowledge acquisition. However, there is a group of students (they should not be underestimated) for whom the exchange of personal experiences and personal and existential relevance played a decisive role. This is the case in the Hamburg and English schools and to some degree in the Dutch and Norwegian sample. Thus, one can suggest that the entire spectrum entails the perspective of school as a place to learn about and to learn from religions. Numerous concrete suggestions for curricular content were forwarded, which can be divided into two broad groups: on the one hand, young people wanted to learn about their own religion; on the other hand (and this aspect takes precedence for most of them), they wished to learn about other religions. They exhibited a markedly stronger interest in encountering and learning about other religions than has been observed before. Although this applies more strongly for those from a religious background and/or affiliation, even those who accorded religion a low significance in their personal lives in many cases showed an interest in religion as a subject of knowledge. Even many non-religious respondents favoured addressing religious questions and issues in a school context. Finally, one remarkable observation we were able to make was that a number of respondents, when asked about the content that religious education should include, did not address what, but *how* they should be taught. This once more reflects concerns about unequal treatment and the undue influence of some religions over others. The respondents favoured an open, impartial form of religious education that leaves room for debate and questions.

Religiosity of the teacher

The teacher's religious affiliation is considered important inasmuch as it affects his/her competence as a teacher. Opinion is divided over whether a firm affiliation is an asset or an obstacle in this respect. Respondents agreed that while teachers should be free to have a personal religious affiliation, they must not allow it to affect their impartiality as educators.

The respondents showed remarkable capacity for critical reflection in their answer to the question of whether religious affiliation was desirable in religious education teachers. They were clear on the fact that religious education functions as a school subject to be studied, tested and graded and that teachers have a key function in that process. Their role, influence and educational competence were regarded as key factors and assessed critically. The responses in this matter did not share a fundamental position but rather proffered arguments for and against, centring on the issue of competence. Three main lines of argument predominated. A large proportion of the respondents held that, as long as a teacher is able to address religious content competently and tactfully, religious affiliation is not an issue. However, those respondents who considered personal religiosity to be a fundamental prerequisite for teaching religion favoured religious affiliation on the teacher's part. But the majority either viewed religious affiliation on the part of the teacher with scepticism or rejected it outright over concerns that it could lead to pressure, proselytism, favouritism or partiality. Teachers may practise a religion personally, but only as long as it does not infringe on the neutrality expected of them in their position as educators. Thus, the position of respondents on the religiosity of teachers was largely rooted in their view of whether such religiosity presents a problem or, conversely, constitutes an essential qualification for a religion teacher.

Model of religious education: separate or together?

There is no one model of religious education that respondents favour. Whether a joint or confessionally separated instruction is favoured depends largely on the past experience of respondents. As long as students had not had negative experiences, such as offence to their personal belief, indoctrination or discrimination, they were in favour of the model with which they were already acquainted. Those respondents without any personal experience were about equally divided between the two approaches.

While preferences regarding the religiosity of the teacher and the contents of religious education seemed to be hardly influenced by contextual setting, their views on whether religious education should take place in mixed or confessionally separated groups were strongly informed by it. There was no one single favoured model, but three different positions predominated: in some cases, a clear majority favoured confessional separation; in others, a mixed class was advocated; in the third case, the respondents were split broadly 50:50 on this issue. Proponents of joint lessons argued from four positions: From a personal perspective, they expressed a wish to (a) learn about other religions and (b) share their views with others and afford them the same opportunity. They further believed that learning together fosters (c) better mutual understanding, which they regarded as (d) vital preparation for life in a modern religiously plural society and a preventative measure against conflicts. Those who proposed confessional instruction in groups separated according to faith or denomination mostly argued that they (1) wished to acquire a thorough understanding of their own religion while they often found others uninteresting or were concerned that introducing differing religious views might confuse them. Separate instruction was also favoured because it (2) led to strengthened religious convictions. Interestingly, they also forwarded arguments similar to those proposed by the opposite position in that they said that (3) separate learning groups ensured a free exchange of views and prevented conflicts. As with positions on the role of the school as a venue for religious education (and experience), the personal experience of the respondents can be shown to have a strong influence here. The majority of students who had experienced religious instruction in heterogeneous groups, as is the case in the Norwegian, the English and the Hamburg samples (and this could, to a degree, also be said of the French case) favoured non-confessional religious education, while those who had been taught in confessional groups (Germany/North Rhine-Westphalia) preferred that model. Those respondents who had not or had only sporadically experienced religious education personally (students from Estonia and from St. Petersburg) were equally divided between both positions. This, too, demonstrates the degree to which the views and positions of young people can be shaped by their contextual settings.

Reflection and interpretation

In the following, we will present an integrated overview of the findings, taking account of the different contextual settings of religion in schools. This is indicated not the least because our analysis of responses has shown that the experiences that young people had, or more importantly did not have, are particularly strong influences on their views, sometimes more pronounced than gender, religious affiliation or migration history. These experiences are, in turn, particularly liable to be influenced by the contextual setting inside the school environment. Thus, we will now interpret the findings not just in the context of individual variables but also especially with regard to the contextually determined ground rules of addressing religion in the school environment.

The regional and national research reports broadly showed three different types of contextual settings for addressing religion in school:

- *An integrative, plurality-fostering approach*. State policy takes account of and favours religious plurality. This is reflected in educational designs aimed at the integration or cooperation of different religions. Religious plurality is actively fostered, and learning from different religions in a dialogic, experience-centred manner is a curricular goal. The dominant intention of religious education can be defined as 'learning from religions'; religious education attempts to integrate cognitive and experiential aspects into a comprehensive whole using the teaching content as a tool for personal development. The best example for this is the English case, but the situation as it was described in the setting of Hamburg and (partly) in the Norwegian sample too approaches this type of contextual setting.
- *A plurality conscious, but separate approach*. The extant plurality of religions in modern society is acknowledged, but no attempt is made to integrate what are conceived of as separate, self-contained entities. This separation may also be reflected in schools segregated by confession. Within a school, it is expressed by separate religious instruction for students of different religious affiliation. Religious plurality may be represented in the subject curriculum, but this is only done in terms of factual knowledge. The subject is often understood as confessional religious instruction, aiming to introduce the students to a given religious tradition. The situation in the Spanish case may be regarded as prototypical for this approach, though the schools studied in the German state of North Rhine-Westphalia followed a similar pattern. The report on the students in the Christian foundation school in the Netherlands describes a broadly similar situation. The survey took place in a Christian school, and students of a non-Christian background hardly figured in it. While being aware of the fact that this Dutch case should not be generalised as typical for the situation in the Netherlands, one has to recognise that the Dutch post-pillarised educational system still incorporates strong traditions of separation by confession that are mirrored in the case analysed in the qualitative study.
- *A strongly secular, traditionally critical approach to religion. Religious education is not a school subject in its own right*. The contents and expressions of religion tend to remain invisible in the scholastic context. Religion and religious plurality may be the subject of study, but only in a context of a neutral presentation of factual knowledge. The dominant aim is to 'teach about religions'. This setting has developed from a long

tradition of separation of church and state in the respective national or regional education systems. The most salient example was given in the French case, though both Estonia and Russia also serve as examples for an approach to religion that does not accord it the status of a traditional subject in its own right.

We have to emphasise again that this categorisation does not serve primarily to make distinctions between nations. Of course, national educational and religious policies are strong influences on the contextual setting of any school, but the approaches outlined above do not define national conditions, but typical constellations which were identified in various places in the course of our research and to which the situations in different national or regional studies conformed to a certain degree. It was possible in the case of some countries, such as Germany and France, to identify regionally very different contextual settings. Our assertion remains that these contextual settings function as a formative background for the experiences individual students have of religion in school. With this in mind, we will proceed to interpret some findings and highlight some of the contextual differences they show.

The greatest degree of unanimity among young people throughout Europe was found on the point that *religion should have a place in school*. This support grows from all three constellations. However, the responses also show a degree of tension. These range between a readiness to embrace religious diversity to a distanced, cautious approach to the perceived dangers of religion. When correlating these poles to the above-mentioned contextual constellations, we find that religion and religious plurality are valued especially in settings where religion is an accepted presence in school settings and personal experience in interfaith dialogue is common, such as in the English sample (Ipgrave and McKenna 2008, 136f.). A more distanced view towards religion as a subject or area of study is found to emerge from different constellations. It is particularly pronounced in settings where religious education has little traditional presence in the school curriculum and environment; such as Estonia (Schihalejev 2008, 266; 2010) or St Petersburg (Kozyrev 2008, 299). However, it can also be rejected when visible religious differences in the school environment are felt to threaten ideals of equality as in the French case (Béraud, Massignon, and Mathieu 2008, 78).

Similar tension becomes evident in the question of the *teaching content* desired. We can see a relatively clear fault line between a *knowledge-based* and an *experiential* orientation, in didactic terms, the difference between *teaching about religions* and *learning from religions*. Here, too, it is evident that the combination of knowledge and experience orientation with the intention of learning from different religious traditions is particularly emphasised in a plurality-fostering, dialogical approach to religion (Ipgrave and McKenna 2008, 138f.; Knauth 2008, 234f.). It does not come as a surprise that this has a home in a traditionally integrative school subject. A more remarkable fact is that a desire for knowledge about other religions is strongly evident in traditionally separate or secular contexts of types (b) and (c) as well. Independent of contextual factors, a consensus that school should teach its students about different religions prevails across all European schools we surveyed.

The question of the *religious belief of teachers is positioned between the poles of 'religious'* versus *'non-religious'*, between an emphasis on *religious experience* and on *pedagogic competence*. It is interesting to note that the structure of responses is similar in all contextual settings. We believe that this is due to the fact that the respondents most strongly reflected the systemic aspects of school when considering the role of the teacher and thus sought to balance competence and equal treatment. The only exception, at first glance, appears to be the French case with a unanimous plea for the strict neutrality of the teacher (Béraud, Massignon, and Mathieu 2008, 75). But a deeper analysis shows that this neutrality is an indispensable part of the teacher's competence. In other words, with regard to the question of whether a religious education teacher should be religious, the different religious and ideological positions and contextual factors are superseded by the common role of school student which all respondents experience and interpret similarly.

The question of *how religious education should be structured*, however, is strongly informed by the contextual setting. Basically, the respondents favoured what they knew, as long as their personal experiences had not been too negative. It is nonetheless worthwhile to look more closely at some regional or national contextual characteristics. Regarding the situation in Spain, we find that the vote for and against confessional religious education follows an interesting religious majority–minority constellation. Muslim students tended to favour separated religious education because they demanded assurances that their religion is represented in a Christian-dominated school context at all and remains visible in a Catholic-dominated society (Dietz, Rosón Lorente, and Ruiz Garzón 2008, 46). The problem in France, conversely, is not the invisibility of Islam in school but its conspicuous visibility that is interpreted as a challenge to a traditionally secular state education system with its strict neutrality requirement in teaching about religious issues (Béraud, Massignon, and Mathieu 2008, 79). The situation as it was described in the St Petersburg case (Kozyrev 2008, 304f.) and in Estonian schools (Schihalejev 2008, 272; 2010), on the other hand, seems to reflect a state of transition in the relatively evenly divided vote on whether religious education should be separate or common. Altogether, these secular settings appear to be characterised by a cautious and distanced approach to the subject: religious education, of whatever kind, is strongly associated with voluntarism. In the Dutch report (ter Avest et al. 2008, 106) and in the Norwegian analysis (von der Lippe 2008, 166f.), as well as for a certain secularised group of German students (Knauth 2008, 238f.), we note, however, that a shared religious education is also valued by young people with a distanced, critical position towards religion. If this group is interested in religion, the non-confessional model offers them the best opportunity to formulate and explore this personal interest because they rather tend to focus on religion as a phenomenon expressed in numerous different traditions.

Students from settings having an inclusive religious education that integrates them from different backgrounds as in Hamburg (Knauth 2008, 239) and the English community schools (Ipgrave and McKenna 2008, 140) especially had a regard for this approach as a model for the much desired peaceful coexistence of religions in school and society, largely based on their own positive experiences. Yet, they shared this vision with respondents who preferred a separate religious education on the grounds that it would be less likely to generate the kind of conflict that could result from confronting religious differences openly.

Conclusion

Our interpretation of the findings in the light of their contextual settings leads us to conclude the following. The views of the majority of students surveyed point towards an orientation that favours religion and plurality and tolerance in religious matters as part of the school curriculum. Young people from eight European countries, coming from a wide range of social, cultural and religious backgrounds, showed themselves to be strongly aware of the increased importance of religion to their life and society. They want to broaden their knowledge of the religious dimension and of different religious traditions because they take religion seriously as a factor for dialogue and conflict and share a strong desire for people from different backgrounds to live together in peace.[3]

However: this shared orientation does not extend to unanimity over the place of religion in school. Our analysis indicates that there can be no unitary solution for bringing religion into schools throughout Europe. This is, as a matter of fact, also true for different contexts within countries and regions. Rather, it seems to be advisable to take careful account of the diverse contextual settings. This publication and the REDCo research overall, however, suggests evidence that the development and support of context-sensitive dialogical approaches to religion into school and society could be a promising endeavour because religious plurality is expected to become an issue of increasing importance in future.

Notes

1. A comprehensive description of the different contexts of religions in school in the participating countries is given in Jackson et al. (2007).
2. Compare the differentiation between introducing into, learning about and learning from as it was introduced by Ziebertz (1994), referring to Grimmitt (1994). The first concept 'introducing into' conforms to a mono-religious orientation aiming at making the students familiar with the traditions and practices of one particular religion whereat religious plurality is acknowledged. 'Learning about' as the second type of religious education complies with a multireligious character by following the idea of providing the students with objective information about different religious traditions in a neutral manner. The third concept 'learning from' targets at giving

orientation and life direction to students for what all religions may serve as source of meaning, while, in practice, this concept is likely to root in one particular religion.

3. This general tendency that young people show a positive attitude towards religious pluralism in school and society could be confirmed by the large-scale quantitative study within the REDCo project. School is expected to function as a place for imparting knowledge, learning the ability for (inter-) religious dialogue and understanding the role religion plays in society, whereas the majority do not wish it to be a place for religious socialisation. This also corresponds to the findings of other research studies in the field of religious education. Nonetheless, it became clear that in plural European societies, different requirements will have to be aligned, e.g., the expectations of Muslim students who wish to a much higher degree that school should not only to be a place for knowledge acquisition but also for leading to religious belief (Körs 2009, 270f.).

References

Béraud, C., B. Massignon, and S. Mathieu. 2008. French students, religion and school: The ideal of Laïcité at stake with religious diversity. In *Encountering religious pluralism in school and society: A qualitative study of teenage perspectives in Europe,* ed. T. Knauth, D.-P. Jozsa, G. Bertram-Troost, and J. Ipgrave, 51–80. Münster: Waxmann.

Dietz, G., J. Rosón Lorente, and F. Ruiz Garzón. 2008. Religion and education in the view of Spanish youth: The legacy of mono-confessionalism in times of religious pluralisation. In *Encountering religious pluralism in school and society: A qualitative study of teenage perspectives in Europe,* ed. T. Knauth, D.-P. Jozsa, G. Bertram-Troost, and J. Ipgrave, 21–49. Münster: Waxmann.

Grimmitt, M. 1994. Religious education and the ideology of pluralism. *British Journal of Religious Education* 16, no. 3: 133–47.

Ipgrave, J., and G. Bertram-Troost. 2008. European comparison: Personal views and experiences of religion. In *Encountering religious pluralism in school and society: A qualitative study of teenage perspectives in Europe,* ed. T. Knauth, D.-P. Jozsa, G. Bertram-Troost, and J. Ipgrave, 375–87. Münster: Waxmann.

Ipgrave, J., and U. McKenna. 2008. Diverse experiences and common vision: English students' perspectives on religion and religious education. In *Encountering religious pluralism in school and society: A qualitative study of teenage perspectives in Europe,* ed. T. Knauth, D.-P. Jozsa, G. Bertram-Troost, and J. Ipgrave, 113–47. Münster: Waxmann.

Jackson, R., S. Miedema, W. Weisse, and J.P. Willaime, eds. 2007. *Religion and education in Europe: Developments, contexts and debates.* Münster: Waxmann.

Jozsa, D.-P., and M. Friederici. 2008. European comparison: Social dimension of religion. In *Encountering religious pluralism in school and society: A qualitative study of teenage perspectives in Europe,* ed. T. Knauth, D.-P. Jozsa, G. Bertram-Troost, and J. Ipgrave, 389–96. Münster: Waxmann.

Knauth, T. 2008. 'Better together than apart': Religion in school and lifeworld of students in Hamburg. In *Encountering religious pluralism in school and society: A qualitative study of teenage perspectives in Europe,* ed. T. Knauth, D.-P. Jozsa, G. Bertram-Troost, and J. Ipgrave, 207–45. Münster: Waxmann.

Knauth, T., D.-P. Jozsa, G. Bertram-Troost, and J. Ipgrave, eds. 2008. *Encountering religious pluralism in school and society: A qualitative study of teenage perspectives in Europe.* Münster: Waxmann.

Körs, A. 2009. Jugend und religion in Europa. Einstellungen zu Religion in Lebenswelt, Schule und Gesellschaft im Vergleich acht europäischer Länder [Youth and religion in Europe. Attitudes towards religion in their lives, school and society by comparison of eight European countries.]. In *Religionsunterricht, Dialog und Konflikt: Analysen im Kontext Europas* [Religious education, dialogue and conflict: Analyses in European contexts], ed. D.-P. Jozsa, T. Knauth, and W. Weiße, 241–86. Münster: Waxmann.

Kozyrev, F. 2008. Religion and education through the eyes of students from Saint-Petersburg. In *Encountering religious pluralism in school and society: A qualitative study of teenage perspectives in Europe,* ed. T. Knauth, D.-P. Jozsa, G. Bertram-Troost, and J. Ipgrave, 279–308. Münster: Waxmann.

Schihalejev, O. 2008. Meeting diversity: Students' perspectives in Estonia. In *Encountering religious pluralism in school and society: A qualitative study of teenage perspectives in Europe,* ed. T. Knauth, D.-P. Jozsa, G. Bertram-Troost, and J. Ipgrave, 247–78. Münster: Waxmann.

Schihalejev, O. 2010. *From indifference to dialogue? Estonian young people, the school and religious diversity.* Münster: Waxmann.

ter Avest, I., G. Bertram-Troost, A. van Laar, S. Miedema, and C. Bakker. 2008. Religion in the educational lifeworld of students: Results of a Dutch qualitative study. In *Encountering religious pluralism in school and society: A qualitative study of teenage perspectives in Europe,* ed. T. Knauth, D.-P. Jozsa, G. Bertram-Troost, and J. Ipgrave, 81–111. Münster: Waxmann.

von der Lippe, M. 2008. To believe or not to believe: Young people's perceptions and experiences of religion and religious education in Norway. In *Encountering religious pluralism in school and society: A qualitative study of teenage perspectives in Europe,* ed. T. Knauth, D.-P. Jozsa, G. Bertram-Troost, and J. Ipgrave, 149–71. Münster: Waxmann.

Ziebertz, H.G. 1994. Religiöse Lernprozesse und theologisches Bewusstsein [Religious learning processes and theological consciousness]. In *Religiöser Pluralismus und Interreligiöses Lernen* [Religious pluralism and interreligious learning], ed. J.A. van der Ven and H.G. Ziebertz, 233–75. Weinheim, Kampen: Dt. StudienVerlag, Kok.

Influences on students' views on religions and education in England and Estonia

Sean Neill[a] and Olga Schihalejev[b]

[a]Institute of Education, University of Warwick, Coventry CV4 7AL, UK; [b]Faculty of Theology, University of Tartu, Tartu, Estonia

Structural modelling offers an overall pattern of relationships; this paper looks at differences in students' attitude structures between England and Estonia. Where different coherent sets of beliefs exist in a national sample, factor analysis, which focuses on sets of responses which differ between groups, should be able to separate them out. England and Estonia differ both in the composition of the factors, indicating differences in the patterns of viewpoints between the students in the two countries, and in the interrelation between the factors and influences. In England, the first factor indicates attitude differences between the religiously *committed* and the uncommitted, but in Estonia this is only the second factor, despite the importance of religion to the 'Russians'. In Estonia the first, *integrative,* factor relates to religious education, which evokes much more divergence of opinion than in the English data. In the structural model, the most striking differences relate to the stronger differences in belief in Estonia, the greater influence of *language spoken* in England and the effect of *RE model* only in Estonia. However, the Estonian data indicate that individual influences on *commitment* reduce the effect of *RE model*, a group-level influence.

Introduction

In the framework of the REDCo (Religion in Education. A contribution to Dialogue or a Factor of Conflict in Transforming Societies of European Countries?) project, a survey among 14–16-year-old students in eight countries was carried out and the results were analysed at a univariate and bivariate level by Valk et al. (2009) (see also Schihalejev 2010, chap. 4). A particular focus of the project was on dialogue and interaction between students who had different beliefs. The different systems of religious education (RE) in different countries, especially in those countries where RE is optional or students within a country have very different RE experiences, may be seen as providing a 'natural experiment' on the value of RE. There are different approaches to RE across Europe; approaches that emphasise religious nurture or the formation of faith, and those that emphasise learning *about* different religions. Some variants on the latter also encourage students to reflect on their learning in clarifying their own personal views (sometimes called 'learning from' religion(s), while others concentrate on the informational side of the subject. The broad similarities across countries in the quantitative survey (Beraud 2009; Bertram-Troost 2009; Valk 2009) overlie marked differences between countries.

In this paper, we compare the responses of students in two countries with divergent histories – England and Estonia. In the 1920s, a new model of RE was introduced and Estonia became one of the first countries with a model of non-confessional RE. Under the Soviet regime (1940–late-1980s) RE in schools was prohibited and in some places courses on scientific atheism were introduced or atheistic instruction took place in various subjects (Remmel 2004). Now, two decades after renewed independence, the majority of students in Estonia acquire their knowledge, attitudes and views about religion by studying religion in their history, civic education and literature courses. Only a few schools offer an elective subject of RE, usually in primary classes or for a year in upper secondary school with the main emphasis on teaching about religions and only a cautious attempts to touch upon students' own personal views (Schihalejev 2010 gives the historical and legislative background).

In England, since the 1970s, most schools follow a similar pluralistic, multifaith curriculum which aims not only to teach children about religions but also encourages them to interpret and reflect on their own personal views in the light of their studies (a combination of 'learning about' and 'learning from' religion; Grimmitt 1987); this replaced non-denominational Christian RE which had developed since the 1870s.

This publication uses structural modelling which offers particular benefits in providing an overall pattern of relationships; the programme fits an overall significance level for the model overall, rather than looking at individual elements. Modelling also allows the effect of specific influences to be assessed after controlling for the effects of other influences.

The different educational value systems act on children who are biologically similar. Neill's (2007) review of the literature suggested that socialised value systems must depend on inborn predispositions, in an analogous way to languages; the wide cultural variety of languages is constrained by children's ability to learn them, and similarly children must value the opinion of those who socialise them to values (damage to the prefrontal lobes of the brain prevents normal socialisation into the values of the society). In formulating a model of how students had responded to their differing experiences, as revealed in their questionnaire answers, we distinguished between:[1]

- 'Ultimate' influences (e.g. *gender*, *language* spoken at home (as defined below) and *model of RE*) – students usually have little control over these.

Language spoken was used as index of integration. For Estonia *language* was classified into Estonian and non-Estonian. For England the 36 languages spoken were classified into four groups: English, English and other (English the main language), other and English, other only. For Estonia only, *model of RE* was also included. This had four ranks according to the respondents' experience of RE: no RE; RE in the primary school only (where the content was usually dealing largely with Christianity and folk festivals); recent RE in the secondary school (where the content is world religions); and an integrated form of dealing with religion (which is usually based on the ecumenical-Christian tradition and so quite different from 'ordinary RE', which is multi-religious);

- 'Intermediate' influence (religious commitment, measured by a question on how important respondents felt religion was to them) – this can be seen as a disposition, arising from the influence of the ultimate causes at a younger age which were outside the individual's control at that age (Neill 2007), which underlies all the proximate outcomes;
- 'Proximate' outcomes (e.g. attitudes) – in adolescents, some responses need to be seen as outcomes, even though they may have been causes of behaviour at an earlier stage, for example whether students have friends from other religious backgrounds.

An important point is that membership of most faith communities entails conforming to a set of beliefs consistent with other members of that faith community (Henrich and Boyd 2001); where different coherent sets of beliefs (either within a religious tradition, or between religious traditions) exist in a national sample, it should be possible to separate them out by factor analysis, as respondents with different sets of beliefs will give different sets of answers in the questionnaire. These factors were then incorporated into a structural model.

Methods

The English sample comprised 421 students across 16 secondary schools. The only school in the sample not following the locally agreed syllabus for RE was one which used a Roman Catholic syllabus. The Estonian sample had 1208 respondents from 21 schools; the selected schools differed in type, size and most importantly, in the models of RE adopted. In both countries students were 14–16 years of age and schools were distributed across the country. Details of the sample and univariate and bivariate analyses for the English sample are given in McKenna, Neill, and Jackson (2009) and for the Estonian sample in Schihalejev (2009). As the questionnaire (Friederici 2009) included 108 questions about behaviour, the first step was to use factor analysis in SPSS to reduce these to a manageable number of factors. The questions had been grouped to reflect that the questions arising from the qualitative phase of

REDCo (Knauth et al. 2008) but, since it is likely that students would not have the same conceptual structure as Knauth et al., all sections of the questionnaire were included in the analysis, to discover the students' actual conceptual structure rather than one imposed by the researchers.

In factor analysis, the highest loadings on each factor are the questions which are answered most differently by groups of people with different views, so the labels given to each factor below are based on these questions, which represent the statistical core of the factor. To compute new factor variables, questions loading at or above .400 on each factor were averaged; negatively loaded questions were summed and subtracted from the summed score for the positive questions. These new factor variables and the hypothesised influences on the outcomes are then correlated to provide guidance on a suitable structure for modelling with AMOS.[2] The English and Estonian data are described in order, followed by comparisons and the conclusion.

Results

England

A preliminary factor analysis with an unlimited number of factors indicated that the initial factors were stable but that, after the sixth factor, the remaining factors contained only small numbers of questions and accounted for small amounts of variance. A six-factor solution was therefore adopted. The first factor was *commitment* to religion, on to which were loaded 26 questions at .400 or above, mainly related to personal religious practice (e.g. 'how often do you pray?') and belief (e.g. 'religion is important to me because I love God'). There were negative loadings for anti-religious questions such as 'religion is nonsense'. A few school-related questions preferring to nurture into religion, such as 'voluntary religious services could be a part of school life', were among the lower loadings, and a few questions about RE at school were among the loadings between .400 and .300; but overall, as the label implies, this factor relates to religious attitudes and practice. As in other countries (Valk et al. 2009), in England Muslims were more committed than adherents to other religions (McKenna, Neill, and Jackson 2009).

The second factor is called *integrative*, following the English multifaith approach to the RE curriculum, which aims to teach about religions in an open and impartial way rather than to nurture pupils into particular religious beliefs (Jackson and O'Grady 2007; QCA 2004). The loadings in this factor (and the corresponding Estonian factor) included a wide variety, integrating religion into relations and into personal life; most of the statements were about the value of being aware of different religions. So, while this does not contradict Alberts' (2007) concept of 'integrative' RE (e.g. 'Learning about different religions at school helps us to live together' would be very consistent with Alberts' concept), the label '*integrative*' is used here only to describe the structure of the factor. The highest loadings on this factor are for 'learning about different religions at school helps us to live together' and 'learn to understand what religions teach'; the emphasis is school-based and pluralistic, though the 32 questions which loaded at .400 or above also included questions about the formation of respondents' own values and self-understanding and their personal relations with peers. Some of the questions which loaded on to both factors 1 and 2, indicate that students who share the *commitment* factor and *integrative* factor are well disposed to talking about religion as a means to shape their own views as well towards living 'peacefully together'. The aspect that the second factor had a greater number of questions loading at a high level on to it, but accounted for less variance than the first, reflects that *commitment* is more polarised than acceptance of the multifaith curriculum approach, which can be accepted both by those who are religiously committed themselves and by those who are uncommitted or antipathetic to religion.

The third factor, which may be labelled *secularisation*, has loadings such as 'without religion the world would be a better place' and 'disagreement on religious issues leads to conflicts'. Some questions, are loaded positively on this factor but negatively on the first *commitment* factor, while others, such as 'there should be no place for religion in school life' are loaded positively on this factor but negatively on the second *integrative* factor. This factor, which has 14 loadings above .400, therefore represents anti-religious intolerance rather than intolerance by one religion towards another.

The fourth factor may be labelled *contact* as the seven loadings above .400 all related to interpersonal contact such as 'at school I go round with young people who have different religious backgrounds'. Where this factor shares loadings with the *commitment* and *integrative* factors, they are in the same direction, while loadings it shares with the *secularisation* factor are loaded in the opposite direction.

The remaining two factors have only a few loadings. The fifth *separation* factor has only three loadings above .400 such as 'pupils should study religious education separately in groups according to which religion they belong'. The factor shares a positive loading with the *commitment* factor, but shared loadings with *integrative* and (as might be expected) *contact* are opposite. The sixth factor may be labelled *uncertainty* as its loadings are for questions such as 'what I think about religion is open to change'.

In the correlation matrix between the factors and the putative causal variables, we may start with the intercorrelations between the factors. As might be expected from the discussion of the factors above, the *commitment, integrative* and *contact* factors are highly significantly intercorrelated with each other and negatively correlated with the *secularisation* factor. The *separation* factor is more weakly, though still highly significantly, correlated with *commitment* but there are no significant correlations between the *uncertainty* factor and other factors. There was a highly significant positive correlation between *commitment* and the importance students attributed to religion and their belief in a

God. The patterns of correlation for the *integrative* factor were similar, though lower but still highly significant. Students with less integrated *home language* showed highly significantly more *commitment* and *integrative* attitudes. Girls were more positive towards the *integrative* approach but there was no gender difference for *commitment.*

Correspondingly, *secularisation* showed a negative correlation to religious commitment and belief in a God and was an attitude less likely to be held by girls and students with less integrated *home language. Contact* showed a similar pattern of correlations to the *integrative* factor except for no gender effect.

The relations between the other two factors and potential causes were weaker; boys, and those who felt religion more important being highly significantly more likely to endorse *separation* and those who believed in a God significantly more likely to do so. However, these correlations were much lower than for the previous factors. Similarly the correlations between *uncertainty* and potential causes were relatively weak, with girls scoring more highly on *uncertainty* and those who felt religion important, believed in a God, or had less integrated *home language* scoring lower on *uncertainty.* It should be pointed out that those who believed in a life force, for example, were only relatively less certain about the existence of God than those who believed in a God, indicating that they were 'searchers' for the meaning of the concept of 'God'.

In building the structural model we assumed that students' attitudes towards the *importance of religion* influence their answers to the other questions; factors which were highly correlated were combined by 'latent variables'. 'Latent variables' may be seen as attitudes underlying the observed factors; *belief* underlying *commitment* and *separation,* and *understanding* underlying *integrative* and *contact. Uncertainty* was omitted because it had weak correlations with other variables and accounted for only a small amount of variance. In the figures, observed variables (including the factor variables discussed above) are displayed in rectangular boxes, the latent variables in oval boxes. Oval boxes are also used for the error estimates; these account for the remaining variance where two variables are not perfectly correlated.

The model (Figure 1) shows *language spoken* is strongly related to *how important* students felt religion was to them, with gender having a negligible effect. Students' views on the *importance of religion* were very strongly correlated with their *'personal' spirituality* or belief in a God. The *importance of religion* was strongly associated with the latent variable of *belief;* this latent variable related almost entirely to *commitment,* its association with *separation* being very weak. *Belief* is also strongly correlated with, and seen as the cause of the latent variable of *understanding;* this latent variable is strongly associated both with *contact* and very strongly with *integrative.* There was, as might be expected, a strong negative correlation between *how important* respondents considered religion, and support for *secularisation,* and also a negative correlation between support for *secularisation* and *understanding.* These two

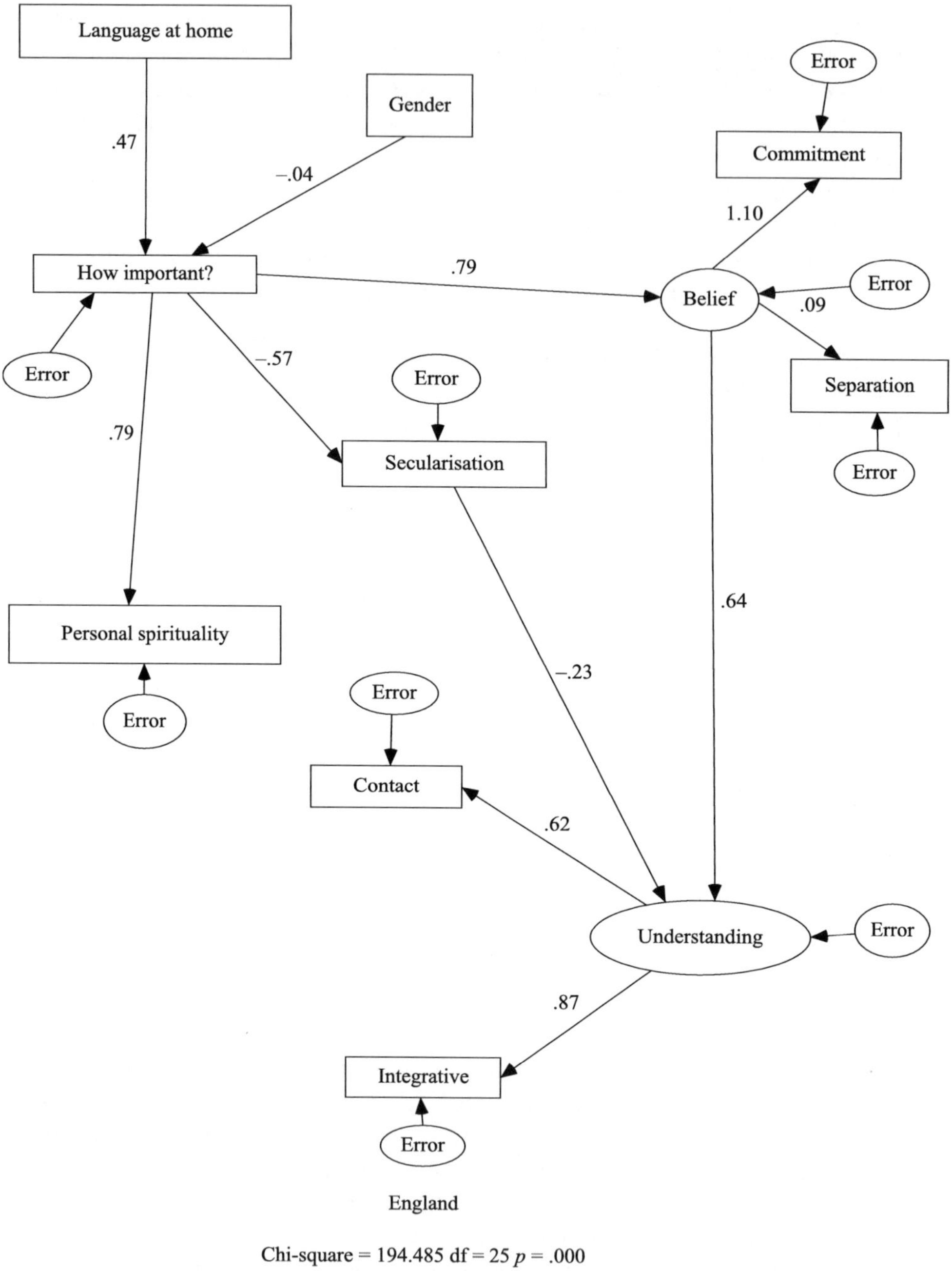

Figure 1. Structural model for England.

negative correlations mean that *how important* and *understanding* are correlated both via *secularisation* and via *belief*; their overall correlation can be calculated by multiplying up the correlations along both pathways.

Estonia

A preliminary analysis indicated that a five-factor solution was appropriate. The first factor, with 34 loadings above .400, focused on *integrative approaches* to RE, labelling positive attitudes towards education about religion at school; an example of the highest loadings was 'I find topics about religions interesting at school'. Although it focused on understanding religions and their place in the world, current events and history, and understanding others, the factor integrated a wide range of aspects, including questions about learning and developing one's own views and respect for and interaction with others. Lower loadings included school support for religion, such as facilities for prayer in school. The label *integrative* is intended to convey that students who responded positively to this factor not only favoured understanding and enquiry about religion for others and themselves, but, at an abstract level,[3] also school support for their religious identity formation. As discussed below, this factor, which accounts for a large proportion of the total variance, reflects a sharp divergence between those who accept and reject RE.

The second factor (with 15 loadings above .400) can be seen as personal *commitment*; it is termed 'personal' because many of the loadings refer to private rather than public practice, such as the highest loading 'read sacred texts for yourself'. The Estonian 'commitment' factor may relate especially to the characteristics of Orthodox 'Russian' (Schihalejev 2009, 2010) respondents. These have a distinctive religious tradition of private religious practice, which was essential to preserve their religious affiliation under the previous Communist regime (see also Kozyrev and Valk 2009).

The third factor can be labelled as belief in *respect*, as it has nine loadings above .400, such as 'respecting the religion of others helps to cope with differences'. There are also lower loadings for school-related contacts, such as for 'at school, I go around with young people who have different religious backgrounds'. Where it shares loadings with other factors, the loadings on this *respect* factor are of the same sign as those for the *integrative* and *commitment* factors. The set of three factors therefore indicate the contrast between the religiously more committed who are generally positive towards RE and other religions, and the not committed, who are negative. However, the fifth factor, discussed below, indicates that some committed students support segregation.

In contrast the fourth factor represents *secular hostility* to religion, with 13 loadings such as 'I and my friends talk about how stupid religion is and what cruelties are carried out in its name'. Where this factor shares loadings with the *integrative* and *commitment* factors these loadings are of the opposite sign.

The fifth factor can be labelled as *separation* and has only two loadings above .400, such as 'pupils should study religious education separately in groups according to which religion they belong'. However there are a considerable number of loadings between .400 and .300, some of which are shared with the *integrative* and *commitment* factors, such as 'religion helps me to be a better person'.

In looking at the correlations between the outcome factors and potential causes, it is again appropriate to start by looking at the intercorrelations between the factors. The *integrative* factor is highly significantly correlated with the *commitment* and *respect* factors, but the latter two are more weakly, though still highly significantly, intercorrelated. Similarly the *respect* factor is more weakly correlated with the *separation* factor than the other two, though in all three cases the correlations are highly significant. This suggests that, while most of the 'committed' preferred a multifaith form of RE, there is a group of religiously committed students who feel more secure with separate studies. Three of the factors (*integrative, commitment* and *respect*) are very highly significantly negatively correlated with the *secular hostility* factor and more weakly with the *separation* factor. In the structural model (below) the factors are grouped to reflect the influence of the *commitment* factor, representing more personal attitudes to religion, and the *integrative* and *respect* factors, representing social interaction, especially at school. *Separation* was omitted from the final model because it had few loadings, accounted for only a small proportion of variance and was rather weakly correlated with other factors. The pattern of correlations between the factors resembles attitudes in other countries in the REDCo survey (Valk et al. 2009) where those who have belief themselves respect those who have other beliefs and support mutual understanding, and those who do not have belief are more negative to all beliefs, but is much more polarised.

Turning to the potential causes, there are strong and very highly significant correlations between the *importance of religion* to students and their *belief in God* and between both of these and the *integrative* and, especially, the *commitment* factors. However, the *respect* factor is more weakly, but still very highly significantly correlated to both. Correspondingly, the *secular hostility* factor is strongly significantly negatively correlated to the *importance* of religion and to *belief*.

Non-integrated *home language* is highly significantly correlated to the *importance* of religion and *belief* – few students had themselves been born abroad or held foreign citizenship but more substantial proportions of mothers and fathers had been born in Russia. Correspondingly, 'Russians' scored highly significantly lower both for *secular hostility* and *respect,* and highly significantly higher for *commitment.* However, there was no significant relationship between *home language* and the *integrative* factor.

The *RE model* experienced (as defined in the 'Methods' section) was very highly significantly correlated to the *integrative* and *respect* factors and significantly correlated to *commitment.* However, it was not correlated to *secular hostility,* the *importance* of religion or *belief in God.*

Girls were highly significantly more likely to consider religion important and to believe in a God; correspondingly they were less likely to show *secular hostility* to religion and rated the positive factors, especially the *integrative* and *respect* factors, higher.

For the Estonian data only one latent variable, *understanding* was used combining the *integrative* and *respect* factors. The variable of *RE model* was added to those used to analyse the English data, because in Estonia, unlike in England, experience varies widely and the correlations discussed above indicated that this had significant effects (Figure 2).

In looking at the relationships in the model, the correlation between the *importance of religion* and *commitment* was strong, and *commitment* was also strongly associated with *understanding. Understanding* was particularly closely associated with the *integrative* factor, but also had a strong correlation with the *respect* factor. *Secular hostility* was strongly negatively related to the *importance of religion,* and in turn more weakly negatively related to *understanding.*

Home language was negatively linked to *respect*, suggesting a more separatist attitude by the 'Russians' which was apparent already in the bivariate data. These, seemingly separatist, views could also be explained by their very private understanding of religion: if religion is not believed to play any role in human relations and belongs only to the private sphere of life, then there is no need for respect (Schihalejev 2009, 112).

The *RE model* experienced was correlated with *understanding*, both directly and via *commitment.* As can be seen from the model, the effects of the *RE model* were relatively weak; this is not unexpected, both by comparison with other systematic research on the effects of teaching approach on attitudes, where the effects, while very highly significant, were small (Smith and Kay 2000), and because the *RE model* is an influence at group level whereas the other 'ultimate' influences in the model, *gender* and *language spoken*, are at an individual level. Individual variation among the students exposed to each type of RE will weaken the effect of the *RE model.* Analysis of RE in Germany (Neill and Josza forthcoming), where there is also variation in RE experience, shows similar effects of the RE model, and a similar interaction between the *RE model* and *home language* (though in Germany religious non-German speakers are mostly Muslims).

Comparison and conclusion

The factor analyses of the English and Estonian data are in several ways similar but we can find important differences as well. For example *integrative* factors share many variables: they both value RE highly as a factor to promote 'peaceful together', communicative skills as well as a place to reflect on

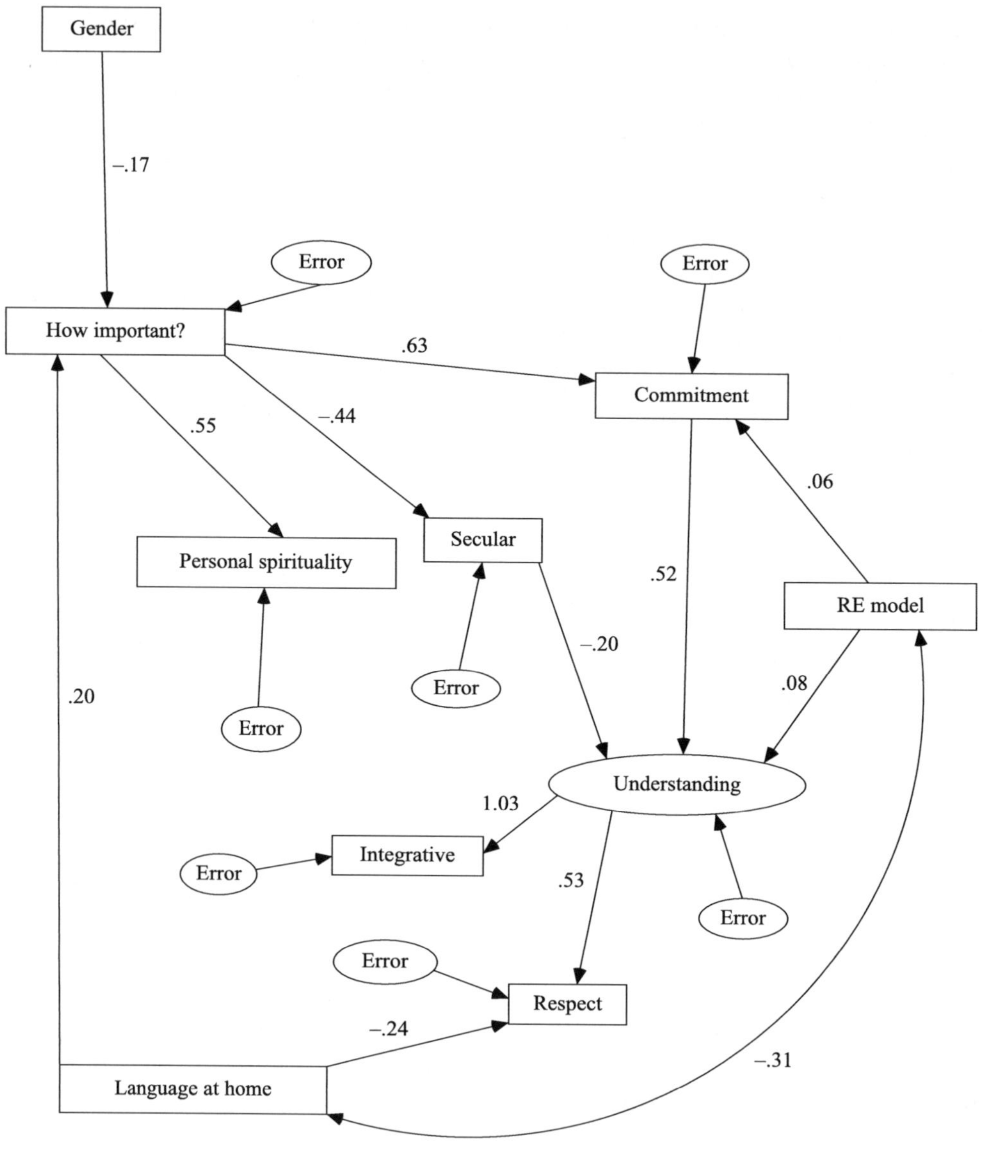

Estonia

Chi-square = 491.256 df = 23 p = .000

Figure 2. Structural model for Estonia.

students' own values and views. The differences between two countries' *integrative* factors are in the lower loadings. Here one can find 'students should be guided towards religious belief' in the Estonian factor, while the English factor included a positive loading for 'respecting the religion of others helps to cope with differences'. The Estonian factor reflects the special significance of RE for students for whom religion plays an important role in their life, while the English factor is more focused on relations.

An interesting difference between the English and Estonian *commitment* factors is that the Estonian factor does not include any negative loadings (such as 'religion is nonsense') and has fewer loadings than the English *commitment* factor. In contrast to Estonia, the English *commitment* factor includes more statements about religions' influence on one's life (religion helps to 'cope with difficulties') and several statements indicating the social effects of religion in general ('religion is important in our history') and also about schools' role in nurturing religious belief. Religiously committed students in Estonia seem to have adopted the practice of keeping religion as strictly private (Schihalejev 2010). As a result, while in England the religiously committed differ from the not committed in valuing the social dimension of religion more, in Estonia the committed and not committed do not differ in this sense, because of the 'private' orientation of the committed.

In England (McKenna, Neill, and Jackson 2009) respondents had experienced RE designed to teach 'about' religions for their entire school careers, but the observantly religious are a minority in a non-observant but generally tolerant society. As a result, the factor analysis, which focuses on identifying the distinctive groups which account for variation in the sample, picks out religious *commitment* as the factor creating the greatest variance in the English sample. In contrast, in Estonia, differing experience of RE leads to strong differences in willingness to understand about religion (Schihalejev 2010) and thus the *integrative* factor has more effect on variance than that related to *commitment.*

The Estonian *respect* factor has some similarities to the *contact* factor in the English data, but it is more theoretical, whereas the English factor includes loadings for actual friendly contacts. The Estonian *secular* factor differs from the *secularisation* factor in the English sample because the high loadings indicate a much stronger level of personal hostile aggressiveness, while the English factor emphasises more strongly abstract statements and statements of religion belonging to the private sphere.

In looking at the relationships in the model, we find that the effects of *importance of religion* and belief in a God were rather weaker in the Estonian than in the English data. This could relate to a bigger hesitation among Estonian students irrespective of their religious affiliation to label the object of their belief as 'God' (Schihalejev 2009). The correlation between the *importance of religion*, *commitment* and *understanding* are strong in both datasets. Similarly in both countries, *secular hostility* was strongly negatively related to the *importance of religion,* and in turn more weakly negatively related to *understanding.*

Overall, there are strong similarities between the factor structure in the two countries; this could be due to an innate basis of morality (Neill 2007) or a shared European culture. However, here we are concentrating on the differences caused by historical and political circumstances. The English policy of a curriculum based on a locally agreed syllabus seems to have created a more tolerant attitude especially among those who are religiously committed themselves and less antagonistic attitudes among their secular peers than in Estonia. In England all community schools must use the locally agreed syllabus as a basis for RE. In drawing up this syllabus consideration has to be given to both local circumstances and different interest groups, for example, representatives of faiths other than Christianity have to have a say in its production. Although RE in Estonia deals with different religions and involves students with different religious and secular backgrounds, it has little opportunity to influence the students with most hostile attitudes because of its voluntary status and restricted time allowance in Estonian educational settings.

We now turn to the opportunities for a more specific assessment of the effects of different types of RE which the Estonian data provide. Baker's (2010) survey of students in independent Christian schools in England offers an interesting mirror image to the Estonian situation where believers are a small minority. About 10% of the students in Baker's schools had no religious affiliation. Their views diverged highly statistically significantly from their Christian peers especially in respect of Christian values, despite being exposed to a curriculum pervaded by a strongly Christian ethos, including creationism in science. Most relevant to the REDCo data is that Baker's non-affiliated students gave significantly less tolerant answers to both questions on immigration than their Christian peers. This and the limited effect of RE on students' personal spirituality as found in the REDCo survey suggests that the concerns of opponents of RE in Estonia such as Villems (2008), that RE makes students religious, are greater than what is justified.

The relative effect of the different types of RE in Estonia accords with previous research. Primary school RE, with an emphasis on festivals, has similarities to the thematic and mixed approaches which Smith and Kay (2000) found less effective in promoting positive attitudes (to the main religions in the UK) than systematic RE; with a thematic approach it was easier for learners to become confused about which religion a component belief belonged to (Kay and Smith 2000). Estonian students with recent RE experience in the secondary school will have encountered the systematic approach, dealing with each religion as a coherent set of beliefs, which is more effective according to Smith and Kay (2000). Additionally, some hostile attitudes towards religion among students who have studied RE in primary school may be due to the fact that their understanding of religion becomes inconsistent with their general affective development if there is no RE input to reshape their understanding as they mature (Schihalejev 2009). The fact that the integrated form of RE, with its ecumenical-Christian basis, appears to have been most effective in promoting *understanding* as well as *commitment* may be explained by an apparent paradox in Kay and Smith's (2002) study of classroom factors and attitudes to world religions. They found that where copies of the Bible were used in the classroom, attitudes to Buddhism, Hinduism and Islam were improved. They suggested an explanation for this surprising finding: because attitudes towards all the religions were correlated, students' realisation that Christianity draws on an authoritative text suggested that other religions might have a similar basis.

Acknowledgements

This paper was originated with, and is dedicated to the memory of, Dr Pille Valk. Dr Ursula McKenna was responsible for the collection of the English data for the REDCo project, which was supported by Framework 6 of the European Commission. The work of Olga Schihalejev was supported by the European Union through the European Regional Development Fund (Centre of Excellence in Cultural Theory, CECT).

Notes

1. Note that here the terms 'ultimate', 'intermediate' and 'proximate' are being used in a different sense to their meaning in religious studies or theology.
2. AMOS is the sub-programme within SPSS for structural modelling.
3. Despite their general appreciation of the subject they would not choose the voluntary RE themselves as they feel it would contribute to their additional marginalisation by fellow students (Schihalejev 2009, 2010).

References

Alberts, W. 2007. *Integrative religious education in Europe: A study-of-religions approach.* Berlin/New York: Walter de Gruyter.

Baker, S.G. 2010. An investigation of the new independent Christian schools: What kind of citizens are they producing? D Phil diss., University of Warwick.

Beraud, C. 2009. The role of religion in students' lives and their surroundings. In *Teenagers' perspectives on the role of religion in their lives, schools and societies: A European quantitative study*, ed. P. Valk, G. Bertram-Troost, M. Friederici, and C. Beraud, 397–408. Münster: Waxmann.

Bertram-Troost, G. 2009. How do European pupils see religion in school? In *Teenagers' perspectives on the role of religion in their lives, schools and societies: A European quantitative study*, ed. P. Valk, G. Bertram-Troost, M. Friederici, and C. Beraud, 409–22. Münster: Waxmann.

Friederici, M. 2009. From the research question to the sampling. In *Teenagers' perspectives on the role of religion in their lives, schools and societies: A European quantitative study*, ed. P. Valk, G. Bertram-Troost, M. Friederici, and C. Beraud, 13–22. Münster: Waxmann.

Grimmitt, M.H. 1987. *Religious education and human development: The relationship between studying religions and personal, social and moral education.* Great Wakering: McCrimmons.

Henrich, J., and R. Boyd. 2001. Why people punish defectors: Weak conformist transmission can stabilise costly enforcement of norms in cooperative dilemmas. *Journal of Theoretical Biology* 208: 79–89.

Jackson, R., and K. O'Grady. 2007. Religions and education in England: Social plurality, civil religion and religious education pedagogy. In *Religion and education in Europe: Developments, contexts and debates*, ed. R. Jackson, S. Miedema, W. Weisse, and J.-P. Willaime, 181–202. Münster: Waxmann.

Kay, W.K., and D.L. Smith. 2000. Religious terms and attitudes in the classroom (part 1). *British Journal of Religious Education* 22, no. 2: 81–90.

Kay, W.K., and D.L. Smith. 2002. Classroom factors and attitude towards six world religions. *British Journal of Religious Education* 24, no. 2: 111–22.

Knauth, T., D.-P. Jozsa, G. Bertram-Troost, and J. Ipgrave, eds. 2008. *Encountering religious pluralism in school and society – A qualitative study of teenage perspectives in Europe*. Münster: Waxmann.

Kozyrev, F., and P. Valk. 2009. Saint-Petersburg students' views about religion in education – Results of the quantitative survey. In *Teenagers' perspectives on the role of religion in their lives, schools and societies: A European quantitative study*, ed. P. Valk, G. Bertram-Troost, M. Friederici, and C. Beraud, 311–49. Münster: Waxmann.

McKenna, U., S. Neill, and R. Jackson. 2009. Personal worldviews, dialogue and tolerance: Students' views on religious education in England. In *Teenagers' perspectives on the role of religion in their lives, schools and societies: A European quantitative study*, ed. P. Valk, G. Bertram-Troost, M. Friederici, and C. Beraud, 49–70. Münster: Waxmann.

Neill, S.R.St.J. 2007. 'The origins of virtue'? Should affective education pay more attention to the 'biology of virtue'? In *Learning beyond cognition*, ed. N. Kryger and B. Ravn. Copenhagen: Danish University of Education Press.

Neill, S.R.St.J., D.-P. Josza and T. Knauth. Forthcoming. Assessing the effectiveness of religious education in Hamburg and Nordrheinwestphalia through structural modeling.

QCA (Qualifications & Curriculum Authority). 2004. *Religious education the non-statutory national framework.* London: Qualifications & Curriculum Authority. http://www.qca.org.uk/6163.html.

Remmel, A. 2004. Ateismi ajaloost Eestis (XIX sajandi lõpust kuni aastani 1989) [The history of atheism in Estonia (from the end of XIX century to 1989)]. MA diss., Tartu University. http://dspace.utlib.ee/dspace/bitstream/10062/916/5/remmel.pdf.

Schihalejev, O. 2009. Options beside *'and no Religion too'* – Perspectives of Estonian youth. In *Teenagers' perspectives on the role of religion in their lives, schools and societies: A European quantitative study*, ed. P. Valk, G. Bertram-Troost, M. Friederici, and C. Beraud, 79–120. Münster: Waxmann.

Schihalejev, O. 2010. *From indifference to dialogue? Estonian young people, the school and religious diversity.* Münster: Waxmann.

Smith, D.L., and W.K. Kay. 2000. Religious terms and attitudes in the classroom (part 2). *British Journal of Religious Education* 22 no. 3: 181–91.

Valk, P. 2009. The process of the quantitative study. In *Teenagers' perspectives on the role of religion in their lives, schools and societies. A European quantitative study*, ed. P. Valk, G. Bertram-Troost, M. Friederici, and C. Beraud, 41–7. Münster: Waxmann.

Valk, P., G. Bertram-Troost, M. Friederici, and C. Beraud, eds. 2009. *Teenagers' perspectives on the role of religion in their lives, schools and societies: A European quantitative study.* Münster: Waxmann.

Villems, R. 2008. Speech of the President of the Academy on General Assembly of Estonian Academy of Sciences. 10 December. http://www.akadeemia.ee/_repository/File/TEGEVUS/ETTEKANDED/RV%2010.12.08.pdf.

European religious education teachers' perceptions of and responses to classroom diversity and their relationship to personal and professional biographies

Judith Everington[a], Ina ter Avest[b], Cok Bakker[b] and Anna van der Want[c]

[a]*Institute of Education, University of Warwick, Coventry CV4 7AL, UK;* [b]*Department of Theology, Faculty of Humanities, Utrecht University, Utrecht, The Netherlands;* [c]*School of Education, Eindhoven University of Technology, Eindhoven, The Netherlands*

This paper focuses on teachers of secondary level religious education in England, Estonia, France, Germany, the Netherlands and Norway. It presents a study of the teachers' perceptions of and responses to the diversity within their classes, in relation to their professional role and their personal and professional biographies. The study employed biographical research methods and 36 teachers were interviewed. Key findings were that, in every country, there was a clear relationship between individual teachers' personal biographies and how they responded to religious and/or cultural diversity and common cross-national strategies for dealing with these aspects of diversity. However, socio-cultural factors within each country (including dominant views of the relationship between religion and education) affected the ways in which the teachers perceived the diversity within their classes and there were national differences in how teachers prioritised aspects of diversity. The study concludes that if teachers of religion are to extend the range of their responses to classroom diversity, they would benefit from opportunities to reflect on the relationship between their perceptions of and responses to religious and cultural diversity, their personal biographies, and national requirements and expectations related to their professional role.

Introduction

The study reported below grew out of a desire on the part of a number of REDCo researchers to balance the project's focus on students with research on those responsible for providing their religion-related education. All the researchers who contributed to this study work with teachers and have a commitment towards teacher-related research. Most of them also had prior experience of biographical research and of drawing on this to promote teacher development. The publication of a European standard-setting document calling for the development of strategies for teaching about religions and beliefs in schools and related teacher training (OSCE 2007) provided an additional motivation to undertake the study.

The research design and question

The research addressed the following question: How does the role of the religious education (RE) teacher and the teacher's personal and professional biography relate to his/her perception of diversity in the classroom and to the development of his/her strategies for responding to this diversity?

Diversity

In line with the REDCo project's focus on pedagogical approaches that 'enhance dialogue and understanding without ignoring tensions between people of different religion, culture and political opinion' (Weisse 2007, 11), the team was particularly interested in exploring the teachers' perceptions of and responses to religious and cultural diversity. However, there was a concern to view these in the context of and from the wider perspective of teachers' perceptions of the diversity within their teaching groups.

As professionals who work with teachers and as researchers who have undertaken studies of RE teachers' professional lives, members of the team approached the REDCo study with an awareness of the kinds of diversity that teachers encounter within their classes. At the research design stage it was agreed that these include differences between students' backgrounds and beliefs/commitments, academic performance and attainment, and learning needs. However, there was also a recognition that, in practice, teachers do not necessarily view their teaching groups in terms of these kinds of diversity or view these as separate matters: for example, a teacher who views every student as unique may respond to each student as a whole person rather than think in terms of differences between students' backgrounds, beliefs or learning needs.

In order to avoid prejudging and/or leading interviewees' responses, it was decided that the interviews should enable the teachers to consider whether they perceive differences between their students, to identify any differences that they considered to be especially significant and, in doing so, to reveal the relative significance of particular kinds of diversity, including religious and cultural diversity. The aim was to allow differences between teachers' priorities to emerge. In this way, the team hoped to build a picture of similarities and differences between 36 teachers' perceptions and related responses and to explore possible reasons for these, focusing on the role of the RE teacher and personal and professional biographies.

RE teachers' perceptions of and responses to diversity in relation to their role and biographies

In designing the research and at stages in its discussions, the team was influenced by Kelchtermans' work on teachers' professionalism. According to Kelchtermans (2000), it is by exploring teachers' biographies in relation to their descriptions of everyday classroom practices that we can learn how they perceive diversity and develop a 'practical wisdom' to respond to this. The Swedish scholar Todd was another influence. Todd (2007) argues that teachers who are confronted with differences in their classrooms are constantly involved in a complex process of decision-making and judging the situation. When negotiating between the particular cultural and religious characteristics of their students and general principles of respect and tolerance, teachers have to make decisions 'on the spot'. In doing so, they often rely on familiar strategies informed by current 'rules', including professional and school regulations and societal expectations. Todd (2007) stresses the importance of teachers undertaking a process of critical reflection on such 'rules' and their underlying values and the role that these play in their decision-making. These theoretical propositions will be returned to in the discussion of findings.

Methodology

Selection of interviewees

Researchers from six of the eight REDCo countries chose to be involved in the study. Interviewees were selected from the researchers' own networks. This made it possible to identify teachers who would be willing and able to talk about their personal and professional lives in an interview situation (Goodson and Sikes 2001, 24).

In each country, six teachers were selected using the same criteria related to age, years of teaching experience and type of training. The intention was to ensure that the data produced for transcription and analysis would be rich but manageable (Goodson and Sikes 2001, 22). Each national group included two teachers of approximately 25, 40 and 55 years, their ages reflecting length of teaching experience, and teachers with 'no formal RE training', 'training in supplementary RE courses' and 'formal RE training'. The criteria used in this 'purposive' approach to selection (Mertens 1997) reflected the research team's experience of working with teachers of differing ages and training backgrounds; their professional view that these differences are evident in teachers' understandings of RE and strategies and a desire to explore if and how such differences might be reflected in the teachers' approaches to classroom diversity.

Semi-structured biographical interviews

The interviews were approximately one-hour long and were loosely structured, using a set of six open-ended questions. These were presented in the 'home language' but in English they were as follows:

Q1. Could you tell me who you are?
Q2. How would you describe the students in your school?
Q3. Thinking about the groups that you teach, are the students generally similar to each other or are there differences between them?
Q4. How do you feel about these differences?
Q5. How do you deal with the diversity in your groups?
Q6. Why do you think that you take this approach/these approaches?

As above, the openness of these questions was intended to allow the teachers themselves to identify significant differences. Elaboration on initial responses was left open and unstructured, enabling the interviewer to follow lines of thinking suggested by these and any emerging themes or patterns. However, a list of guidelines supported the interviewer in exploring the relationship between the teacher's personal and professional biography and between biography and perceptions of and strategies related to diversity.

Analysis of data

There were two phases of analysis. In the first phase, researchers in each country transcribed and analysed the six interviews. Analysis involved close, interpretative reading of each transcript in order to identify relationships, themes and patterns within and between the interviewees' responses (Denzin and Lincoln 2000, 633–43). All six transcripts were then read together, with the aim of identifying themes common to the six teachers.

In the second phase, researchers met to discuss the national themes and to agree a set of categories for selecting from and organising national data to produce English language 'portraits' of each teacher. A comparative cross-national analysis using 36 teachers' portraits was then undertaken. Again, this involved close reading and here the aim was to explore differences between the national 'groups' as well as identify commonalities and the themes suggested by these. The research was published in book form (van der Want et al. 2009).

Research findings

This section begins with a brief outline of RE in each of the countries. We then offer a country-by-country summary of findings related to teachers' perceptions of and responses to classroom diversity. Finally, we focus on teachers' biographies giving an indication of the key biographical themes that relate specifically to responses to religious and cultural diversity.

School-based religious education

The interviews provided data on the teachers' own understandings of their role but each researcher also provided contextual information on the status and nature of RE in his/her country. A brief summary of this is offered below: an extensive examination of RE in the REDCo countries can be found in Jackson et al. (2007).

RE occupies different positions in the countries in which the research was conducted. Whereas Norway, Germany, France and England have a prescribed national or regional curriculum, the Netherlands does not. In Estonia, the national RE syllabus is advisory and schools decide if RE will be included in the curriculum. In France, the teaching of religion(s) is governed by the concept of *laïcité*, meaning that all state 'services', including education, must be strictly neutral in religious matters (Williame 2007). RE is not a subject in its own right: 'religious facts' are taught in a number of subjects (such as philosophy and history) and teachers have a degree of freedom in judging where and how to introduce aspects of religions.

In England, Norway and Estonia RE is a non-confessional subject, that is, it does not seek to nurture students in a religious faith. In Germany and the Netherlands RE can be either non-confessional or faith based. In Germany the religious communities in each 'state' are responsible for the content of RE. In the Netherlands each school is free to shape RE in accordance with its formal religious identity and there is no legal requirement for its inclusion in the curriculum. RE is a compulsory subject in England and Norway and in German state schools although there is a legal right of withdrawal. In highly secularised Estonia, only 10% of schools offer RE as an optional subject.

Teachers' perceptions of diversity and related classroom strategies

Here we offer a summary of findings, presented country by country. The intention is to offer a picture of the differences and commonalities that emerged at the stage of cross-national analysis and to introduce the relationship between teachers' professional and personal lives.

Reflecting on the diversity within their classes, the English teachers focused initially on socio-economic differences. They related these differences to students' classroom performance, aspirations and attainment. Several teachers also referred to ethnic differences and some talked about students' racist attitudes and their efforts to deal with these. In terms of strategies, all of the teachers wished to avoid drawing attention to students' religious affiliations and the differences between these, as summed up in the claim: 'I treat them all equally.' Teachers were opposed to using students from religious backgrounds as a source of information and wished to avoid embarrassing them. One teacher related this to her daughter's experience of being 'picked on' to talk about her Christian faith in RE lessons and subsequent rejection of her Christian identity.

Teachers were also concerned that drawing attention to the 'difference' of students from minority groups would create or exacerbate divisions within their classes. However, all spoke of encouraging students who volunteer to talk about their beliefs and experiences and of seeking ways of encouraging those who were more reticent including creating a 'safe' and supportive classroom atmosphere.

Estonian teachers rarely made reference to the religious background of their students but all recognised differences in students' attitudes to religion and RE. Although negative attitudes could result in bad behaviour, the teachers were generally positive about the diversity of students' attitudes as these made lessons lively and interesting and could be used as a learning resource. However, there was agreement that the beliefs of students with religious commitments were rarely addressed in lessons, given their reluctance to make explicit statements about religion in front of their classmates. Some teachers used their own religious beliefs to encourage such students, whilst others avoided personal disclosure as inappropriate in school. A number of the teachers expressed concern at the vulnerability of students with religious commitments and a desire to respect their privacy. Relating this approach to her personal life, one interviewee explained: 'Teachers denigrated my little sister in front of others in the class, then it was awkward for others to start a friendship …'

The French teachers' first response to the question of classroom diversity was to refer to students' academic performance and learning needs. Socio-economic inequalities were a second aspect of diversity referred to and there was particular concern about the impact of poverty and family problems on students' learning. However, teachers also talked of the ways in which they responded to cultural and religious diversity, within the constraints of laïcité. One philosophy teacher explained that she did not enquire about students' religious backgrounds, 'because they have the right not to be assigned an identity', but waited for them 'to bring up religion'. When they did so, she employed a conversational strategy to encourage the expression of personal views and the ability to listen to and learn from alternatives. She felt that her upbringing in a mixed faith (Jewish–Catholic) family enabled her to feel more comfortable with the expression of religious beliefs than many other philosophy teachers.

Participation in *'Religion für Alle'* (*Religion for All*) was a characteristic of the Hamburg teachers' situation and refers to RE lessons that are attended by students from differing religious backgrounds and in which there is an explicit focus on religious diversity. Although the neighbourhoods in which the teachers worked were either predominantly Christian or Muslim, all of the teachers felt that the religious diversity within their groups enriched RE lessons. Reference was also made to differences in students' academic performance and knowledge of religions. Some teachers saw lack of knowledge as a problem but others felt that it resulted in greater openness, especially towards studying the Bible. All of these teachers viewed interreligious dialogue as a long-term goal of RE and encouraged students to express their own beliefs and to respond to those of others with openness and respect. Most also referred to the importance of creating a 'safe' classroom environment for such sharing to take place. For one teacher this involved openly sharing her own religious beliefs but ensuring that there was no pressure on students to do so. She explained that these were strategies that she had valued as a school student and that her memory of them became influential in her decision to teach RE.

The Dutch teachers focused initially on students' religious backgrounds and denominations. Implicitly, all of these teachers took their own Christian 'position' as a point of reference and some talked about 'us' in contrast to 'them'. All reported that students have a positive attitude towards RE if the teacher's approach and strategies were appropriate. The 'flavour' of the Christianity taught should not be too strong and the lessons should match the students' learning levels and styles. Class discussion was popular and teachers considered it to be a valuable strategy for responding to the diversity of students' backgrounds and views. One teacher spoke of the importance of providing opportunities for students to learn about and discuss a range of religious beliefs and to make up their own minds about these. Reflecting on the relationship between his strategies and personal life, he referred to 'a development in my own thinking about religions and world views' that began with a decision to become a Christian and moved on to a realisation that he had questions about other religions and needed to learn from them in order to develop his understanding of 'who God is'.

The Norwegian teachers recognised ethnic, religious and social dimensions of diversity. However, all focused on differences in students' knowledge of religions and in their learning styles and attainment. There was also a concern that students have become increasingly reluctant to admit to or express religious convictions. Activities used to address this included formal debates and role plays but the teachers emphasised the need for caution when discussing personal beliefs and students' right to privacy. Most teachers spoke of their attempts to create a classroom atmosphere of trust and confidence and one teacher was clear about the relationship between her approach to this and her life experiences: 'I believe that I am the teacher I am because I grew up with two cultures at home and because I have lived abroad and moved; I have learned to respect other people and to be more humble'.

Relationship between teachers' perceptions of and responses to religious and cultural diversity and their personal biographies

The findings presented above provide evidence of national differences in the teachers' perceptions of the most significant aspects of classroom diversity. These will be discussed in the penultimate section. However, there were teachers in every country who recognised religious and/or cultural differences between their students, and analysis of interview data indicated a relationship between their perceptions of and responses to this aspect of diversity and their personal biographies. Cross-national comparison suggested commonalities and a number of key biographical themes; these are presented below.

Family background

When talking about their perceptions of and responses to diversity there were teachers in all countries who recognised the influence of their family background. Three kinds of 'influence' were particularly apparent.

The teachers came from differing socio-economic backgrounds but in each country there were interviewees who referred to the influence of family members who were teachers or scholars. In other cases, coming from a minority ethnic and/or religious background was identified as most influential. Illustrating both points, an Estonian teacher described her parents as scholars who, having little time for their children, left her to assume a parental role. Although she had tried to conceal her Jewish background she felt that this explained her lack of childhood friends and she was grateful to the few who were 'brave' enough to befriend her. As a teacher, she valued differences amongst students and admired those who stand up for 'outsiders'. She hoped to 'inspire love', not despite differences, but because all can contribute, through their uniqueness, to make life better for everyone.

Other interviewees referred to the influence of ethnic/cultural diversity in the areas in which they had grown up. An English teacher explained: 'Having grown up in Africa ... I've always been used to having people of different backgrounds around and being comfortable about asking questions and wanting to know about the differences.'

Experiences as school and higher education students

Interviews undertaken in all countries provided evidence that teachers had chosen to employ teaching strategies that they had enjoyed as school students or that had been influential in their personal struggles with religion. For example an Estonian teacher recognised that her preference for activities that encourage a free exchange of views about religion was related to the value that these had had in her own schooldays, especially in finding her own 'freedom'. Reference has already been made to the Dutch teacher who recognised a connection between his strategies for engaging students in the study and discussion of religions and his personal quest to understand 'who God is'.

Pre-teaching experiences of diversity

For a significant number of the teachers, awareness and appreciation of religious and/or cultural diversity began when travelling or working abroad. For example, a German teacher argued that interreligious classroom dialogue can only be meaningfully entered into once important terms and their connotations in different cultures are clarified. During interview, he recognised a connection between this view and his experiences of living in Latin American countries where he had struggled with the fact that people do not always understand the meaning and intention of an outsider's efforts to communicate, even when using the national language.

Personal beliefs

Teachers in all countries recognised or indicated a relationship between their personal beliefs and their diversity-related perceptions and strategies. All but one of the Estonian, German, Dutch and Norwegian teachers described themselves as Christian. The English and French teachers subscribed to a range of religious and secular world views including those of an agnostic and a political orientation.

Religiously committed teachers emphasised that religion is important to them and saw this as an asset in promoting respect for and understanding of religious beliefs and people. However, all were concerned to avoid imposing their own views on their students. For example, when reflecting on the relationship between his personal beliefs and teaching, an English Muslim teacher stated:

> Service to God. *That's* what it is … That's my job. That's my purpose in life and I believe that it's everybody's purpose in life. But it's not my job to tell everybody to do it or not. I just have to influence others to do good and gain respect for each other.

Some of the religiously committed interviewees felt that their students should not be aware of their teacher's personal beliefs, whilst others believed that they had good reason to be open about their faith. This was the case for the Muslim teacher quoted above, who explained that, because his (largely agnostic/atheist) groups were aware that there is 'always a Muslim at the front of the class', issues of diversity were constantly at the forefront in his lessons. Whilst this teacher made use of his own 'otherness', there were interviewees who defined their students as 'other' in relation to their own beliefs and affiliations. For example, two of the Dutch teachers spoke in terms of 'the other' when referring to students from Protestant denominations that differed from their own.

Amongst the teachers with no religious commitment, there were some who did not hide this fact from their students. However, most felt that students should not be aware of their teachers' personal views, and there was a concern to avoid influencing their thinking.

Influence of higher education and teacher training

All of the teachers had undertaken degree level studies, although not all in theology or religious studies. Training ranged from specialist masters level courses to generalist courses without an RE component. Despite these differences, there were few references to the teachers' studies or training in the interviews. In general, the language that the teachers used to describe their strategies was everyday language rather than didactical, pedagogical or theological language and explanations were often introduced in personal terms, as in 'I try to ...' or 'I feel that ...' There also appeared to be a relationship between the ways in which the teachers talked about these matters and their personal biographies. For example, a French teacher who was a member of a left-wing anarchist trade union, described herself as a 'fire-fighter' when talking about her efforts to defuse tensions within her ethnically diverse classes. Despite an academically rigorous university education and training, she justified her strategies by saying: 'that calms them down' and 'that makes them feel good'.

Discussion of key findings and implications for future research and development

National differences between teachers' perceptions of diversity

When undertaking our cross-national analysis we found differences in the hierarchy of national perceptions of diversity. We suggest that these differences are related to the national contexts in which the teachers have grown up and been educated and trained. In this respect, there is an interesting relationship between individual biographies, the role that is adopted as a teacher of RE and socio-cultural factors, including dominant views of religion, the relationship between religion and education and RE.

In Hamburg, where religion is central to the 'Religion for All' approach (Knauth 2007), and in the Netherlands, with a history of organising society along religious dividing lines (ter Avest et al. 2007), religion was first in the teachers' hierarchy of perceptions. In contrast, the Norwegian teachers referred to religion as only one aspect amongst others and focused on differences in prior knowledge, learning styles and attainment. Although these teachers worked in schools with visible religious diversity, their wider context is one of religious and cultural homogeneity and this, together with a deep-seated cultural commitment to a concept of equality that emphasises 'sameness' (Johanssen 2009), may have influenced the teachers' responses to the question of diversity. Academic performance was the first aspect of diversity referred to by the French teachers, followed by socio-economic differences. The concept of *laicité*, with its emphasis on strict neutrality in relation to religious matters, appears to have been influential in interviewees' prioritisation of differences, despite their awareness of and efforts to work with the cultural and religious differences within their classes. The English teachers prioritised socio-economic differences. This may be related to a heightened awareness of 'class difference' in England, especially in relation to education (Dunne and Gazeley 2008) and to the fact that these teachers worked in 'secular' state schools and within a system that draws a clear distinction between 'secular' community schools and those with a religious character. Estonian teachers focused initially on students' attitudes to religion and RE and the impact of these on motivation, behaviour and classroom interaction. In a society in which RE and more generally, religion and its place in education have been at the centre of fierce debate for the past 20 years (Schihalejev 2010; Valk 2007), it is perhaps unsurprising that the diversity of students' attitudes to these were particularly significant for the teachers.

Thus, we suggest that the teachers' perceptions of diversity and the significance that religious and cultural diversity had for them were related to how they understood the role of the RE teacher and that this understanding was not simply a matter of accepting legal and professional definitions or of pursuing aims and commitments derived from personal biographies. Dominant socio-cultural 'themes' and concepts related to the influence of religion and education and are reflected in the role that teachers are required to adopt *and* in the role that they create from and for themselves. There appears to be a complex and dynamic relationship between personal, professional and socio-cultural factors and further research is needed to explore these elements.

Common strategies for responding to religious and cultural diversity

Although the significance that these matters had for the teachers varied from country to country, almost all were aware of differences between their students that were related to religious and/or cultural diversity. Most recognised differences in students' backgrounds and personal beliefs and commitments; some highlighted differences in students' attitudes to religion or religious diversity without specifying the reasons for these. However, wherever religious and/or cultural diversity was recognised this was viewed positively and teachers could describe the strategies that they used in relation to it. Cross-national comparison suggested some similarities in these responses and strategies.

All the teachers emphasised the importance of enabling students to express their own beliefs, views and experiences. There was a common concern that the teacher's beliefs and views should not be an obstacle to this or to enabling students to develop the ability to think for themselves. Classroom discussion was viewed as a key strategy for achieving these aims. However, there was also a widespread concern (less evident in the German and Dutch interviews) to respect students' privacy and to avoid drawing attention to differences between them. Strategies included avoiding direct questions about students' religious/cultural backgrounds or beliefs and activities that would require them to reveal such matters, especially if this would involve revealing their 'difference' in relation to peers. In positive terms, most teachers spoke of creating an inclusive classroom atmosphere that would enable all students to feel valued and sufficiently safe to share and discuss personal matters.

The identification of strategies that appear to be common to interviewees in all countries requires further research but should be of value in future studies, including those related to the development of Europe-wide principles for the training of teachers of RE (OSCE 2007).

Relationship between teachers' personal biographies and their responses to religious and cultural diversity

Whilst our study indicates that there were some common strategies for dealing with religious and cultural diversity, the reasons that the teachers gave for using these differed and there were some strategies that were idiosyncratic. In both respects we found a relationship between strategies and individual biographies. The possible implications of these findings for teachers' professional practice and development are considered below.

In many respects, the relationship between the teachers' personal experiences and beliefs and their professional attitudes and strategies appeared to be a positive one and many viewed their personal lives as a valuable source of professional commitment and insight. However, there were aspects of this relationship that appeared to researchers to be potentially problematic and to raise issues for teachers' professional practice and development.

Three issues will be introduced below, but as an overarching point, we return to the theoretical propositions referred to in the introduction: the need for teachers to become aware of and to reflect on their reasons for making decisions and adopting particular strategies, given that decisions must often be made 'on the spot' and that the factors that influence these may not have been thought through or even recognised.

In responding to religious and/or cultural diversity, a number of interviewees showed a tendency to employ teaching strategies that, as students, they had enjoyed or valued in their personal struggles with religion. A considerable body of research indicates that a tendency to reproduce the kind of teaching experienced as a school student is common amongst teachers. However, such research also highlights the danger that the largely unconscious reproduction of approaches that were valued in earlier years can block the exploration of the wide range of teaching styles needed to respond to pupils' differing backgrounds and learning needs (Knowles 1992). We recommend that teacher development programmes provide opportunities for critical reflection on familiar or routine strategies in light of the biographical factors that may underlie the use of these.

Many of our interviewees were concerned to create an inclusive classroom atmosphere by playing down differences. This included avoiding activities that would expose differences amongst students but also keeping the teacher's own beliefs and views hidden. In some cases there was evidence that this latter concern was related to negative incidents in the teachers' personal lives; in others the teachers spoke of the need to adopt a 'neutral' position and to avoid indoctrination.

Research on teachers' lives and professional development has drawn attention to the dangers of attempting to compartmentalise personal and professional lives and to the importance of creating bridges between these (Goodson and Sikes 2001, 73). RE teachers who are able to move backwards and forwards between their personal and professional lives are able to reflect on the relationship between these and to make judgements about when and how to bring their own beliefs, views and experiences into the classroom (Everington and Sikes 2001; Sikes and Everington 2001). Cooling (2002) offers a similar analysis in relation to RE teachers having a commitment to a religious faith. Drawing on a long debate about RE teachers' 'neutrality', he urges teachers to recognise that they cannot 'bracket out' their personal beliefs in their professional lives. However, by reflecting on the ways in which their personal faith can support and give meaning to their professional responsibilities, teachers can develop an awareness of when and how to draw on this for the benefit of their students and when they should exercise 'restraint' in bringing their own beliefs and commitments into the classroom (Cooling 2002, 54). We suggest that teachers would benefit from opportunities to consider such research and to engage in the kinds of reflection recommended.

When explaining and justifying their strategies, most of our interviewees made reference to practical or personal matters and talked in terms of 'I decided to …' or 'I wanted to …' Very few referred to their national contexts and the impact or influence of legal/professional requirements or policies and socio-cultural-political factors. This situation may provide some evidence for Todd's (2007) claim that teachers often rely on familiar strategies that are informed by 'unconscious obedience' to current 'rules', including professional and school regulations and societal expectations. Todd argues that if teachers are to develop their strategies to meet students' differing needs, they must embark on a process of critical reflection on such 'rules' and their underlying values and the role that these play in their decision-making. Johanssen (2011) presents a related argument when he draws on Norwegian scholarship and his own research to highlight the importance of RE teachers' knowledge of national and local politics and of the socio-cultural context in which they work, in their ability to effectively plan for and manage teaching about religious and cultural diversity and in classes where such diversity is represented. Again, we suggest that teacher development programmes should encourage reflection on these matters.

Conclusion

In this paper, we have introduced our study of teachers' perceptions of and responses to classroom diversity in relation to their personal and professional biographies, and highlighted findings related to religious and cultural diversity. As this is a qualitative study involving 36 teachers, we recognise its limitations but offer our findings as a contribution to the growing body of research that is concerned to recognise RE teachers' experiences, beliefs and commitments as well as their practice. As the study involved teachers and researchers from six European countries we hope that our findings can be viewed as indicative in future Europe-wide research on teaching about religious and cultural diversity and in classrooms where there is religious and cultural diversity. In particular, we hope that our study will be drawn upon in the training and development of teachers to undertake this work.

References

Cooling, T. 2002. Commitment and indoctrination: A dilemma for religious education? In *Issues in RE,* ed. L. Broadbent and A. Brown. London: Routledge.

Denzin, N., and Y. Lincoln, eds. 2000. *Handbook of qualitative research.* 2nd ed. California: Sage.

Dunne, M., and L. Gazeley. 2008. Teachers, social class and underachievement. *British Journal of Sociology of Education* 29, no. 5: 451–63.

Everington, J., and P. Sikes. 2001. I want to change the world: The beginning RE teacher, the reduction of prejudice and the pursuit of intercultural understanding and respect. In *Towards religious competence: Diversity as a challenge for education in Europe,* ed. H.-G. Heimbrock, C.T. Scheilke, and P. Schreiner, 180–203. Münster: Lit Verlag.

Goodson, I., and P. Sikes. 2001. *Life history research in educational settings: Learning from lives.* Buckingham: Oxford University Press.

Jackson, R., S. Miedema, W. Weisse, and J.P. Willaime. 2007. *Religion and education in Europe: Developments, contexts and debates.* Münster: Waxmann.

Johanssen, O. 2009. Sameness as norm and challenge – Norwegian teachers and religious diversity. In *Teachers responding to religious diversity in Europe: Researching biography and pedagogy,* ed. A. van der Want, C. Bakker, I. ter Avest, and J. Everington, 95–110. Münster: Waxmann.

Johanssen, O. 2011. Forthcoming. Contextual knowledge for an inclusive RE. In *Context in religious education research,* ed. G. Skeie, J. Everington, I. ter Avest, and S.. Meidema. Münster: Waxmann

Kelchtermans, G. 2000. *Reflectief ervaringsleren voor leerkrachten, een werkboek voor opleiders, nascholers en stagebegeleiders*, Cahier voor didactiek 10. Wolters Plantyn Educatieve Uitgevers [Learning from experiences by reflection on action. An exercise book for teachers and coaches in teacher education. Exercise book no. 10. Wolters Plantyn Educatieve Utigevers].

Knauth, T. 2007. Religious education in Germany. In *Religion and education in Europe: Developments, contexts and debates,* ed. R. Jackson, S. Miedema, W. Weisse, and J.P. Willaime, 243–66. Münster: Waxman.

Knowles, J.G. 1992. Models for understanding pre-service and beginning teachers' biographies: Illustrations from case studies. In *Studying teachers' lives,* ed. I. Goodson, 99–152. London: Routledge.

Mertens, D.M. 1997. *Research methods in education and psychology: Integrating diversity with quantitative and qualitative approaches.* London: Sage.

OSCE (Organisation for Security and Co-operation in Europe/Office for Democratic Institutions and Human Rights). 2007. *Toledo guiding principles on teaching about religions and beliefs in schools.* Warsaw: OSCE.

Schihalejev, O. 2010. *From indifference to dialogue? Estonian young people, the school and religious diversity*. Münster: Waxmann.

Sikes, P. and J. Everington. 2001. Becoming an RE teacher. *British Journal of Religious Education* 24, no. 1: 8–19.

Ter Avest, A., C. Bakker, G. Betram-Troost, and S. Miedema. 2007. Religion and education in the Dutch pillarised and post pillarised educational system: Historical background and current debates. In *Religion and education in Europe: Developments, contexts and debat*es, ed. R. Jackson, S. Miedema, W. Weisse, and J.P. Willaime. Münster: Waxmann.

Todd, S. 2007. Teachers judging without scripts, or thinking cosmopolitan. *Ethics and Education* 2, no. 1: 25–38.

Valk, P. 2007. Religious education in Estonia. In *Religion and education in Europe: Developments, contexts and debates,* ed. R. Jackson, S. Miedema, W. Weisse, and J.P. Willaime, 159–80. Munster: Waxman.

van der Want, A., C. Bakker, I. ter Avest, and J. Everington, eds. 2009. *Teachers responding to religious diversity in Europe: Researching biography and pedagogy*. Münster: Waxmann.

Weisse, W. 2007. The European research project on religion and education 'REDCou: An introduction. In *Religion and education in Europe: Developments, contexts and debates,* ed. R. Jackson, S. Miedema, W. Weisse, and J.P. Willaime, 9–25. Munster: Waxman.

Williame, J.P. 2007. Teaching religious issues in French public schools. In *Religion and education in Europe: Developments, contexts and debates,* ed. R. Jackson, S. Miedema, W. Weisse, and J.P. Willaime, 57–66. Munster: Waxman.

Russian REDCo findings in support of dialogue and hermeneutics

Fedor Kozyrev

Institute for Religious Pedagogy, Russian Christian Academy for Humanities, St Petersburg, Russia

REDCo findings question the ideal of neutrality of the teacher on ethical, epistemological and didactical grounds showing in particular that the exposure of the teacher's personal commitments and beliefs stimulates students to participate in dialogue. The findings support hermeneutical approaches to the empirical studies in education showing that quantitative methods are to be used in a wider framework where there is a hermeneutical process of revisiting given data in the light of the new data. Qualitative methods and international and interdisciplinary cooperation are of high value in this process.

Introduction

This publication does not provide a systematic presentation of REDCo (Religion in Education: a Contribution to Dialogue or a Factor of Conflict in Transforming Societies of European Countries) results but rather an attempt to highlight the findings that changed, reinforced or influenced my personal vision of the problem under study as I coordinated REDCo in Russia during three years of research. In some sense this informal kind of a summary may be more efficient than a systematic one, for it is precisely the formation of attitudes and visions for which projects like REDCo should be intended. The statistics obtained in the course of study tell little by themselves. Of course they are valuable, and I support the idea that the collected field data call for launching a new project that would deal only with analytical processing of sets of empirical data available after the completion of REDCo and some other European projects such as RaLP at the University of Wurzburg (Ziebertz and Kay 2005). But that would be another study, different from what we experienced in REDCo.

The interesting thing with complex projects like REDCo is that they are intended to give new knowledge for outsiders (other scientists, politicians, managers, practising educators, etc.) but in fact it is mostly the researchers themselves who can learn from the results. It is hardly expectable that somebody else will spend months or years going into the matter deeply enough to deal with results as with an integrated body. More probably one will take a piece of this body to bring to one's own nest. Those who would like to be more objective and more devoted to holistic approach can either trust the researchers as first hand witnesses of the case or take their time and read the whole story themselves. Juxtaposition of these first-order and second-order readings may give a more stereoscopic picture of the results and disclose some presuppositions of the first-order reader while loading the picture with new presuppositions and judgments. In any case the vision of the researchers is one of the basic elements in the construction of meanings and this is how my voluntaristic approach to the topic in this publication can be justified.

In what follows I will focus first on three selected findings that are of particular interest for me as questioning the ideal of neutrality on ethical, epistemological and didactical grounds. Then I will turn to methodological reflections that resonate with these findings if tuned to the problem of neutrality and objectivity. Seen from these two different perspectives, the main outcome of my REDCo experience can be described as a shift of vision towards a better appreciation of hermeneutical and dialogical approaches to both education and research.

Selected findings: three arguments against neutrality

REDCo policy recommendations presented to European institutions were based on agreed conclusions that were recognised by all national teams as relevant to their contexts. One among these basic findings seems to be less predictable and more challenging than the others in the context of Russia. Thus, it is more valuable. 'Students for whom religion is important in their lives are more likely to respect the religious background of others and value the role of religion in the world' (Weisse 2009, 13). In fact, in this statement one can find a partial answer to the main REDCo question about religion in education as a factor of peaceful coexistence. If religious education succeeds in making religion more important in students' lives, one can expect that they will be 'more likely to respect the religious background of others'. It is quite contrary to what we have been used to hearing in Russia for two decades of public debates about the admissibility of RE. We heard that religion should in no way be part of school life because no religion can tolerate another. An argument of intolerance of religious people became so familiar that participants in the debates usually did not notice that it ought to be empirically proven. Now REDCo has disproved it.

In the Russian quantitative dataset, the phenomenon observed by different national teams was present clearly and repeatedly. It allowed us to formulate the following conclusion independently of the other teams:

> Comparison between students with and without religious affiliation showed religious students to be more open to dialogue and in some respects more tolerant than non-religious students. Religious students have more positive attitudes towards religion and show more respect towards other believers. They are more informed about and more interested in the religious views of the others around. They do not show any more dislike of people from other religions than non-religious students and advocate freedom of religious expression more intensely. Based on the bi-variate analysis of the data, one may portray religious students in our sample as quite open-minded persons, accepting their religiousness with the same level of inner freedom as the students who refused to affiliate themselves with a religious tradition. In more general terms, the data obtained give empirical grounds to consider the religiousness of students as a positive factor for their citizenship and their communicative competences to live in a plural society. (Kozyrev and Valk 2009, 347)

As for secular societies like the one we have in Russia, where the non-religious worldview is traditionally considered as the model of neutrality, I consider this finding as the first argument against such neutrality, putting into question its sustainability *on ethical grounds*. If belonging to a particular religious worldview which is a priori different from another religious and non-religious worldview helps young people to respect others, and the illusion of being neutral by standing beyond religious differences helps on the contrary to cherish the feeling of superiority, then is the ideal of neutrality compatible with the tasks of moral education?

There is another finding agreed in the REDCo research group that questions the ideal of neutrality from another point of view. 'Students generally favour the model of education about religion with which they are familiar' (Weisse 2009, 13). This correlation was most pronounced in the case of Germany. Students from the Münster and Hamburg samples, who experienced respectively separated and integrated RE, showed contrasting views on the preferable model. Each group liked the model they had and some respondents from both sides expressed their convictions unfalteringly. The regularity was also clear when the national samples were compared to each other. English students favoured non-confessional multi-religious RE, French and Russian students, more than the students in other countries, were consolidated around the ideas that there should be no place for religion at school and that there is no need for the subject of religious education. In short, students were found to be quite conservative, and this finding challenges a widespread notion of young people as less stuck to habits than their elders. It shows how effectively attitudes of students towards RE can be shaped by school experience and this finding, by the way, may have some practical consequences for policy making in education. But I would like to emphasise here a more theoretical aspect.

The idea that our judgements and interpretations are unavoidably charged with presuppositions, as presented for instance in the hermeneutics of Gadamer, questions the sustainability of neutrality *on epistemological grounds*. The mentioned REDCo findings bring empirical support to this idea, showing statistically and vividly how life experiences and horizons of understanding shaped by these experiences serve as factors determining judgements. This forms the next question. If judgements are so obviously dependant upon experiences, what will ensure the higher level or, let's say, the better quality of neutrality? The more alternatives we see and are able to take into account, the more balanced should be our choices, the less preconceived our opinions and thus the more neutral our positions. Let's underline this point: we talk first of all about the existential type of experiences that are not translatable in the form of abstract knowledge but rather in the form of participation. Paradoxically it means that, in order to develop a neutral view, let's say on religion, a school should provide existential experience of being religious. At least it should make efforts to provide students with opportunities for grasping the meaning of being religious. Distant and critical knowledge is certainly able to contribute as well. For instance, the very argument we develop here should resonate with an open-minded student and make him think about the problem of neutrality before any existential stimuli are received. But we believe it to be a stimulus in itself for the student to seek participating and existential forms of knowledge and understanding.

The third finding deals with the neutrality of the teacher. In the list of key results underpinning REDCo policy recommendations, teachers are mentioned only once, when it is said that 'dialogue is a favoured strategy for teachers to cope with diversity in the classroom' (Weisse 2009, 13). This statement is made in the context of a further warning that 'in practice, not all students are comfortable with the way diversity is managed in schools' and apparently in connection with the following recommendation to 'train educators in methods that support and encourage students to be comfortable with difference and to engage with the diversity of their personal experiences' (Weisse 2009, 14). How to create better conditions for dialogue and what role neutrality of the teacher may play in achieving this task is not explained in the document, partly because the main target group of REDCo research were students, not teachers. Nevertheless, in the framework of REDCo, a group of researchers collected, analysed and presented extensive empirical material on different teachers' strategies to deal with diversity (van der Want et al. 2009). Not being a part of the group, I would like to approach the question here through the other set of empirical data that I dealt with personally and that appeared revealing for me.

I am referring to incident analysis during research on classroom interaction (ter Avest et al. 2009). The Russian group was active in this aspect of the research and managed to videotape and analyse four examples of classroom interaction on different religious topics and in different settings, each 45–90 minutes long. We found the method of incident analysis very efficient and able to show, as if under a microscope, details of the fabric of the school teaching and learning process. There were several unexpected findings from this work. For instance, we found the issues of communication and 'proper behaviour' in difficult situations to be of vital importance for adolescents, awakening much more enthusiasm and passion in them than the 'ultimate' problems offered for discussion. We observed how the most delicate way of conversation established by a teacher did not succeed in involving students in dialogue until he or she switched to a provocative and attacking way of interaction. These were single observations but there were also some repeating patterns of classroom interaction detected in the course of study that allowed us to draw several conclusions.

Among these conclusions supported by the all material available for the analysis there was one about neutrality. This is how it was formulated in the report:

> The level of mutual trust and respect, long-term interpersonal tensions and problems, the teacher's commitments and perception of them on the part of the students all constitute an organic component of interaction and contribute essentially into its quality and course. Dialogue becomes more natural, intensive and consequently more productive when the teacher addresses students *personally*. This inter-personal element of the teacher-student interaction seems to be an unavoidable prerequisite of dialogue either in a confessional or a non-confessional framework. It means that the ideal of neutrality of a teacher in religious as well as in all other types of educational interaction is hardly compatible with a dialogical approach. (Kozyrev 2009, 215)

The conclusion may be regarded in our view as an empirical argument questioning the sustainability of the ideal of neutrality *on didactical grounds*.

The concept of neutrality of the teacher becomes remarkably less popular in the official language of international documents on religious education. The Toledo Guiding Principles are illustrative, clearly differentiating between the obligation of state 'to maintain a posture of neutrality' and the situation of teachers 'enjoying the freedom of thought, conscience and religion' and called to 'approach their task in a balanced and professional fashion' (OSCE 2007, 36–7). Instead of imposing neutrality upon teachers, the document recommends them to encourage *empathetical* attitudes among learners about religions and beliefs and insightfully assumes that 'being open about one's own beliefs can serve as an invitation to others to do the same' (46). The last sentence is amazingly congruent with the conclusion drawn by us from our REDCo experience. It gives hope that the results of our empirical work will strengthen the trend in policy making that creates better conditions for religious dialogue in the classroom.

Reflections on methodology (I): triangulation

One of the most fascinating features of the REDCo methodology was the multiplicity of methods corresponding to the multidimensional nature of the research. I would not call it a system of methods, for in the choice and usage of methods we felt more flexibility than a 'complete system' would suggest, but it rather was a well-organised sequence allowing us to try different tools and to evaluate their efficiency and compatibility. Taking into account intensive communication among researchers being intrinsic to a large, collaborative project, REDCo, besides its direct goals, may be regarded as a long-term methodological workshop where researchers from different countries could exchange their methodological competences and experiences and get practice in developing common standards. To summarise, it appeared to be a good international laboratory for the methodology of complex research. In countries with secular models of education, where religion as a subject of learning has been withdrawn from the pedagogical discourse or – like in Russia – substituted by antireligious propaganda, experience of that kind may considerably broaden the horizon of the researchers and help them to see that the multidimensional nature of religious phenomena calls for an interdisciplinary approach to them.

The combination of qualitative (open questionnaires and interviews) and quantitative (Likert-scaled questionnaires) surveys was the main chain in the sequence. In my view, it was also one of the most successful decisions in the research design. The practice of making pre-tests, or 'pilot studies', is common but usually these studies are done in precisely the way the main study is planned. Thus the method of the main study is corrected or refined by the pilot study. In REDCo we had something more, for it was clear from the beginning that qualitative and quantitative surveys are different in method; but it was not clear till the end how they relate to each other and how we might work with this ambiguity. In at least one practical sense the qualitative research did work as a preparatory stage for the quantitative one. Using Markus Friederici's words:

> … on the basis of the reactions of students to the qualitative questionnaire and its open questions, we chose quotations from their answers for formulating statements which we placed as items in the quantitative studies. In other words: the students in the quantitative survey had to fill in to what degree they agreed or disagreed with the quoted views of their (European) peers. (2009, 19)

However, the qualitative study stood for itself as regards its results. There had been conclusions drawn on its basis and fixed in the collection of articles published before the quantitative survey was launched. The brave decision to publish it created a challenging situation of 'no step back' for any researchers who were too hasty with some of their conclusions on the qualitative stage. It may even have created a temptation to interpret new quantitative results in a way that ensured good correspondence with previous conclusions. And it surely created a perfect and almost unprecedented condition for analytical work focusing on purely methodological issues of reliability of empirical methods. Thus the *triangulation* of results obtained by different methods became a key and distinct term of REDCo.

Strictly speaking the term 'triangulation', borrowed from geodesics, may be applied to the case of REDCo only as a metaphor. No one could expect that the process of putting the results together will result in mapping the situation with religion in education in Europe as accurately as may be done with the mapping of earth by means of geodesic triangulation. So the process would be better described in terms of a hermeneutical circle than in terms of a geodesic triangle. REDCo methodology was extremely sensitive to this hermeneutical dimension of research activities and this quality was not surprising since the methodology was based on the Warwick interpretive approach (Jackson 1997, 2002). Oscillation between the historical and cultural context of the societies and communities under study, individual self expressions of the interviewed students and teachers, statistical data on the average attitudes toward religion shown by different samples and sub-samples of students, observations of classroom interaction, consultations with experts in different fields involved in the project, as well as between other sources of knowledge and understanding, was far too complicated process to be depicted in a linear way. Indeed, as already noticed above, the whole process looked much more like a revision of a story in the light of newly found details than a step-by-step discovery of an unknown land. Constructivist ideas sounded much more sensible to me after experiencing REDCo.

The hermeneutical nature of the research activity dealing with rich and multidimensional objects may be expressed not only through the image of oscillating movement between parts and the whole in a circle. Wilna Meijer in her article on hermeneutics of religious education shows how the concept of the *wandering viewpoint* (*wandernde Blickpunkt*) coined by the theorist of reception-aesthetics Wolfgang Iser is applicable not only for literary fiction but for a wider spectrum of texts:

> Without an overall view of the entire text, the reader moves through the text and gradually forms an image of the meaning. A 'wandering viewpoint': the eye of the reader moves, travels through the text ... What has already been read forms the expectation of what is still to come. If the text that follows meets that expectation, the reader will be able to follow the rest of the narrative and trace his course through the text. But if something unexpected happens, if he experiences surprise at the course of events in the story, he will then have to re-think the meaning of earlier passages which have kindled the mistaken expectation. The 'wandering viewpoint' therefore, does not merely refer to travelling through the text from beginning to end, but also includes revisiting parts of the text read earlier in order to place them in a new perspective, to see them in new ways, to interpret them differently. (Meijer 2007, 36)

This description corresponds very well to what was done by REDCo researchers when they revisited previous results in order to place them in a new perspective created by newly found data.

Remarkable and distinctive for REDCo was the integration of quantitative methods, and their innate logic, into the wider methodological frame of hermeneutics with its contextual, situational and participative way of learning. It is still an unusual pattern. More common and more suitable to scientific standards are situations when (inter-)subjective elements of the research, such as working hypotheses and insights, sporadic observations, qualitative evaluations, personal interpretations and judgements, and descriptions of concrete situations, visions expressed in a non-formalised language, perform their function while being subordinated to quantitative objective evaluation and are thus doomed to die off as soon as the latter is achieved. With REDCo that was not the case. Its quantitative survey, although being the most laboursome and thoroughly prepared part of the project, was not its only valuable part. I dare say it was not the most important element. In this sense REDCo methodology may be considered as a way into postsecular or postmodern science in which an 'objective picture' resulting from research will not be presented as something unquestionable and entirely free from the intentions and cultural presuppositions of the researchers and receivers of knowledge, but rather as something insufficient without qualitative (and hopefully thick) descriptions.

This is not to undermine the merit of objectivism in empirical studies. Whether it be a result of objectivist education or not, today one can hardly feel comfortable with a picture of reality deprived of 'the dry facts of statistics'. For me personally, one of the revealing moments during my participation in the project was my attempt to scrutinise articles in the volume presenting results of the qualitative research (Knauth et al. 2008). The authors contributing to the volume had been asked to avoid any quantitative evaluations like percentages or average meanings. Although the recommendation was obviously correct from a methodological point of view, I have found in practice that the more an author of a chapter tried to be obedient to the rule, the less integrated was the picture his or her report was able to produce. The chapters could highlight very interesting facts, situations, problems and phenomena that exist in particular circumstances, but they could not give me a sense of the whole that could be compared or even juxtaposed with another whole. Figures expressed either in a 'permitted' form (like 'a half', 'one third', etc.) or baldly in percentages, made concrete, keeping the fragments of reality together; or rather they were like a scaling tool bringing each piece to its 'natural size' before it was combined with others.

Maybe I wanted too much from the qualitative research, but I think it is what we always want from any research. We want research to contribute to our vision and the level of our open-mindedness determines the extent to which we allow empirical data to change our previous visions and prejudgements. The metaphor of a wandering viewpoint fits perfectly with a rich scientific inquiry engaging different methods and dealing with living and changing reality. When the project is over, the book is over. One cannot add to it simply because the reality to study is now different from what was there before. But many people besides the authors can participate in the story through reading it. They may follow the same path after the researchers and may feel it necessary to re-read both the book and their own narratives to achieve better integrity if something unexpected happens and their expectations of reality are not met with new data. Analytical procedures, governed by logics, are tightly implicated in this process with synthetic operations of reconstruction, and the criteria of statistics, with their levels of reliability and rules for representation, are too poor a tool to distinguish between right and wrong. Hermeneutics, able – in Paul Ricoeur's view (2007) – to arbitrate between systems of interpretation and to mark the borders within which each system establishes and follows its own criteria of validity and standards of thinking, evidently provides a more inclusive and more adequate framework for meaning construction. It gives room to statistics among other data types but does not allow them to throw out other systems of interpretation from the common nest.

Reflections on methodology (II): statistics and hermeneutics

Now I will give several examples from the REDCo experience of why we should not neglect qualitative methods, and how they can complement statisitics and help us to achieve a more critical interpretation of empirical data. First I would like to draw attention to a comment made by a female respondent from our quantitative study: 'Almost every day I think about religion, but I can't say for sure if I believe in God or not' (Kozyrev and Valk 2009, 343). The girl who left this comment was identified in our survey as non-religious according to the criteria used. And surely this fact juxtaposed to her comment challenges the routine approaches to the 'measurement of religiosity'. During recent decades, much has been done to overcome the simplistic dichotomy of believers and non-believers in empirical studies. Now different forms and levels of religious commitment are taken into account and the former group of 'atheists' is found too heterogenous to be regarded as one group. H.-G. Ziebertz and W. Kay, for instance, distinguish between naturalism, cosmology, agnosticism, criticism and atheism as distinct forms of non-religious worldviews, asuming, at the same time, that 'no hermetically sealed border between religious and non-religious worldviews exists in reality' (Ziebertz and Kay 2009, 43). According to their classification, the quoted comment can be clearly identified as agnostic, since it is a statement 'in which doubts about the existence of religious truth are formulated', and 'the doubt stands between acceptance and denial' (44). But what a difference lies between the worldviews and life orientations of this type of agnostic who thinks about religion 'almost every day'and an agnostic who has decided that doubt is a most comfortable state of mind and does not think about religion any more! And, if even such an advanced typology is not sensitive enough to meet this difference, what about splitting the group of 'agnostics' further and so on *ad infinitum*? The methodological task, in the face of this problem, is to identify the objects, cases and situations in which the 'typological' approach ceases to work at all. It does not work when we deal with literary characters in fiction. We need to show reserachers when it is better to switch to purely hermeneutical approaches that are more relevant for grasping the rich reality under study.

According to REDCo policy recommendations, the school population includes a sizeable group of students 'who hold a variety of occasionally fluctuating positions' in their attitudes toward the importance of religion (Weisse 2009, 13). Taking into account the instability of views responsible for this fluctuation, another methodological problem besides the efficiency of typology is connected with the existence of unaccounted attractors that determine the choice of answers in these situations of fluctuation and hesitation, at points of bifurcation, so to speak. As these situations seem to arise often, the influence of these attractors to the results may be crucial. The most common kind of influence is through personal involvement of a researcher or especially a teacher present in the classroom during questioning. It is a specific problem of pedagogical surveys, for children as respondents are used to asking questions even if the guidelines written for them are clear and detailed. One word of recommendation can change the results. Special attention was given to this problem in REDCo and several documented situations showed the effect of the readiness of the respondents to follow the advice of the adults. As mentioned in our article on the quantitative study, in one of the St Petersburg schools several students, while answering a question about their religious affiliation, asked their teacher: 'What is the name of *our* religion, the one we have in Russia?' and one student in another school asked if he should put his *official* religion or not (Kozyrev and Valk 2009, 315) and this question made all the other respondents puzzled about the proper way of answering. The experience of group interviews we had in our Russian survey showed us also that interrelations among peers is a factor no less influential than the influence of adults. We recorded a situation in which a girl who agreed to give an oral interview after written questioning changed her view on the admissibility of RE at school, probably under the influence of another girl interviewed together with her – one who had a much more negative attitude toward the public role of religion. Our video camera recorded how during the whole interview the first girl examined the face of the second one as if trying to guess her reactions.

Among examples of evidence of the influence that teachers and peers can produce on the individual answers of students is the difference found in the attitudes toward RE of two class-groups of the same age within one and the same school, chosen for study in St Petersburg. Reflecting on the results of our qualitative study, we explained this difference as a result of 'the cumulative effect' that takes place when religious experiences are shared in a community of learners (Kozyrev 2008, 308). The quantitative study gave new grounds to support this view and led us to a conclusion that:

> direct and indirect personal influences of teachers and other active agents of the educational process, producing negative and/or positive experiences with religion and religious diversity, may be the key force that affects students' religious

perceptions and attitudes. The school 'membership groups' (Jackson 1997), constituting learning communities, may also influence their members through 'the collective micro-societal standards of values and norms functioning as criteria for judgments about different forms of behaviour and religious expression. (Kozyrev and Valk 2009, 348)

Situations vary not only from one particular group to another, but they also rapidly change with time. One example illustrates how fragile and ephemeral might be the conditions that are proposed to exemplify a broader and presumably more stable context in empirical studies. Three schools in St Petersburg participated in both qualitative and quantitative surveys. During the qualitative study, students in one of these schools were characterised as 'expressing much less motivation to talk about religion in peer groups' (Kozyrev 2008, 298) and 'having certain difficulties with the expression of their perceptions ... The lack of knowledge about religion was more evident in their vocabulary. They also referred more often to this lack of knowledge in their answers' (Kozyrev 2008, 290). A year later this very class-group of students occupied one of the highest ratings among nine schools in showing most the positive attitude toward religion in general (Kozyrev and Valk 2009, 339) and being identified as one of the most 'religiously educated' groups according to a good number of criteria (Kozyrev and Valk 2009, 345). The change was clear also in comparison between the three schools that had been compared a year before and between the results of two surveys when we considered the group alone. The group seemed to undergo miraculous transformation.

This case illustrates the value of thick description (Geertz 1983; Jackson 1997). Luckily we knew what happened in the school between the two surveys. First, the literature syllabus for that year was 'packed' with a Dostoevsky novel and it gave students opportunity to pay more attention than before to religious issues during literature classes. Second, we knew that, besides focusing on the religious aspects of Dostoevsky's writings, the literature teacher gave a series of classes on the Bible between the two surveys. That could be the main reason why so many students declared that they read sacred texts and listed school among the important sources of knowledge about religion in the quantitative survey. Third, a selection took place in this class-group because of the transition to the higher school level, and a good number of students with lower capacities left the school. Finally, as we summarised in our chapter, the previous participation of a number of the respondents in the qualitative research made them feel in a way more 'familiar' with religion and thus stimulated more positive reactions (in the other two schools all respondents were new).

This is not the only example from our sample. Just to mention one more, among the 403 questionnaires analysed, the only two expressions of open chauvinism came from one group of students. Was it a coincidence or not? We know that a bloody ethnic conflict had taken place in the neighbourhood around the school a year before.

The high responsiveness of the subjects of pedagogical studies to external influences means that when these studies are planned and their results are interpreted, multiple factors should be carefully taken into account and analysed. It is doubtful if any results of selective observations may be generalised, unless they are accompanied by thicker descriptions of procedures (particularly accounting for how confidential and independent choices were ensured), of background and of socio-demographic context. Consultation between the researchers with teachers/tutors, and other actors knowing the situation in the classroom 'from inside', seems to be a necessary prerequisite of sampling and of the proper analysis of empirical data. And from the stage of planning onwards, hermeneutical processes come into play; for seeing 'from inside' and 'from outside' are the two necessary points of reference that, in the interplay of interpretations, pave the way to understanding.

Conclusions

The old-fashioned manner of presenting the results of quantitative studies of complex phenomena as a 'final word' meets neither postpositivist epistemological standards nor postmodern general scepticism about scientific neutrality. The proper way of meeting these challenges may involve not the devaluing of quantitative studies but rather putting them into a wider framework of hermeneutical process. Researchers' and readers' experiences of revisiting data may become more worthwhile if perceived and arranged not in the form of the control governed by the rigid statistical criteria of reliability, but in the form of re-reading of the story for better interpretation.

The adequacy of interpretation in pedagogical studies strongly depends on the knowledge of situations under study 'from inside'. That is why dialogue with 'insiders' as well as deep inquiries regarding procedures of study, background and socio-demographic context are necessary elements of the research. Thick field notes and materials based on these dialogues and observations may help scholars revisiting data to fulfil the hermeneutical principle of better reading. Qualitative methods are of high value in this respect.

Applied to pedagogical practice, this reconceptualisation of the research activity calls for dialogical approaches to teaching and learning processes focused on the problem of interpretation. The development of students' critical thinking and of their ability to be neutral should encourage not only encounters with the fact of plurality of interpretations but also reflections on their own presuppositions as well as on their experience of having personal commitments and beliefs. As soon as this dialogical relationship is established, the exposure of the teacher's personal commitments and beliefs stimulates students to more active and comfortable involvement in the exchange of interpretations. The recognition of personal commitments and subjective forms of knowledge in classroom discourse leads to a better quality of objectivity and neutrality based on awareness of the variety of forms of knowledge and is more relevant to the changing standards of scientific research.

References

Friederici, M. 2009. From the research question to the sampling. In *Teenagers' perspectives on the role of religion in their lives, schools and societies – A European quantitative study,* ed. P. Valk, G. Bertram-Troost, M. Friederici, and C. Beraud, 13–22. Münster: Waxmann.

Geertz, C. 1983. *Local knowledge.* New York: Basic Books.

Jackson, R. 1997. *Religious education: An interpretive approach.* London: Hodder & Stoughton.

Jackson, R. 2002. *Religious education: An interpretive approach.* London: Hodder & Stoughton.

Knauth, T., D.-P. Jozsa, G. Bertram-Troost, and J. Ipgrave, eds. 2008. *Encountering religious pluralism in school and society – A qualitative study of teenage perspectives in Europe.* Münster: Waxmann.

Kozyrev, F. 2008. Religion and education through the eyes of students from Saint-Petersburg. In *Encountering religious pluralism in school and society: A qualitative study of teenage perspectives in Europe,* ed. T. Knauth, D.-P. Jozsa, G. Bertram-Troost, and J. Ipgrave, 279–308. Münster: Waxmann.

Kozyrev, F. 2009. Dialogues about religion: Incident analysis of classroom interaction in St. Petersburg. In *Dialogue and conflict on religion: Studies of classroom interaction in European countries,* ed. I. ter Avest, D.-P. Jozsa, T. Knauth, J. Rosón, and G. Skeie, 194–224. Münster: Waxmann.

Kozyrev, F., and P. Valk. 2009. Saint-Petersburg students' views about religion in education: Results of the quantitative survey. In *Teenagers' perspectives on the role of religion in their lives, schools and societies: A European quantitative study,* P. Valk, G. Bertram-Troost, M. Friederici, and C. Beraud, 311–49. Münster: Waxmann.

Meijer, W.A.J. 2007. The hermeneutics of (religious) education: Reading and interpretation as a model for the educational process. *Journal of Religious Education* 55, no. 3: 34–8.

OSCE. 2007. *Toledo guiding principles on teaching about religions and beliefs in public schools.* Warsaw: Organisation for Security and Co-operation in Europe, Office for Democratic Institutions and Human Rights. http://www.osce.org/item/28314.html.

Ricoeur, P. 2007. *The conflict of interpretations: Essays in hermeneutics.* Evanston, IL: Northwestern University Press.

ter Avest, I., D.-P. Jozsa, T. Knauth, J. Rosón, and G. Skeie, eds. 2009. *Dialogue and conflict on religion: Studies of classroom interaction in European countries.* Münster: Waxmann.

Van der Want, A., C. Bakker, J. Everington, and I. ter Avest, eds. 2009. *Teachers responding to religious diversity in Europe: Researching biography and pedagogy.* Münster: Waxmann.

Weisse, W., ed. 2009. The relevance of interreligious dialogue for intercultural understanding: REDCo. Documentation of a public event in the Council of Europe (March 2009). http://www.redco.uni-hamburg.de/cosmea/core/corebase/mediabase/awr/redco/research_findings/REDCo_Strasbourg_Doc.pdf.

Ziebertz, H.-G., and W.K. Kay, eds. 2005. *Youth in Europe I: An international empirical study about life perspectives.* Münster: Lit Verlag.

Ziebertz, H.-G., and W.K. Kay. 2009. Analytic tools and methods. In *Youth in Europe II. An international empirical study about religiosity,* ed. H.-G. Ziebertz and W.K. Kay, 33–56. Münster: Lit Verlag.

Investigating the impact of religious diversity in schools for secondary education: a challenging but necessary exercise

Gerdien D. Bertram-Troost

Faculty of Psychology and Education, Department of Theory and Research in Education, VU University Amsterdam, Van der Boechorststraat 1, 1081 BT Amsterdam, The Netherlands

Both in academic and public discussions, there is an ongoing debate about the pros and cons of religious diversity in education. Until recently, many arguments used in this debate have not had a strong theoretical basis and often lack empirical underpinning as well. In this paper I go further into the reasons why researching the impact of religious diversity in education is so complicated. Reflections on the findings with regard to religious diversity in education from a European research project on religion, education, dialogue and conflict are taken as a starting point to explore further, both from a conceptual and an empirical perspective, why it is so difficult to answer the question about the impact of religious diversity in education. Among the aspects discussed are the fact that a single definition of 'religious diversity' cannot be given. This problematises empirical studies on the impact of religious diversity, since the less clear research concepts are, the higher the risk is of making misinterpretations. A further complication is that the influence of school cannot be strictly separated from other factors of influence. The paper concludes with practical implications for empirical research on religious diversity as possibilities to overcome the difficulties described. Special attention is paid to making use of the perspective of students themselves.

Introduction

From time to time there are serious debates in the Netherlands on the tenability of the education system and the right of parents to send their children to faith schools.[1] These debates often focus on the advantages and disadvantages of religious diversity in schools for both individual pupils and for society as a whole. One of the arguments used is that homogeneous religious schools do not prepare pupils adequately enough for life in a diverse society. Additionally, there are quite positive and optimistic beliefs about the effects of schools where pupils do meet religious diversity. However, such arguments often lack the support of empirical evidence (e.g. Grace 2003). This could result in decisions with regard to the educational system that are inadequate for society as a whole or for individual young people. What would happen, for instance, if the decision were made to forbid the establishment of segregated faith schools, such as Islamic or Orthodox Christian schools? One might intuitively think that this would result in more contact between young people of different religions, which might increase social cohesion in society. However, it might also be the case that young people could become more confused about their own (religious) identity and therefore feel even less secure in interacting with religious others.

To establish the effects of religious diversity in secondary education and to avoid too hasty conclusions with regard to the education system, more insight is needed into the actual effects of religious diversity in education and schools on how pupils are prepared for a life in a diverse society. However, it is very difficult to investigate the impact of religious diversity in education.

In this paper I will go further into the reasons why researching the impact of religious diversity in education is so complicated. In order to do this, I will review parts of the recent European research project on religion, education, dialogue and conflict (REDCo) in which I was involved as part of the Dutch team. The REDCo project involved nine universities from eight countries[2] and consisted of several sub-projects including both a qualitative and a quantitative study on teenagers' perspectives on the role of religion in their lives, schools and societies (Knauth et al. 2008; Valk et al. 2009). After describing some REDCo findings with regard to the impact of religious diversity in education on the degree to which pupils express tolerance and openness to dialogue, I will explore, both from a conceptual and an empirical perspective, why it is so difficult to give a proper, well-founded, answer to the question: 'What is the effect of religious diversity (or the absence of it) in secondary schools on the development of young people?' In the conclusion, I will propose a research approach which at least takes into account the difficulties described and which tries to overcome them.

Some empirical findings as an example of conceptual and empirical confusion

As part of the REDCo project a quantitative study was carried out among European young people aged 14–16 years (Valk et al. 2009). Although the main research questions did not focus explicitly on the role and impact of religious diversity in education,[3] some of the additional hypotheses did and were meant to explore the data further and to identify tendencies which are worth investigating in further research. Two very relevant hypotheses were: 'Students who have encountered religious diversity in education are more tolerant' and 'Students who have encountered religious diversity in education are more open to dialogue on religious issues'. On the basis of the analysis of the questionnaires completed by pupils in their country, national research teams were asked to reflect on these hypotheses. However, it turned out that, on the basis of the available REDCo material, it was very difficult for the national teams to give well-founded comments on these hypotheses (Bertram-Troost 2009). On the basis of the reflections of the national teams, I distinguished three main reasons for this.

In some participating countries the most important reason why it was impossible to give a well-founded conclusion was that it was very difficult to differentiate between schools where pupils meet religious diversity and schools where they do not. This was the case, for instance, in England where, in most schools which participated in the quantitative REDCo study, religious diversity is just a given (McKenna, Neill, and Jackson 2009). Also in Estonia it is difficult to make a differentiation between schools where pupils meet religious diversity and schools where pupils do not. This is related to the fact that 85% of the Estonian respondents said that they do not have a religious affiliation or that they cannot define it (Schihalejev 2009). In the Estionian sample, 'religious diversity in education' as such was not meaningful.[4]

In some countries, however, it was possible to distinguish schools with a relatively high versus low degree of religious diversity among pupils. Nevertheless, it was also the case in these countries that the researchers found it very difficult to draw conclusions with regard to the hypotheses about the impact of religious diversity. The Russian researchers clearly state that one needs to be cautious not to draw illegitimate conclusions about the effects of religious diversity on the basis of the data findings as we have them now (Kozyrev and Valk 2009). They make it clear that it is very difficult to separate the influence of school from the many other contextual influences pupils are confronted with. Also the Norwegian researchers indicate that, on the basis of the current data, it is impossible to separate influencing factors (Skeie and von der Lippe 2009). They find that pupils of the school with the highest degree of religious diversity are also the pupils who are very tolerant and who attach importance to dialogue. However, at this school, there are many pupils to whom religion (especially Islam) is important. This could also have an effect on the extent to which pupils are tolerant and/or open to dialogue.

A third reason, related to the second reason, for why it is so difficult to draw conclusions on the impact of religious diversity in education, is that information is lacking to check the interpretations researchers make on the basis of the data. Béraud et al. (2009) compare the reactions of pupils who attend private schools (relatively small religious diversity) and pupils who go to public schools (bigger religious diversity). They indicate that pupils of the private schools seem to be less open-minded. However, no further arguments to explain this are given. The German researchers underline the need for further data exploration. They indicate that it is their impression that the impact of personal contacts that pupils have (both inside and outside school) is more important than the presence or absence of religious diversity in the school itself. However, they stress that this is just an impression which cannot yet be substantiated (Josza, Knauth, and Weisse 2009). In the Dutch context, no significant differences were found between pupils who have experiences with religious diversity in school and pupils who (relatively) lack this experience with regard to the extent to which pupils respect other pupils who believe (Bertram-Troost et al. 2009). However, on the basis of just the quantitative questionnaire, there are many ways to interpret the findings.

With regard to the hypothesis on openness to dialogue, national teams had similar difficulties in providing well-founded interpretations. From the REDCo study it appears that the important question of the impact of religious diversity on the individual and social development of young people in itself is very difficult to answer. In the remaining part of this paper, I would like to explore why this is the case, both from a conceptual and an empirical perspective. I will elaborate on the reasons mentioned so far. In the conclusion, I will go further into possible ways to overcome the conceptual and empirical difficulties.

Lack of conceptual clarity

When exploring the impact of religious diversity in school on the individual and social development of young people (as citizens of a plural society), one needs to have some clarity about the main research concept 'religious diversity'. What is meant by 'religious' or 'religion'? What can be understood by 'diversity'? However, these fundamental questions are hardly mentioned in publications. Although religious diversity is, nowadays, a very common term, authors hardly explain what they really mean by it. As an actual example of this I refer to the contribution of Breen (2009) in this journal. In his very interesting and valuable article on 'Religious diversity, inter-ethnic relations and the Catholic school', he describes an ethnographic case study of how a single faith school in England was *responsive* to religious and ethnic diversity within its social/spatial surroundings, he does not express what he understands by 'religious diversity'. From the article the reader gets the impression that religious diversity is described on an institutional level as the focus is on how Catholic young people (learn to) mix with Muslim, Hindu and Sikh children. No attention is paid to the fact that within the 'single faith' (Catholic) school there can also be religious diversity to some degree. There are good reasons to doubt that there is really no religious diversity at a single faith school (see, for instance, Bertram-Troost 2006). This issue is even more interesting when we take into account the fact that religious attitudes of young people especially can be characterised as individualised (see Schweitzer 2007). One of the characteristics of individualised religion is 'the adolescents' distinction between their own faith and the faith maintained and taught by religious institutions' (91). From that perspective, it could very well be the case that a school which is labelled by researchers as being without religious diversity is described by the pupils themselves as a school where religious diversity is present. This could especially be the case with confessional schools. In the framework of the REDCo questionnaire, we did not ask the teachers how they looked upon religious diversity in their school, but we have good reasons to presume that they themselves also perceived differences related to religion between the children (Bertram-Troost 2006; van der Want et al. 2009). An important question therefore is: 'In the eyes of whom is there religious diversity at school or not?' It is clear that research on the impact of religious diversity on the development of young people should at least take into account to what degree and how they themselves experience religious diversity at their school.

Apart from the fact that the possible different perspectives of researchers, teachers and pupils should be taken into account, it is also necessary to have a clearer focus on what is, conceptually, meant by 'religious diversity' and to distinguish this from other categories, such as ethnic diversity. Williams and O'Reilly (1998) describe diversity as refering to differences between individuals on any attribute that may lead to the perception that another person is different from the self. Lieberson (1969), with the (empirical) question of how one could measure population diversity in mind, describes it as: 'The probability of obtaining unlike characteristics when two persons are randomly paired.' When formulating a definition for 'religious diversity' one might be inclined to simply add the adjective 'religious' to these definitions. One could state, for instance, that religious diversity is 'the probability of obtaining unlike religious characteristics when two persons are randomly paired'. However, it is still not clear what is meant by the term 'religious'. Above, I have already made clear that it is important to take into account differences between institutionalised religion and individualised religion. If one only looked at institutional diversity, the picture might be very 'black and white'. However, if individualised religion and the personal fulfilment people (pupils) give to 'religion' is central, there is the risk that 'religious diversity' becomes an empty concept. In this case, since everyone would have his/her own 'religion', there would always be religious diversity as soon as two people came together.

Elsewhere Bertram-Troost and Miedema (2009a, 2009b) described how European pupils answered the question: 'What does the word 'religion' mean to you?' On the basis of the answers, several categories were distinguished: 'Belief in God', 'Belief in something', 'Guidance in life', 'Elements/forms of religion', 'Group identities/culture', 'Conflict potential'. And it is not only the pupils themselves who have different interpretations of what 'religion' is. Also in research, policy, media, etc., different meanings and interpretations are given to the concept 'religion'. In many countries, an additional difficulty is that there are several words which are closely related but still have different connotations. In many of the countries, the word 'religion' (or its equivalent in the relevant languages) has different meanings, depending on the specific context in which the word is used. Bertram-Troost and Miedema came to the important conclusion that there 'is no universally accepted and standardised version of the term (see Smaling and Hijmans 1997, 15–25)' (2009a, 38). In philosophy, such terms are characterised as 'essentially contested concepts' (see Gallie 1956; van der Kooij, de Ruijter, and Miedema, in preparation). In such cases, the varieties of connotations cannot be reduced to one single, exclusive or essential meaning. Following this line of thought, it is also not possible to give a single definition of 'religious diversity'. As a result of that, especially when using the concept in empirical research, one should be very cautious and try to give as clear a stipulative definition as possible depending on the (research) context which is at stake and on the research questions which are to be answered. Also, when reading and interpreting studies on (the impact of) religious diversity, one should be very much aware of the complexity of this term and try to sort out how authors use it. The risk of drawing invalid conclusions is very high, especially if terms are not used explicitly.

Empirical confusion

Now I have described the most important conceptual difficulties in relation to 'religious diversity', I will show in this section that there are also empirical challenges when it comes to investigating the impact of religious diversity in education on the development of young people. Of course, the conceptual and empirical components are interrelated. A piece of empirical research which is based on weak conceptual elaborations is doomed to fail. Ideally, empirical research should be closely interwoven with a strong theoretical elaboration of the main research concepts or should intend to generate an adequate theoretical framework. However, even if this is the case, there is no guarantee that research findings are clear and really useful when it comes to answering the question of the impact of religious diversity in education. One of the most important reasons is that interpreting research data is, again, another challenging exercise. It is often difficult to check if data are interpreted correctly, especially when using questionnaires. This is a common problem with (written) questionnaires (Brinkman 2000), but the problem is even bigger when research concepts (like in this case 'religious diversity') are not strictly defined. What might appear to be a straightforward question addressed to pupils can be loaded with many of the researcher's presuppositions. As an example I will take one of the statements used in the REDCo quantitative questionnaire on religion in education. Pupils had to indicate, on a five-point scale, to what degree they agreed with a number of statements. One of these statements was: 'At school I go around with young people who have different religious backgrounds.' How can we know how the pupils read and interpreted this question? Did they think this question was about contacts with pupils who have another belief? Pupils who go to another church? Pupils who have other customs? Pupils who belong to another (ethnic) culture? Probably, there is no one single answer to this question, which makes the matter, of course, even more difficult. One can imagine that pupils who have a religious background themselves might interpret this question differently from pupils who do not identify themselves with a certain religion (or world view). In any case, when working with questions like this one, there are several moments of interpretation: first, the person (in this case a pupil) who completes the questionnaire makes an interpretation of what is meant by the question. Then, when analysing the data, the researcher makes an interpretation of what the answers of the pupils might mean. And, finally, people to whom the research findings are presented also make their own interpretations. The less clear the research concepts are, the higher the risk of making misinterpretations at one or more of the several interpretation moments (the risk of 'double misinterpretations'). Although different interpretations can never be completely eliminated, the risk of drawing illegitimate conclusions can be reduced by making the research steps and conceptual decisions as concrete as possible.

Another difficulty which should be faced, when empirically studying the impact of religious diversity in education, is that the influence of school cannot be strictly separated from other factors of influence. This is the case for every social study on the effects of school (even for the effects of grammar and mathematics lessons), but is especially relevant for studies on attitudes and behaviour. As Petty and Green (2007, 68) put it: 'A long-standing problem has been to find ways to measure student progress or achievement that identify the school's contribution separately from other factors, such as student ability, prior schooling and background and the school's socioeconomic environment'. Most studies on the effects of school focus on examination results. These results can be seen as a measure of academic learning, but do not give a complete picture with regard to the effectiveness of a school, and give little information about non-academic outcomes. In his article on school effectiveness and the 'other outcomes' of secondary schooling, Gray (2004, 186) poses some very relevant questions: 'What do we know about differences between schools in terms of other pupil-related outcomes of schooling beyond academic results? What factors need to be taken into account in interpreting such differences?'.

Gray suggests that young people's commitment to education might be a key factor of influence which needs more investigation. Here, a link can be made with the very interesting contribution of Petty and Green (2007) who introduce the idea of the perceived curriculum from the student's viewpoint. Information on the learning process collected by the students themselves might be a good way to gather insight into the process of education and the relationships between what a school does and the long-term outcomes for individual students (68). This might also be a very good 'method' when trying to investigate the impact of religious diversity in schools. Especially when aspects of 'learning for life' are at stake, it might be good to focus on process indicators instead of outcome measures. Pupils' satisfaction with their educational experiences and pupil–teacher relationships can be two of these process indicators (see also Gray and Wilcox 1995).

Petty and Green developed an instrument 'The Essential Skills Access Test' to measure the opportunities pupils have (from their own perspective) to learn the Essential Skills of their school curriculum. Pupils have to indicate to what degree certain statements apply to them. Some examples of statements, which could also be related to citizenship education, are: 'At school I am taught to be kind to others,' 'The people at my school respect each other' and 'I will be a better citizen because of things I learn at school.' Especially because it is very difficult 'objectively' to separate the influence of school on how young people learn to be citizens of a plural society from other factors of influence, it might be very helpful for our research topic to make use of the pupils' own perspectives. Pupils are often clearly aware of what is going on in school (de Winter 1997); they are the ones par excellence to involve in the research on the impact of religious diversity in education as well.

In the quantitative REDCo study on religion in education, pupils themselves are in fact the most important informants. Some of the statements in the questionnaire they were asked to complete were: 'At school, I learn to have respect for everyone, whatever their religion,' 'Learning about different religions at school helps us to live together' and 'At school, I get knowledge about different religions.' These items are of the same type as the items proposed by Petty and Green. However, in the REDCo questionnaire there were only a few of these questions and, as mentioned earlier, there is a substantial risk of (double) misinterpretation.

Petty and Green's first analyses of their instrument suggest the usefulness and validity of 'using students' perceptions to provide a quantitative measure of school effectiveness, related to the students' experiences at school' (2007, 83). However, closer investigation is needed, also in terms of statistical analysis. Next to that, Petty and Green also recommend further qualitative study in order to better understand patterns of response that emerge. I will come back to this in the final section of this contribution.

Apart from the fact that it is difficult to separate school effects from other factors of influence, and that this is probably even more complicated when measuring non-cognitive school outcomes, it is important to realise that the variance accounted for by school (which indicates school effects) is normally between 10% and 15%. For fields of learning which belong less exclusively to the domain of the school, such as language skills, the contribution of school is often even smaller (e.g. Dijkstra 2002). It is realistic to imagine that the overall effect of school on how young pupils learn to live in a diverse society (which is even a less school specific task) is even smaller. So, when investigating the impact of religious diversity in education, one should not expect impressive statistical numbers. Bosker and Scheerens make clear, however, that 'school effects might be moderate or low in terms of percentage of variance accounted for; they may still have quite significant societal consequences' (1989, 746).

Conclusions and implications

I have made clear that one needs to be very cautious in drawing strong conclusions on the basis of studies on the impact of religious diversity in education. The quantitative REDCo research, which was primarily exploratory by nature, was a very important step in the research on the role and impact of religion in education. On the basis of the study, the three research questions (see note 3) could be answered (Valk et al. 2009). However, the REDCo study also raised various questions and generated hypotheses which need further investigation. Reflections of the REDCo quantitative study on young European people and religion in education made clear that there are several reasons why it was impossible to give well-founded comments on the relation between religious diversity in education and tolerance and openness to dialogue. Among these reasons are the fact that in some countries it was very difficult to differentiate between schools where pupils meet religious diversity and schools where they do not. In other countries, researchers found it too difficult to separate the influence of school (and the influence of religious diversity in school in particular) from many other contextual influences pupils are confronted with. Further, at a certain point, information is missing to check whether data findings are interpreted correctly.

There are various conceptual and empirical traps which enlarge the risk of drawing illegitimate conclusions on the basis of empirical study of the impact of religious diversity in education. With the reflections on the REDCo quantitative research as a background, both the conceptual and empirical traps are further explored in this contribution.

I have shown that it is very difficult to define ‘religious diversity’. As the concept ‘religion’ has several meanings in different contexts, one should be very much aware of the particular meaning given to religion in a specific piece of research. There are also various uncertainties about how to measure the impact of religious diversity. One needs to be very precise about how both individual and social development can be described. Further conceptual elaboration of terms in combination with concrete operationalisations is needed here as a preliminary to conducting empirical research.

Apart from the fact that, on the level of concepts, a lot of work still needs to be done, it is also the case that, with regard to empirical work, efforts are needed to improve the research on the impact of religious diversity in education. The risk of making incorrect interpretations is quite high, especially when using quantitative questionnaires. Another complicating factor is that the influence of school cannot be strictly separated from other factors of influence.

Although I have already given some suggestions to overcome these difficulties, in the last part of this paper I will outline some more practical implications for empirical research on religious diversity. There are good reasons to take the perspectives of the pupils very seriously in order not to focus strictly on the outcomes (if possible at all), but also to pay attention to the learning process as perceived by the students. Especially, as it is very difficult objectively to separate the influence of the school from other factors of influence, it is instructive to learn from the pupils themselves what they think about the impact of religious diversity in school. In addition, especially since the concepts which are dealt with are 'essentially contested concepts', it is necessary to make clear which interpretation is given to terms in a particular context. This means that questions in a questionnaire need to be as concrete as possible in order to reduce the risk of 'double misinterpretations'.

Apart from using questions that are as concrete as possible, in the whole research process, methods also need to be found to check how questions are interpreted by pupils and to ascertain what pupils think about the ways researchers interpret their answers. Therefore, it is very important to make use of a pilot test prior to the final data collection. A short oral interview or a group discussion with the persons who filled in the questionnaire should be part of this. The researcher could, for instance, ask: 'You answered the question whether you have contacts with pupils from different religious backgrounds with "yes". Can you explain more about what you mean by this?' Ideally, pupils should also be asked to reflect on the (summaries of) research outcomes. Do they recognise themselves in the interpretations of the researcher or not? The possibilities for supplementing quantitative work with this kind of interview need to be explored.

In line with the conceptual and empirical challenges described in this paper, it should also be concluded that large quantitative studies are not adequate enough to deal with the important question of the impact of religious diversity in education. The large quantitative study has been very important in order to explore the field and to give an outline of the general context, but appears to be too 'general' to get to a closer view at the 'micro-level'. Ethnographic case studies are necessary to get a closer view of what is really happening in classrooms, on how religious diversity is dealt with in schools and on how this influences young people. To some extent, the qualitative study of REDCo (Knauth et al. 2008) does give more insights on this micro-level. However, within the framework of the REDCo research programme, the qualitative study was used as an exploratory survey in preparation for the quantitative survey (Bertram-Troost et al. 2008). Although this was a very important and useful strategy, I argue that the findings of the quantitative study can be deepened by a follow-up qualitative study which can be more focused than the qualitative study as described in Knauth et al. (2008).

In addition, one should take into account that 'the influence of school' can never be seen on its own. There is always interaction with other factors of influence, among which are family, friends, religious communities and other aspects such as the 'personal character' of pupils. One should be very much aware of this, in order not to exaggerate or underestimate the role of education in preparing pupils for a life in a religiously diverse society.

Finally, it is important to take into account that the (relative) absence or presence of religious diversity in education can have both a direct and an indirect effect on the (individual and social) development of young people. The mere presence or absence in schools of pupils with different religious backgrounds can have an impact on individual pupils (for instance, via personal contacts). However, the influence can also be indirect, namely via the way shape is given to citizenship education in general and the way attention is paid to religious diversity in particular. As stated earlier, the (perceived) religious diversity within both the staff and pupil populations can influence the way attention is given to religion in school and the way pupils are prepared for life in a religiously diverse society. Therefore, the question of the impact of religious diversity in education can only be fully answered when close attention is paid to citizenship education as well.

Notes

1. See, for instance, discussions in national daily newspapers like *Trouw*, *Nederlands Dagblad* and *Reformatorisch Dagblad* (November–December 2009) on the role of religion in education and the right of existence of Orthodox Christian schools.
2. I was a member of the research team from the Netherlands.
3. Central questions were: 'What role has religion in pupils' life and in their surroundings (important others, peers, family)?', 'How do pupils see religion in school and the impact of religion in education?', 'How do pupils consider the impact of religions in society?'
4. For this reason, analysis on the Estonian data focuses more on differences between pupils with regard to the model of religious education pupils have experiences with (and for how many years).

References

Béraud, C., B. Massignon, S. Mathieu, and J.-P. Willaime. 2009. The school – An appropriate institution in France for acquiring knowledge on religious diversity and experiencing it firsthand? In *Teenagers' perspectives on the role of religion in their lives, schools and societies: A European quantitative study,* ed. P. Valk, G.D. Bertram-Troost, M. Friederici, and C. Béraud, 131–63. Münster: Waxmann.

Bertram-Troost, G.D. 2006. *Geloven in bijzonder onderwijs. Levensbeschouwelijke identiteitsontwikkeling van adolesenten in het voortgezet onderwijs* [Belief in denominational education. Religious identity development of adolescents in secondary education]. Zoetermeer: Boekencentrum.

Bertram-Troost, G.D. 2009. How do European pupils see religion in school? In *Teenagers' perspectives on the role of religion in their lives, schools and societies: A European quantitative study,* ed. P. Valk, G.D. Bertram-Troost, M. Friederici, and C. Béraud, 409–23. Münster: Waxmann.

Bertram-Troost, G.D., S.A. de Roos, and S. Miedema. 2009. The relationship between religious education and religious commitments and explorations of adolescents: On religious identity development in Dutch Christian secondary schools. *Journal of Beliefs and Values* 30, no. 1: 17–27.

Bertram-Troost, G.D., J. Ipgrave, D.P. Josza, and T. Knauth. 2008. Encountering religious pluralism in school and society: A qualitative study of teenage perspectives in Europe – Background and contextualisation. In *Encountering religious pluralism in school and society: A qualitative study of teenage perspectives in Europe,* ed. T. Knauth, D.P. Josza, G.D. Bertram-Troost, and J. Ipgrave, 11–19. Münster: Waxmann.

Bertram-Troost, G.D., and S. Miedema. 2009a. Semantic differences in European research cooperation from a methodological and theoretical perspective – Translation and terminology. In *Teenagers' perspectives on the role of religion in their lives, schools and societies: A European quantitative study,* ed. P. Valk, G.D. Bertram-Troost, M. Friederici, and C. Béraud, 29–41. Münster: Waxmann.

Bertram-Troost, G.D., and S. Miedema. 2009b. Semantic differences in international comparative research on religious education: An EC-funded project as example. *Panorama: Intercultural Journal of Interdisciplinary Ethical and Religious Studies for Responsible Research* 21: 133–47.

Bertram-Troost, G.D, S. Miedema, I. ter Avest, and C. Bakker. 2009. Dutch pupils' views on religion in school and society: Report on a quantitative research. In *Teenagers' perspectives on the role of religion in their lives, schools and societies: A European quantitative study,* ed. P. Valk, G.D. Bertram-Troost, M. Friederici, and C. Béraud, 221–60. Münster: Waxmann.

Bosker, R.J., and J. Scheerens. 1989. Issues in the interpretation of the results of school effectiveness research. *International Journal of Educational Research* 13: 741–51.

Breen, D. 2009. Religious diversity, inter-ethnic relations and the Catholic school: Introducing the *responsive* approach to single faith schooling. *British Journal of Religious Education* 31, no. 2: 103–15.

Brinkman, J. 2000. *De vragenlijst* [The questionnaire]. Groningen: Wolters-Noordhoff.

de Winter, M. 1997. *Het alziend oog van de leerling. Een impressie over opvoeding, normen en waardering op school* [The all-seeing eye of pupils. An impression of education, norms and assessment at school] (Trouw-lezing Nederlandse Onderwijs Tentoonstelling, Utrecht 24-1-1997). Amersfoort: CPS.

Dijkstra, A.B. 2002. *Werelden apart? Leefstijlen van middelbare scholieren. Een vergelijkende studie naar de leefwereld van jongeren op gereformeerde scholen* [Separated worlds? Lifestyles of secondary pupils. A comparative study of the life world of adolescents in reform schools]. Assen: Koninklijke Van Gorcum.

Gallie, W.B. 1956. Essentially contested concepts. *Proceedings of the Aristotelian Society* 56: 167–98.

Grace, G. 2003. Educational studies and faith-based schooling: Moving from prejudice to evidence-based argument. *British Journal of Educational Studies* 51, no. 2: 149–67.

Gray, J. 2004. School effectiveness and the 'other outcomes' of secondary schooling: A reassessment of three decades of British research. *Improving Schools* 7, no. 2: 185–98.

Gray, J., and B. Wilcox. 1995. *Good school, bad school: Evaluating performance and encouraging improvement.* Buckingham: Open University Press.

Josza, D., T. Knauth, and W. Weisse. 2009. Religion in school – A comparative study of Hamburg and North Rhine-Westphalia. In *Teenagers' perspectives on the role of religion in their lives, schools and societies: A European quantitative study,* ed. P. Valk, G.D. Bertram-Troost, M. Friederici, and C. Béraud, 173–212. Münster: Waxmann.

Knauth, T., D.P. Josza, G.D. Bertram-Troost, and J. Ipgrave, eds. 2008. *Encountering religious pluralism in school and society: A qualitative study of teenage perspectives in Europe.* Münster: Waxmann.

Kozyrev, F., and P. Valk. 2009. Saint-Petersburg students' views about religion in education – Results of the quantitative survey. In *Teenagers' perspectives on the role of religion in their lives, schools and societies: A European quantitative study,* ed. P. Valk, G.D. Bertram-Troost, M. Friederici, and C. Béraud, 311–49. Münster: Waxmann.

Lieberson, S. 1969. Measuring population diversity. *American Sociological Review* 34, no. 6: 850–62.

McKenna, U., S. Neill, and R. Jackson. 2009. Personal worldviews, dialogue and tolerance – Students' views on religious education in England. In *Teenagers' perspectives on the role of religion in their lives, schools and societies: A European quantitative study,* ed. P. Valk, G.D. Bertram-Troost, M. Friederici, and C. Béraud, 49–70. Münster: Waxmann.

Petty, N.W., and T. Green. 2007. Measuring educational opportunity as perceived by students: A process indicator. *Effectiveness and School Improvement* 18, no. 1: 67–91.

Schihalejev, O. 2009. Options beside 'and no religion too' – Perspectives of Estionian youth. In *Teenagers' perspectives on the role of religion in their lives, schools and societies: A European quantitative study,* ed. P. Valk, G.D. Bertram-Troost, M. Friederici, and C. Béraud, 79–120. Münster: Waxmann.

Schweitzer, F. 2007. Religious individualization: New challenges to education for tolerance. *British Journal of Religious Education* 29, no. 1: 89–100.

Skeie, G., and M. Von der Lippe. 2009. Does religion matter to young people in Norwegian schools? In *Teenagers' perspectives on the role of religion in their lives, schools and societies: A European quantitative study,* ed. P. Valk, G.D. Bertram-Troost, M. Friederici, and C. Béraud, 269–301. Münster: Waxmann.

Smaling, A., and E. Hijmans, eds. 1997. *Kwalitatief onderzoek en levensbeschouwing* [Qualitative research and world view]. Amsterdam: Boom.

Valk, P., G.D. Bertram-Troost, M. Friederici, and C. Béraud, eds. 2009. *Teenagers' perspectives on the role of religion in their lives, schools and societies: A European quantitative study.* Münster: Waxmann.

van der Kooij, J.C., D.J. de Ruijter, and S. Miedema. In preparation. 'Worldview': The meaning of essentially contested concepts and the impact on RE.

van der Want,, A., C. Bakker, I. ter Avest, and J. Everington, eds. 2009. *Teachers responding to religious diversity in Europe: Researching biography and pedagogy.* Münster: Waxmann.

van Houten, M. 2009. De nieuwe schoolstrijd [A new school funding controversy]. *Trouw, De Verdieping,* November 18.

van Soest, A. 2009. Uitzonderingsclausule SP'er gunt refoschool slechts uitstel van executie Minaretten [Exceptional provision: Socialist permits reformed school only postponement of minarets execution]. *Trouw, De Verdieping,* December 22.

Vroegindeweij, G. 2009. Mijn tolerantie is begrensd [My tolerance is limited]. *Reformatorisch Dagblad,* November 28.

Williams, K.Y., and C.A. O'Reilly. 1998. Demography and diversity in organizations. *Research in Organizational Behavior* 20: 77–140.

Index

Page numbers in *Italics* represent tables.
Page numbers in **Bold** represent figures.